"Chloë's subtle voice work opens the heart. Sh[e]
teaching art. She is at the core of a fascinating
individuals to find their truth and freedom t[.]
voice and sound."

—COLEMAN BARKS, author of *Rumi: Soul Fury*

"Chloë has perfected a unique and empowering vocal technique accessible to everyone. In all my research with nonviolent and creative communication skills, I have never experienced this ability to effortlessly generate such a range and depth of human feeling and expression with such spontaneity, courage, and compassion. Chloë is dedicated to recovering the wisdom of the human spirit, in a way that is profound and unique for our times."

—DR. SCILLA ELWORTHY, Niwano Peace Prize Winner and
Nobel Peace Prize nominee, author of *Pioneering the Possible*

"Chloë Goodchild has a voice of mesmerizing purity. She possesses one of the freest spirits I have seen on stage."

—JULIET STEVENSON, actor

"Chloë Goodchild's teaching has opened up my true voice for theatre."

—JERRY HALL, actor and model

"*The Naked Voice* book radiates the power of hope and love from each page. Chloë Goodchild transforms the world into a brighter place. Her sheer positivity interweaves a truly practical guide where you will learn to express yourself in ways you never dreamed of. On a personal note, working with Chloë and her amazing voice was magical. She transformed my simple notes into something magnificent and wild and heartrendingly beautiful. No other singer has ever matched her performance for me."

—ELIZABETH PARKER, film and television composer,
former member of the BBC Radiophonic Workshop

"Chloë Goodchild's music is a new force for peace."

—BEN OKRI, author of *The Famished Road*

"Chloë Goodchild's clarity of tone—both in her music and in her book—penetrates to the bone. I revel in both her songs and words, especially when she surrenders to the mystery of devotion. In the West we usually shy away from pure devotion, often for legitimate reasons. But Chloë evokes the open, trembling, courageous heart of devotion that more deeply invites us into the danger of living. I celebrate and recommend her work."

—GANGAJI, spiritual teacher and author of
Hidden Treasure: Uncovering the Truth in Your Life Story

"Out of nowhere, Chloë Goodchild's naked voice, soaring with a range that one would have believed impossible."

—THE TIMES LITERARY SUPPLEMENT

"Chloë looks like a nun, but she sings wild!"

—ANGELO BADALAMENTI, film composer

"For many years now, through a time in which the sound of the soul has been largely muted by the din of the world, Chloë Goodchild's characteristic optimism and joy have encouraged it to raise its voice in song. Her work has touched and opened many lives, and the light and beauty of her truly liberating spirit shine throughout the pages of this book."

—LINDSAY CLARKE, author of
The Chymical Wedding and *The Water Theatre*

"Chloë Goodchild is one of the foremost proponents of the voice as a therapeutic instrument for healing spirit, mind and body. In *The Naked Voice* she shows herself to be an inspirational teacher who projects her commitment and enthusiasm to opening up hearts and minds through the vibration of our voice. She captures the readers' imagination, showing us that there is no one who cannot open up their voices to transform their lives. *The Naked Voice* will stand alongside those books that have become classics in the field of voice education and sound healing."

—JAMES D'ANGELO, PhD, founder of therapeutic vocal sound program
Soundspirit and the author of *The Healing Power of the Human Voice*

"[A]n exciting book, exploring dimensions and connections little known to most of us ... Based on her many years of singing and teaching experience and the stories of her own life, Chloë Goodchild writes with much passion about the foundational power of the human voice, the development of self-awareness through sound-awareness, the discoveries to be made and the wisdom to be gained by an in-depth encounter with the music within us and the music of life. It makes your heart sing and your body connect in surprisingly new ways."

—URSULA KING, professor emerita of theology and religious studies, Bristol
University, UK, and author of *The Search for Spirituality*

"Chloë Goodchild lives and breathes song. Her lifework, articulated in her inspirational and practical book, *The Naked Voice: Transform Your Life through the Power of Sound,* is a gentle, disarming, and convincing call to all souls ready to return to the authentic power and beauty of their natural voice."

—MICHAEL STILLWATER, founder of
Inner Harmony and Song Without Borders

"Chloë's work is joyful and a source of liberation. Singing with Chloë is a way of returning to original mind. She shows us how to find our authentic voice. It is the voice we need to sing out from and save this dazzlingly beautiful world."

—CHINA GALLAND, author of
The Bond between Women and *Love Cemetery*

"Chloë's voice is primordial. She is a paradisal singer and teacher whose pure being ignites a sound from the source of creation, graced with love...."

—GREG TRICKER, mystic sculptor, visual artist, and author

"The simple purity of Chloë's recurring melody line sparks a whole series of core emotions too long buried."

—LORD DAVID PUTTNAM

"In *The Naked Voice* Chloë Goodchild not only lifts us high above the terrifying cacophony of our time, she stirs the essence of a new creation to rise out of each one of us. She teaches us all how to liberate the voice for own most intimate questing and to bring our resonance to a new day for an awakening humanity."

—JAMES O'DEA, author of *The Conscious Activist*

"[I]n this lyrical yet practical book, Chloë Goodchild invites us to discover, perhaps for the first time, our original song of the soul. As a voice teacher and performer, Chloë has transformed thousands of lives around the world with the potency of sound and song, and here, in the written word, the wisdom of her teachings resonate through every page. Her words provide a map—a songline—directly into the compassionate heart that lies beneath rational thought to reveal who we really are, literally attuning us to our own inner peace, passion, and the divine bliss that is our birthright. Each chapter effortlessly weaves together inspirational stories of healing and transcendence, ancient spiritual knowledge and cutting-edge science with practical exercises and vocal practices, to give us a treasured companion on the road to awakening."

—NICOLA GRAYDON, journalist and author of *The Ancestral Continuum*

"Chloë Goodchild's pure and melodic voice is a healing force for harmonic transformation."
—ALEX DOMAN, coauthor of *Healing at the Speed of Sound*

"I was the girl who was told to 'just mouth the words' in sixth-grade choir and was afraid to sing for decades thence. Chloë Goodchild reconsecrated my voice, tenderly and fiercely drawing it forth until I knew in my cells that my singing was not only a matter of my own healing and pleasure, but a profound invocation into a multidimensional singing field that has the power to serve not only my own awakening, but that of the planet as a whole. Now Chloë has done the miraculous: she has written her unique transmission into the pages of this book. Read it and hear the original, awake, alive and utterly unique naked voice sing free within you. It will heal your body, open your mind, and transform all your relationships."
—KIM ROSEN, author of *Saved by a Poem*

"Chloë Goodchild has written a book that is a major contribution to our understanding of the power of sound and music. From her personal experiences as a singer to the many decades she has worked to empower people through their voices, she has discovered the deep truths inherent in coming into our true, authentic voice and nurturing our souls. This book is a must-read for sound healers, music therapists, physicians, and therapists. It is an astonishing accomplishment."
—Barbara J. Crowe, board-certified music therapist,
Arizona State University director of music therapy, and author of
Music and Soulmaking: Toward a New Theory of Music Therapy

"Even the most solid of material objects is ultimately a dance of constantly changing energy patterns. Ultimately it is all rhythm, all music, the world is sound—Nada Brahma—as the classical Sanskrit philosophers put it. Chloë Goodchild's magnificent book gives us keys to this universe we contain within our own voices. If practiced, the reader will know an inner and outer transformation that is both miraculous and true."
—Jean Houston, PhD, author of *The Wizard of Us*

The Naked Voice

The Naked Voice

*Transform Your Life through the
Power of Sound*

Chloë Goodchild
Foreword by Andrew Harvey

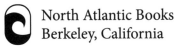

North Atlantic Books
Berkeley, California

Published by
North Atlantic Books
Berkeley, California

Cover art by Kazuaki Tanahashi, brushmind.net
Cover and book design by Mary Ann Casler
Translations of poems by Rumi courtesy of Coleman Barks
The poem "Anyone Can Sing" by William Ayot is reprinted by permission of the author
Photo on page 94 by Aliki Sapountzi, www.aliki.co.uk

Printed in the United States of America

The Naked Voice: Transform Your Life through the Power of Sound is sponsored and published by the Society for the Study of Native Arts and Sciences (dba North Atlantic Books), an educational nonprofit based in Berkeley, California, that collaborates with partners to develop cross-cultural perspectives, nurture holistic views of art, science, the humanities, and healing, and seed personal and global transformation by publishing work on the relationship of body, spirit, and nature.

North Atlantic Books' publications are available through most bookstores. For further information, visit our website at www.northatlanticbooks.com or call 800-733-3000.

Library of Congress Cataloging-in-Publication Data
Goodchild, Chloë.
  The naked voice : transform your life through the power of sound / Chloë Goodchild.
     pages cm
  Summary: "Going beyond traditional vocal training guides, this book will appeal to anyone wishing to encounter themselves at a primal level through the medium of the voice. Those who wish to expand their possiblities for self-expression, in particular singers, actors, teachers, public speakers, and presenters, will also take note"— Provided by publisher.
  ISBN 978-1-58394-877-4 (paperback) — ISBN 978-1-58394-878-1 (e-book)
  1. Health. 2. Sound—Psychological aspects. 3. Mind and body. 4. Healing—Psychological aspects. I. Title.
  RA776.5.G67 2015
  613—dc23   2015001727

3 4 5 6 7 8 9 10 11 12 KPC 26 25 24 23 22 21 20 19

This book includes recycled material and material from well-managed forests.
North Atlantic Books is committed to the protection of our environment.
We print on recycled paper whenever possible and partner with printers
who strive to use environmentally responsible practices.

*I dedicate this book
to my mother,
Jean Helen Mary Ross Goodchild,
and
to my daughter,
Rebecca Hannah Goodchild Nash*

Contents

Part I Transform Your Listening: Sound Awareness

Chapter 1: Your Secret Voice

Chapter 2: Your Instinctual Voice

Chapter 3: Your Still Voice

Part II Transform Your Communication: Sound Intelligence

Chapter 4: Your Heart Voice

Part III Transform Your Life: Sound Wisdom

Chapter 6: Your Naked Voice

Illustrations

Part III

Foreword

C hloë Goodchild is a great friend, one of the world's seminal sacred singers and a magnificent teacher who has led with wild courage and tender encouragement thousands of people all over the world into the discovery of their true voice and the freedom that discovery makes possible. Her work has always been—for me, and for many others who have had the privilege of listening to her or working with her—a tremendous beacon of hope and source of peaceful and passionate sacred energy, especially in a terrible time like ours when so many of us are paralyzed by the violence and misery we see erupting everywhere.

The book that you are holding in your hands is her wise and beautifully constructed manifesto: the crystallization, in easy-to-follow instruction, language, and exercises, of a lifetime's dedication to the secret power of music to unlock our inner divinity and release us into the energy that floods us when we claim the humble authority of our unique selves, and dare to voice that authority with naked vulnerability and truth. Music's sacred power to illumine and inspire has of course been known and employed in all the great mystical systems. What Chloë has done in this fine book is to make this inspiration available to everyone whatever their faith (or lack of it), and in a time when everyone is challenged by the drastically worsening conditions to step forward and put personal love and compassion into public action on behalf of all sentient beings, now terminally endangered, as we are, by humans and our hubris.

Chloë writes, "As your voice is redeemed, a spontaneous aliveness returns, awakening your heart as you journey toward your True Self. By learning to listen to your voice, by learning to understand, honor, accept, and express its message, you begin to discover an inner freedom and to carry it into the world."

The Naked Voice is not a book to read quickly. As the great piece of verbal music it is, it needs and quietly demands the deepest savoring attention. In Chloë's words, "*The Naked Voice* brings you essential sonic codes, maps, templates, and keys with which to unlock the song of your life. . . . Please be aware when you read this book how the space between the words I write are just as important as the spaces, or musical intervals, that exist between the notes of a song. This space invites silent reflection within, between, and beyond the words themselves. Silence is the essential key of this book. So if possible, don't rush your way through it. Allow for space, silence, and the nourishment of deep listening."

If you read *The Naked Voice* in this way you will, I guarantee, have a life-changing experience. The contrapuntal skill with which Chloë Goodchild weaves together (as in one of Bach's late fugues and *The Art of Fugue*) personal mystical experience, galvanizing stories of the healing effect of her work, and lucid exercises and practices that anyone who sings in the shower can do, is for me not only proof of her great gifts as a writer, raconteur, and humble helpful teacher, but also a sign that the message of radical empowerment through music which she is uniquely qualified to bring us has been thought through, lived, and integrated.

With Russill Paul's great book *The Yoga of Sound*, this becomes one of the two most important books on the liberating glory of music that we now have, and its publication is a literary and spiritual event of the highest order. I shall not only treasure *The Naked Voice* but use it myself, and share it with all those I teach at the Institute of Sacred Activism. For me, as for so many others, music is the greatest of all the arts, the closest to direct divine transmission. It sustains those who wish to serve and love with a vibrancy, a celebratory energy, and peacefully passionate determination to keep going in hope and joy, whatever now happens in the world.

As I write this, the log cabin where I live in Arkansas is ringing with the voice I myself have been most galvanized by, the voice I discovered with amazement and rapture fifty years ago, that of Maria Callas. I can still remember the moment at nine years old when I first heard Callas sing *Vissi d'Arte (I lived for art)* from Puccini's opera *Tosca,* erupting like an avalanche of molten lava from the tiny turquoise radio that was my most treasured possession and my door into a wonderland of music of all kinds. I had never heard anything like her, and until I heard her, I had no idea that a human being could be so naked, wild, vulnerable, and ultimately brave and passionate. This discovery was nothing less than an earthquake in my life, a revelation to me. I now realize the volcanic power of my own repressed sacred feminine, of my own secret and unsuspected longing to live unfettered by convention or any kind of system or philosophy that limits the limitless truth and the honest passion of my and everyone's true self.

In all the years that have followed that first revelation, Callas's voice with its ragged fierce glory has been my touchstone of authenticity for myself and others, a constant luminous gold within my spirit, urging it relentlessly toward an ever greater fearlessness and surrender. Whenever I sit down to write or stand up to speak I hear Maria in the ear of my heart, challenging me to kick away all the props and masks and disguises, and just sing out my truth whatever the cost or effect. Callas keeps open for me a door into the astounding and sacred sound world of grand opera, a world in which I continue to experience the soaring and sometimes terrible but always supremely beautiful truths of divine human emotion and divine love. Years later when I encountered the poetry of Rumi and the impassioned crystalline outpourings of other great mystics of love, I realized that my whole being had been prepared through Callas's naked voice to begin the long journey that has been my life, to embrace and incarnate the truths and responsibilities of divine love and wisdom.

May this wonderful book guide you to find and celebrate your own masters of the naked voice, and to recognize them as messengers to you of the wild and holy voice that lives within you and is longing to pour through you in all you are and all you do, without false pride or vanity. "Gesang ist Dasein" wrote Rilke in his *Sonnets to Orpheus*. "Song is Being." Let your being sing in its own irreplaceable unique way. The world and the universe and all the sages and prophets and bodhisattvas and angels and the divine Self are waiting with bated breath for the moment you risk and surrender enough to let your whole life become one uninterrupted music of prayer and praise and gratitude and, above all, celebration of the glorious gift it is to be alive.

You are being summoned here by *your* naked voice, to transform *your* life through the power of sound, to resound with truth and justice for all sentient beings.

—ANDREW HARVEY, Founder of Sacred Activism,
author of *The Hope: A Guide to Sacred Activism*

The Song of Your Life: An African Legend

There is a remarkable story of the Himba people in Namibia, who live on the banks of the Kunene River. It is said the Himba are one of the few cultures that consider the birth date of their children to be not the day they are born, nor the day they are conceived, but the day the mother decides to have the child. The Himba understand that every child's soul resonates or "sings" its unique flavor and purpose. So when a Himba woman decides to have a child, she goes off and sits under a tree by herself, and she listens until she can hear the song of the child that wants to be born. Once she has heard this song, she comes back to the man who will be the child's father and teaches him the song. And then, when they make love to conceive the child, they sing the song as a way to invite the child to come. When the woman becomes pregnant she attunes to the child's song and sings it out loud to the midwives and the old women of the village so that when the child is born, they too can sing the child's song in welcome.

As the child grows up, the other villagers are taught the child's song. If the child falls or gets hurt, someone picks him or her up and sings the soul song to restore well-being. Whenever the child does something wonderful, or travels through transitions such as puberty, the village community honors the child by singing his or her song. There is one other occasion when the child's song is sung to him or her: if the child commits a crime or does something contrary to Himba social norms, instead of punishing the child, the villagers call him or her to the center of the village and form a circle around the child. They then sing the child's "soul song" once again.

The Himba's corrective response to antisocial behavior is led by love and the remembrance of identity. For when you recognize your own song, you have no desire or need to do anything that would hurt another. Such singing restores an open heart, self-worth, sound values, and a clear conscience. As children grow up, their songs are the theme of their lives. In marriage, the songs of the two people are sung together. Finally, when the child, as an adult-elder, prepares to die, all the villagers gather to sing his or her song as the soul transitions into the next life.

Overture:
About This Book

This book will wake you up to a new relationship with who you are as revealed through the power of your voice. Your voice will engage every part of you: breath, body, heart, mind, and soul, pulling the carpet of self-doubt from under your feet. It will relax your rational mind, unwinding your old life, opening your ears, eyes, and imagination to the pleasures and benefits of expressing yourself in ways you never thought possible. There is a unique voice inside you, waiting to be heard: the voice of your true identity and being.

You might well ask: *How can a book on finding yourself through your voice possibly give me the direct experience I long for?* You will soon find out. Throughout the book I share my own direct experience of the transformative power of sound as a catalyst for inner-outer change. I relate some of the life-changing stories that were central in shaping my own teachings of the human voice as a healing and wisdom tool for personal discovery and collective wisdom. These stories are interwoven with accessible vocal practices that will take you deeper into the invisible mystery of your own sound, before self-consciousness and inhibition have time to get in your way. You will be able to experience the transforming benefits that deep listening, spontaneous sound, energy movement, and meditative and structured voice-work can bring to consciousness and life. An effortless dialogue then begins between your inner and outer life in which nonjudgmental listening is the bridge and your voice the messenger. Your ears become sensitive antennae tuning in to the subtle messages flowing back and forth to and from your inner thoughts. In no time, you will be expressing yourself in an embodied, authentic way. As you begin to listen and express yourself more deeply, such questions as "Who am I?" "Who is singing?" and "Where did that sound come from?" will enable you to remember the forgotten or neglected dimensions of yourself, lost in the unconscious cracks between sound and silence. As your voice is redeemed, a spontaneous aliveness returns, awakening your heart as you journey toward your True Self. By learning to listen to your voice, by learning to understand, honor, accept, and express its message, you begin to discover an inner freedom and to carry it into the world.

This book aims to transform your life in the following ways:

Revolutionize the way you listen.
Restore respect and honor to your ears.
Strengthen your auditory consciousness.
Deepen self-awareness through sound awareness.
Empower you to witness and listen without negative judgment.
Assist you in finding your authentic voice.
Integrate your contemplative, creative, and compassionate voice.
Inspire caring and compassionate relationships.
Integrate voice as a metaphor for life and a healing art form.
Introduce transformative vocal skills for conflict resolution.
Introduce the singing field for creative community-building.

The book is divided into three parts:

Part I   Transform Your Listening—Sound Awareness
Part II   Transform Your Communication—Sound Intelligence
Part III   Transform Your Life—Sound Wisdom

Each part combines:

- Teaching and instructional components
- Experiential vocal or movement practices
- Music listening and sing-along sections
- Personal stories related to the chapter theme.

The Naked Voice brings you essential sonic codes, maps, templates, and keys with which to unlock the song of your life. *Sound awareness, sound intelligence,* and *sound wisdom* provide three resounding foundation stones for a "sound-led" way of life, inspiring those three critical qualities of discernment. There is a strong chance that by sharing and exploring this book with another person you will continually find new ways to express the music of your soul, ultimately accessing a depth of communication where there is only ONE of us.

Please be aware when you read this book how the space between the words I write are just as important as the spaces, or musical intervals, that exist between the notes of a song. This space invites silent reflection within, between, and beyond the words themselves. Silence is the essential key of this book. So if possible, don't rush your way through it. Allow for space, silence, and the nourishment of deep listening.

Before you dive deeper, let's reflect on the question that visited me when I was in the early stages of writing: *How can written words on a page possibly capture the nuances of sound and singing, and how can they inspire a direct experience of your authentic voice?*

At first, this book had a "mission impossible" feel to it. Having thrived for most of my singing life on live, sound-led, interactive experiences with other practitioners, I too wondered how it was possible to achieve the same direct communication without access to each other's voices. I knew I needed to try; I welcomed the challenge of giving the invisible new clothes, to express the inexpressible.

The only way forward was to develop a writing style and to offer content that would somehow open your mind to the unexpected through sound, especially *yours.* I see *The Naked Voice* as a musical offering, bringing sound awareness into the foreground of our everyday lives: sometimes it can be quiet, minimalist, and melodically spare; other times it becomes an improvisation, a dynamic stream of consciousness expanding into ecstatic joy and passion. Or it might plummet into the subterranean depths of a dark storyline, only to leap back into staccato spoken song. I seek to catch you unawares, with the continual aim of energizing you and your vocal experience.

I have inserted lyrics or poetic quotes at the opening of most sections that highlight specific music tracks from my solo albums and music collaborations recorded over the last two decades. I invite you to find time to listen to the music accompanying these lyrics in order to more fully comprehend what I'm exploring with you.

Note: Links to my online music are available at the end of this book.

During my travels to Africa, India, Europe, Mexico, and North, Central, and South America, I collected many chants that have inspired my own compositions. Singing these simple healing melodies opens up the contemplative, creative, and compassionate use of sound and reveals the profound impact and healing that ancient chants can offer our modern lives.

I've integrated many personal stories into this journey because, even though they are past, they have been the landmarks and wake-up calls that highlighted and shaped the Naked Voice teachings, drawn from my life as singing pilgrim, mother, and teacher. Given there is nowhere to hide once the "naked voice" is accessed, I enjoy confiding in you with the intimacy of a soul friend, trusting that you will at some point, if not already, dare the same edge of openness and courageous uncertainty with yourself and others. This storytelling dimension is often missing in my live vocal courses and trainings, as there is rarely the time and space to share this level of give and take.

The great cultural historian Thomas Berry encapsulates the evolutionary nature of the Naked Voice journey in his book *The Great Work*: "Just as in the human order, creativity is neither a rational deductive process, nor an irrational wandering of the undisciplined mind, but the emergence of beauty as mysterious as the blossoming of a field of daisies out of the dark earth."

The bottom line is that this book is in your hand for a purpose. Your naked voice is about to wake up the energies of love inside you, and inspire the song of your soul to come out and play. Ideally the book will provide a conduit within which you can engage and cook your own naked-voice experience, as well as enjoy discovering how the art of self-inquiry and deep listening leads to a direct expression of your authentic voice and true authority. The only way we can transform what is "out there" is to transform who is "in here." The best way I know to engage the process of transformation is to utilize my favorite naked-voice practices. In my effort to introduce these practices I weave them into the tapestry of my personal experience to help reveal the infinite gift and grace that this magical naked voice is. It will, if we allow it, transform life as we know it.

If this book can assist you in discovering your whole life as music, it will have achieved its intention. Just as there are no two voices alike, so I hope that you will interpret the meaning hidden within the melodic messages in your own way, letting my thoughts land in your mind like harmonies of some ancient memory, holy love affair, or quiet prayer. However they land, may they lead you home to the unique song of your life.

Naked in Our Song

One is one and one world turning
Naked in our song
One is one the heart is burning
Naked in our song

You and I our voices calling
Naked in our song
You and I defenses falling
Naked in our song

Inside outside all around us
Naked in our song
Laughing crying living dying
Naked in our song

—"Naked in Our Song," *Fierce Wisdom*

Introduction

The Naked-Voice Experience

Since childhood and throughout my life, my voice has been my conscience and guide, providing me with an in-built "sonic laboratory" for self-inquiry. In 1990, following a transformative experience in India, I discovered my voice as my very own self. My singing voice became the messenger of this awakening. I called it my *naked voice,* for it arose from an unconditional source far deeper than my personality or ego could fathom. It touched a place of wisdom and oneness (nonduality) within me that opened vast new fields of perception and presence, which dissolved my rational mind.

I was thirty-seven. From that moment I dedicated myself—through my music recordings, workshops, trainings, and "singing field" events —to an exploration of the human voice as a catalyst for spirit and a gateway into the deepest regions of the human soul. My work with individuals, communities, and organizations worldwide has revealed that there are as many unique voices as there are souls. Your voice is as unique as your twelve-stranded DNA. However, many don't know how to access it. Our schools and social conditioning don't offer many clues. Yet the human voice is everyone's birthright. It is a universal *given,* a bridge between the worlds, the soul's messenger, a gift of spirit capable of inspiring evolutionary shifts in consciousness.

Both ancient wisdom and the latest advances in science agree that every particle of matter, every phenomenon you experience, is a form of resonance or vibration. Your voice is the mouthpiece of this experience. There is nothing more personal, more tied to your identity than your voice. It is a primal means of expression—something true about us that precedes rational thought and conceptualization.

Yet we live in a visually dominated culture that places more importance on our eyes than our ears. The great pianist, conductor, and musical ambassador for peace Daniel Barenboim describes the human ear as "the most intelligent organ in the body." He explains in his talk for the UK Reith Lectures (2006) called "In the Beginning Was Sound" that our ears not only absorb sound or noise into the body, they also send it directly to the brain, thereby setting in motion the whole creative process of thought that a human being is capable of.

Our ears are unique in helping us recollect and remember who we are behind all the artificial layers of self-consciousness catalyzed by the personality or ego. Our ears started operating on the forty-fifth day of our mother's pregnancy. This means that we began to use our ears inside the womb, seven and a half months before the eyes! Yet once born, the significant role and purpose of ears can be seriously neglected, as the eyes assume more and more dominance over the other senses.

Have You Found Your Note?

The person who has found the keynote
of his own life has found
the key of his own life.

—HAZRAT INAYAT KHAN,
The Mysticism of Music, Sound and Word

How do you feel about your voice? Does your voice express who you are and what you really want to say? Does your voice express the real you? What do you most love about your voice? If you were to write a vocal self-portrait, the story of your voice, what would your voice have to say? When is your voice most hidden and unexpressed, and when is it most alive and authentic?

I am not just asking about your singing voice, I am inquiring about your everyday voice in all its forms. The voice you use at home, the voice you present at work, your social entertainer and diva voice, the voice that lets rip in the shower or the car. Maybe you are a voice of protest, an urgent activist, a change-maker, a revolutionary voice? Maybe you never speak up at all? And what about your voices of longing and yearning? When and with whom do they show up? Do they hang out in the shadows with your hidden shy voice, or are they outspoken with the masses? Is there a still voice, a place of sanctuary, where your inner self is nourished and at home?

Research shows that more than two thousand messages move through the brain even before words come out of one's mouth. People pick up on these unspoken voices inside us, carried in the vibration and tone of what we say. So many voices, and yet most of them conceal a deeper longing to be seen and heard, not just for what we have achieved, but simply for who we truly *are*. Paradoxically, the way we express ourselves in everyday life is largely determined by how safely or adventurously we wish to live and play. Our personality habits are sustained by lifelong, ingrained, taken-for-granted assumptions about what is good and bad, right and wrong. This hypnosis of the mind derives from a life of inhibition, separateness, unfulfilled dreams, fear, and a belief that duality is the only reality, leaving us no choice but to spend our lives struggling between the oppositions of pleasure-pain, success-failure, happiness-sadness, win-lose.

However, there is a deeper, wiser you behind the warring polarities of your rational mind and ego-self. This deeper you is found in the landscape of your soul. Your soul is your unconditioned self, the messenger of your spirit, and it is forever free and unaffected by everyday survival and stress. As the great Sufi mystic and poet Rumi has said, your soul is simply here for its own joy, and it is most easily accessed through your heart rather than your head. Which is why getting out of your head and into your heart makes communicating so much easier. It's essential.

Singing offers a fast and effective way to open your heart and embody what you really want to communicate. Despite what your mind would have you believe, your soul loves to sing.

Your authentic singing voice is the muscle and mouthpiece of your soul. As unique as your fingerprint and DNA, your soul has a melody, a rhythm, and a resonance that is yours alone. You are the only one who can embody your voice. Your true or *naked* voice can access your soul song, and this resonant song reveals your authentic nature, who you really are.

Expressing your soul song is easy if you are willing and committed to listening, to hearing, and to acknowledging it without judgment of any kind. Once heard, your soul song will take you on the journey of your life beyond social conditioning and all your self-limiting beliefs of right-wrong doing. It's an adventurous journey supported by new communication skills, inspiring a metamorphosis, from bug to butterfly, from entropy to syntropy, from a fear-driven persona to a transparent, courageous, compassionate human being resonating with the energies of unconditional love.

As you learn to listen to and accept yourself without judgment, you will soon discover how to engage with the voice of your personal calling and what really matters to you. When your naked or authentic voice is firing on all cylinders, your whole body starts to vibrate with an aliveness that resonates in every cell of your body.

It's a well-known fact that the Australian Aborigines believe *the whole world was sounded into Being*. Scientists researching the earliest known archaeological sites on the Australian continent—using thermo-luminescence and other modern dating techniques—have pushed the date for Aboriginal presence in Australia to at least 40,000 years. Others point to 60,000 years. The hallmark of Aboriginal culture is "oneness with nature" and all beings. Prominent rocks, canyons, waterfalls, islands, beaches, and other natural features, as well as sun, moon, visible stars, and animals, have their own stories of creation and interconnectedness. To the traditional Aborigine they are all sacred: environment is the essence of Australian Aboriginal godliness. Out of this deep reverence for nature Aborigines learned to live in remarkable harmony with the land and its animals.

Paban das Baul, one of the Bauls of Bengal, a wandering group of mystical minstrel singers from Bengal, India, once told me at "The Sacred Voices" Festival in London that the Bauls describe the human body as God's "house of song." The great Indian philosopher Hazrat Inayat Khan reminds us that "harmony is the source of all manifestation," unifying earth and heaven *(The Mysticism of Music, Sound and Word, The Sufi Message)*. The unique melody of your soul is a sonorous medicine that resonates through your body temple with a sound map for your life.

Find Your True Voice and Your Life Will Change in Ways You Never Imagined Possible

For more than thirty years I have been facilitating people's discovery of their authentic voices, primarily through their natural sound and singing—that is to say, singing with the intention to transform, not perform. Singing to express, not impress. There is something intrinsic about authentic singing that transcends everyday words. Singing from your soul connects you with a wondrous power inside you. It bypasses the rational mind, opens your heart, and takes you directly to what you most care about in your life.

Singing has an immediate and unpredictable impact. As soon as sound is pouring out of your mouth, you are brought into the present moment, face to face with yourself, and there is nowhere to hide. It's like falling in love. Singing ignites the entire electromagnetic field of your heart, switching on the whole light bulb of the brain, and awakens your soul into a way of being where all and everything is possible. Everyone knows that when you sing, musical vibrations move through you, altering your physical and emotional landscape.

Sound is the invisible music of matter. Your sound is the invisible architecture and geometry of your emotions, expressing the relative resonance or dissonance of your relationship with Earth, humanity, heaven, and the whole universe. Music, as shared by humans, is a delicate arc of audible frequencies that harmonize and unify us, transforming our negative emotions into deeper positive feelings. The musical molecules of our emotions play a significant part in clarifying our perceptions and inspiring caring relationships, thus offering our children a far greater chance of evolving consciously.

Science is trying to explain why singing has such a calming yet energizing and wholesome effect on people. Researchers are beginning to discover that singing relaxes your nerves and lifts your spirits at the same time. The elation may come from endorphins, a hormone released by singing, which is associated with feelings of pleasure. For example, the hormone oxytocin is released during singing, which has been found to alleviate anxiety and stress, and to enhance feelings of trust and bonding, which may explain why a range of research shows that singing lessens feelings of depression and loneliness in significant ways.

TED.com has produced an animated educational video created by Anita Collins and Sharon Colman Graham that demonstrates how music directly affects the instrumentalist's brain:

> Did you know that every time musicians pick up their instruments there are fireworks going off all over their brains? On the outside, they may look calm and focused, reading the music and making the precise and practiced movements required. But inside their brains, there's a party going on. How do we know this? In the last few decades, neuroscientists have made enormous breakthroughs in understanding how our brains work by monitoring them in real time with instruments like FMRi and PET scanners. When people are hooked up to these machines, tasks, such as reading or doing math problems, each have corresponding areas of the brain where activity can be observed. But when researchers got the participants to listen to music, they saw fireworks. Multiple areas of their brains were lighting up at once, as they processed the sound, took it apart to understand elements like melody and rhythm, and then put it all back together into unified musical experience. And our brains do all this work in the split second between when we first hear the music and when our foot starts to tap along. But when scientists turned from observing the brains of music listeners to those of musicians, the little backyard fireworks became

a jubilee. . . . The neuroscientists saw multiple areas of the brain light up, simultaneously processing different information in intricate, interrelated, and astonishingly fast sequences. But what is it about making music that sets the brain alight? The research is still fairly new, but neuroscientists have a pretty good idea. Playing a musical instrument engages practically every area of the brain at once, especially the visual, auditory, and motor cortices. And as with any other workout, disciplined, structured practice in playing music strengthens those brain functions, allowing us to apply that strength to other activities.*

If the brain is activated in these ways when you play a musical instrument, it is activated—all the more so—when you start singing. And it's not just the human brain that is "lit up" by song and sound.

The Song of Your Soul

How do you communicate with your soul? Or more importantly, how does your soul communicate with you? And what part may sound and singing play in these courageous conversations with yourself? You will find out as your voice explores the practices within this book.

The Naked Voice is an experience inviting you to take responsibility for rediscovering the song of your soul, thereby liberating your life and the lives of those around you. You are no longer the singular living organism that you have been calling "me." You are an interconnected community of trillions of living cells called "we." I call this "we" a singing field: a resonant polyphonic field of sound, an electromagnetic vibrating constellation of musical molecules, an omniverse of elemental sounds and frequencies ranging from dense, earthy, and dark to etheric, heavenly, and luminous. Humanity has barely begun to fathom the infinite resources available to us through our "house of song." A new and different language of consciousness, a harmonic resonance, awaits us here.

---

* TED.com URL link: http://ed.ted.com/lessons/how-playing-an-instrument-benefits-your-brain-anita-collins

Melody is the medium within which my soul hears something from your soul, and together we drink water from a secret spring whose current of sound moves immensities inside us, from the marrow of our bones through the singing hairs in our ears, awakening the heart through the music of our emotions while our thinking mind surrenders to a deeper intuition. The nervous system is conductor, the heart is the conduit, and love is the source.

> What was in that candle's light
> that burned and consumed me so quickly?
> Come back my love
> The form of our love is not a created form
> There was a dawn I remember when my soul
> heard something
> from your soul.
> I drank water from your spring
> And felt the current take me
>
> —RUMI (COLEMAN BARKS TRANSLATION)

Responding to the Call

In our world when the emphasis is put on success and all that, the song is rarely heard and all too often forgotten. That's missing the Call . . . On the other hand, if you stay open, you'll not only hear the song, but you'll hear it in its great symphonic composition as you go on . . . behind the surface play of duality. Behind all these manifestations is the one radiance which shines through all things. The function of art [and song] is to reveal this radiance through the created object.

> —JOSEPH CAMPBELL, *An Open Life*

The anthropologist James Cameron once told me of an Australian who knew that one day he would receive "the call" from his Aboriginal forefathers. It would show up as a knock on the door. When that time came he would have to totally surrender his old life and follow his Aboriginal calling. We each have the chance to respond to an essential inner calling. It doesn't have to be as literal as the vocational calling to join a monastic or shamanic tradition. As tempting as those traditions were earlier in my life, the transformative calling I received while in India showed up in more unpredictable ways than my ordinary mind could ever have imagined.

If someone had told me that I was going to have a dream in my early thirties—while sleeping on a beach in Crete—about one of India's greatest woman saints, that I would then travel to India, encounter spiritual and vocal masters, have a life-changing *no-mind* experience, then return to the United Kingdom to record ecstatic love poetry and sacred mantra and world chant while simultaneously bringing up my daughter and pioneering a spiritual school of sound called The Naked Voice, I would have split my sides laughing.

Looking back, I see that the universe was simply responding to my intense hunger for meaning. So it tailor-made an unconventional way of life designed to seize my spiritual longing and shape it into an integrated practice of devotional voice, energy movement, silence, and self-inquiry.

THIS PRACTICE HAS THREE PILLARS:

- Sound Awareness:
  How to live in harmony with your true nature.
- Sound Intelligence:
  How to communicate creatively with conscience.
- Sound Wisdom:
  How to transmit the wisdom of your spirit.

Your voice is a highly effective place to begin exploring your relationship with your own personal calling. The following chapters offer stories, vocal practices, and links to my musical recordings where you can learn a range of simple songs, chants, and anthems to enhance your journey to the source of your very own naked voice.

Whatever form it may take, you can guarantee that your own inner call will certainly turn up in the form of a restlessness followed by questions, either gentle or fierce, that won't leave you alone—questions about who you are, why you are here, and what is the point or purpose of your life. Have you heard your true voice yet? If so, have you found a way to connect with it? If not, how hungry are you to find it?

Consider stopping right now and take a moment to ask yourself: *Who am I? Why am I here? Where does this sound come from? What is it calling for?*

The more we start to inquire who we are and where our sound originates, the more quickly we shift from a self-conscious state, where we are trying to impress others, to a more balanced state, one in which we can listen to ourselves in a nonjudgmental way and express ourselves naturally, authentically, effortlessly.

Many hear the call but ignore or resist it out of a lack of trust or confidence. Many others never get the chance to respond to the call at all, due to circumstances literally beyond their control: natural disasters, political oppression, poverty. There are of course those remarkable individuals who wake up and respond to the leadings of their true voice with a conscience and a courage that arises from the adversity of their upbringing. Many others are born in supportive circumstances, yet due to the seduction of consumerism, greed, and false needs, they don't bother to question who they are or what they truly want. Some people begin to seek out a more conscious way of life but then give up due to fear, self-doubt, social opposition, obsessive insecurity, loss of face, and loneliness.

A growing number of people are responding to the call of an authentic life and will travel a long way along the line. However, they may well withdraw at a critical moment in their evolution, sabotaging their quest due to a powerful and primal fear of *visibility*. We seem to naturally recoil from standing up against all odds for what we believe, from the willingness to take responsibility for what's going on, from embodying the truth. Are we afraid of what we want most?

There remains a relatively small yet growing number of people who are hearing the call for an evolutionary consciousness and who are following it unswervingly, regardless of the consequences. I have heard it said that this growing number of human beings has been "wired" or programmed differently from the majority of humanity that remains hypnotized by the lure of entropy. The conscious "breed" of human beings knows they certainly cannot follow the status quo. They have absolutely no choice but to discover the essential awareness skills and conscious communication tools that will enable them to embody and voice values and ways of living based on the emerging new paradigm.

How I Found My Voice

What is this river, calling me home?

—"This River," *Contemplative Devotion*

Early Years

I have long had a love affair with sound and silence. My early life was influenced by a period of partial deafness following an unsuccessful operation on my tonsils at the age of four. This, together with some other life-threatening illnesses in my early teens, ignited a life-long fascination with the essential role that our whole voice plays as a catalyst for true communication.

As a questioning teenager and student at secondary school, I first happened upon the delights of shared sound and song when I volunteered to conduct our annual inter-form singing competitions. Performative singing was regarded by my peers as being a soft inferior pastime, or too specialist for access. It was therefore left in the hands of a minority group of "classical singer" trainees. However, this more informal singing project became the highlight of an otherwise lackluster school life. Following a near-death bout of pneumonia during which I was taken away from school for several months, I had lost interest in academic life. It was the annual singing competition that gave me a temporary sense of pleasure and purpose each year, as I galvanized thirty "nonmusical" teenagers to sing in exquisite multipart harmonies, astonishing the ears of all our teachers.

Choral singing was one of the greatest joys in my childhood. I later studied music and education at Cambridge University, and had by then decided to change the world through music. As a trained music-drama teacher, my first job was in one of north London's most dangerous city schools, where my predecessor had been stabbed. This first teaching year was enough to deflate all hopes of changing anything within the school environment. The complex politics, the excessive focus on rational thinking, rote learning, and competition, together with the low status given to music education were devastating for me. To maintain my sanity while there, I directed and conducted a Choral Music Festival, bringing together hundreds of young children from twelve multicultural schools in North London.

My marriage soon took me away from London to a music teaching job as second-in-command of a dynamic music department at a school in a deprived area of Bristol. There, despite a positive head of music and an extremely well-resourced music department, the focus was primarily on training an elite minority of instrumental musicians in theory, harmony, and performance. I resigned from this position to seek more effective contexts for the empowering application and use of voice and sound beyond the confines of music as entertainment and performance.

Peace Education

I left formal music teaching altogether in the early eighties to explore the deeper structural and institutional issues that were somehow preventing the effective use of creative music-making *for everyone* in schools. To achieve this aim I realized that I would have to create an entirely new approach if I was to actually change an educational system that prioritized competitive academic study at the expense of in-depth experiential learning inspired by creative expression through music, drama, and the arts.

I cofounded The Avon Peace Education Project in Bristol in 1982. Our goal was to provide supportive contexts for secondary school children and teachers to explore issues of peace and conflict together. We introduced vocal and choral techniques, spoken and sung voice to assist in conflict resolution, mediation initiatives, and other nonthreatening ways in which teachers and pupils could learn to listen to each other cooperatively without judgment.

The intensity of this change-making was becoming exhausting, and my own musical life had taken a back seat. I realized I needed to nourish myself by focusing more on my own singing expression once more. So I began to look out for voice trainings that could help me develop a more embodied and spontaneous relationship with my voice than my classical choral upbringing had provided. North Indian voice teacher Gilles Petit and Cumbrian natural voice teacher Frankie Armstrong came to my rescue, urging me to let go and unleash a passion in my voice across the whole vocal and emotional range.

I was thirsty for a new understanding that I couldn't find in my own Western culture. So I traveled to India in search of deeper ways to integrate my spirit through voice and sound. I began to study the ancient vocal philosophy and musical styles of India. This was a groundbreaking moment in my life, as I realized that Indian culture regarded the human voice as the supreme musical instrument of the human spirit. As I inquired more deeply I began to meet spiritual masters of *advaita*, or nonduality, a Sanskrit word translated as "not separate" or "not two." These spiritual teachings, together with classical Indian vocal music, provided me with both a self-inquiry and a singing practice that I had been searching for all my life. I began to discover how singing as self-inquiry could instill a quality of intention and concentration, leading to a depth of devotion that opened my heart into a direct experience of oneness or peace through the subtle musical mastery of the emotions.

In 1990, while in India, I felt a deep union within me that shattered my old self-identity, opening the doors ever wider to the potential of sound, voice, and silence as a spiritual practice and a direct way to embody and express my whole self.

From Me to We

From the unity experience in India, I began to understand the powerful role that our authentic voice can play in liberating the struggling rational mind from the negative dispersion of reactive thought and feelings of separateness. On my return to the UK I founded a voice-training program called The Naked Voice, which later became The Naked Voice Charitable Foundation, which aimed to help people from all areas of life find their authentic voice, through a direct experience of wholeness, and to express it courageously and compassionately in the world. The Naked Voice has since become an international community for workshops, seminars, and interactive musical events.

For thirty years, I have facilitated thousands of individuals and groups worldwide. They sound, chant, and sing in ways that shift attention from a reactive and separate "me-first" way of communicating to an all-inclusive "we-centered" existence. I now provide online individual sessions, called voice lines, along with vocal seminars, trainings, and in-depth retreats that inspire ways to build positive sound values at an individual, local, and global level. Over the last two decades, The Naked Voice has grown into an international community of practitioners, facilitators, and collaborators who are bringing its principles and practices into the home, workplace, health and healing centers, hospices, and educational, medical, religious, and corporate institutions.

Many people who have experienced the life-changing power of their own authentic voice share with me the sheer JOY of expressing themselves freely without self-sabotage. They are often startled by how much simpler it is than they anticipated. It is as simple as breathing. Once found, it relaxes your mind, reduces stress, opens your heart, and inspires practical, mindful, and courageous ways to give voice and live in the world. The naked voice has gracefully and gradually revealed its gifts to me over the years, enabling me to share these gifts with others like you. They offer many blessings, most notably a place of inner sanctuary supported by an alchemy of self-inquiry, healing breath-work, deep listening, energy movement, devotional chanting, spontaneous utterance, and multipart singing. These practices constellate into a conscious-communication tool kit that opens the portal to the full spectrum of human consciousness: total aliveness and presence in every cell of your being. That presence brings a remembrance of the true inheritance that is yours to receive.

If you walk with me down this path, you will soon find yourself breathing deeper, relaxing, and sounding out in ways that you never imagined possible. With committed practice and determination, your naked voice can unearth that language of wisdom inside you, older and deeper than the polarity of all conflict. Yet conflict is a welcome component and catalyst of your vocal adventure into the deepest seams of your creative life. Conflict is, after all, the essence of all music. Without conflict there is no music, no resonance, dissonance, chaos, no inner-outer relationship, harmonic resolution, no push and pull, no engagement with the interconnected sonic web of life that we are. So whether you are meditating alone, diving deep into a challenging soul friendship, meeting an intimate stranger on the bus, or communicating with an audience of thousands, your naked voice is always present, ready to share the unique melody, rhythm, soul song, and essence of your being. The naked voice is your birthright, your unique language, and your prerogative. It is the sound of your self—prior to religion, politics, and law—ready to reveal to you the whole of your life as music.

Sound Principles

Omnipresent Sound

I am, you are, we are, the whole world and this omniverse we inhabit is sound. This eternal sound is forever arriving from and returning to its source: silence. Its source is unchanging: stillness, the realm of the unmanifested world. This sound has no beginning or end. It is timeless and all-pervading. Its one singular note is the bridge between our visible and invisible, audible and inaudible worlds. It is the vibration and resonance of being itself. This one unchanging note is the source of all sounds, vibrations, rhythms, and resonances. Its presence is prior to all thought. For the most part we have forgotten to listen to this original sound-before-sound, and so we have lost connection with ourselves and the source of our existence. This unchanging sound awakens our remembrance of who we are. Self-remembrance enables us to listen to ourselves and others with unconditional ears without fear. Such deep listening calms the nervous system and emotional body and is the fastest, most efficient way to bypass the rational mind and bring you home to source. This omnipresent sound of oneness, nonduality, is the bedrock of your naked-voice experience.

Silence: The Unstruck Sound

Sound has an inextricable relationship with silence. Without silence there is no sound. In Indian music philosophy, silence is described as "the unstruck sound." This *unstruck sound* is a dynamic living presence, and it calls for immense respect and reverence within all music and soundmaking. Silence plays a central role in bringing the vocalist into an intimacy with his or her own unique sound. Silence is the source of your sound, or *shabdha brahma,* Sanskrit for "inner sound."

Sound as Polarity

As your sound awareness and listening practice deepen, you will become increasingly sensitive to the many changing voices of your inner-outer life. You will become more aware of the juxtaposition between the conditioned and unconditional universe you live in. You inhabit a world of duality made up of corresponding or opposing forces: light and dark, particle and wave, happy and sad, active and receptive, absolute and relative, empty and full, masculine and feminine, vertical and horizontal. Life is a dance. As you learn to navigate these apparently *opposing* forces of existence with increasing awareness, you will discover them to be *complementary.* For example, it is possible to express yourself passionately about an issue or activity as well as be entirely free of attachment to its outcome. This koan of living in duality and oneness *simultaneously* strengthens, releases, sustains, and ultimately liberates us to embrace our lives and communicate with each other in balanced, creative ways.

Sound Awareness and Self-Acceptance

As your appreciation of silence deepens, your self-observing mind or *witness consciousness* will also strengthen within you. As that happens you will find that your reactive mind calms down, and you will begin to be more accepting of everything going on around you with a spacious awareness that dissolves the usual obsessive emotional identification with your choices, decisions, and general "doership." This new sound awareness brings an all-inclusive acceptance of what is occurring. We are not born with this nonjudging sound awareness. However, it is a wisdom that we can learn and develop with loving concentration. Your witness consciousness transforms outworn communication patterns based on an "us-them" and "right-wrong" divisive reality into an expressive and cocreative awareness that honors and interacts with all the voices involved in an embodied and grounded way. The witness consciousness is a largely forgotten wisdom on planet Earth. Yet without it there is little chance for the creative and conscious resolution of conflict. Without the witness, we constantly fall victim to the reactivity of our negative emotions, with little hope of transforming them into deeper positive human feelings. Hence the destructive plight of individuals, communities, and nations.

Sound of Discernment

The questions "Who am I?" and "Who Sings?" are two everyday mantras that magically shift our attention into a deeper self-inquiry, focusing our awareness to a reality far greater than the tight shoe of our mind could ever imagine. Discernment is the fruit of the self-observing mind. The witness consciousness brings a compassionate listening that ignites an effortless wisdom. Learning to discern which voices are true, what is their nature (instinctual, intuitive, or insightful), as well as the motivation driving them is key for authentic sound and voice work. Discernment ignites a depth of listening and sound awareness, anchored in the unchanging sound, that is capable of interacting courageously with all the moods, modes, and music of our emotional dramas.

There is often an experience in hearing your true voice for the first time: that an old outworn self-identity is dying, and this can be terrifying to let go of. Yet once your naked voice is heard, everything changes. Old wounds begin to surface and heal, the sky of the mind begins to clear. You find yourself standing in the presence of something far greater than you ever imagined. Your sound awareness accesses the unfathomable spirit within: the song of your soul.

Wonder is an experience of life often associated with the innocence of childhood, or the early stages of first love. Yet your true or naked voice expresses an ageless and loving aliveness. Wonder connects you with the most essential vibration and resonance of your being. Its eternal magic can be ignited, harnessed, and explored through the many sounds and voices of our emerging naked song.

Your naked voice is a universal inheritance. It does not therefore derive from one single religion, system, doctrine, or political path. On the contrary, your naked voice derives from an inner security that is grounded, confident, and intentional. Awakening and embodying your true voice catalyzes a bubbling aliveness within you. Your naked voice is rooted in the wisdom of uncertainty. And from the music of this uncertainty arises the fearless music of your heart, no longer driven by a love of power and domination, but by the power of love and compassion.

Conflict is an essential, life-generating force in the evolution of conscious communication with self and others. Conflict is the impassioned music of the human heart. Without conflict there is no music, no life-force, no energy, no melodic flow, rhythm, or harmony happening in our relationships. Once heard and engaged with for what it is, the conflicts we face can reveal within their own dissonance the deeper music of their true resonance. Your naked voice will introduce you to masterful and musical ways to express, harness, and navigate your emotional conflicts in unexpected and nourishing ways.

Sound as a Healing Medicine

Your naked voice is a healing medicine, transforming the melodies of your negative emotions into deeper positive feelings, always nourishing and restoring your singing soul.

Your naked voice is uninterested in the obsessions of your ego or personality voice except to the degree that your personality's many voices are willing to become the wrathful deities of the soul, challenging you to change and to grow. The holy fool is an essential ingredient of your sound playtime. It invites you to drop your outworn masks of respectability and let go the entire control panel of your mind; to slough off all the cozy agonies that defend your precious isolated life; and finally, to face the intense hunger and longing that has been driving you toward the one who has been loving you all your lives—your very own self.

As you learn to listen and to express your true sound—and the feelings of your soul—you begin to access ways to navigate your own depths and the voices of your unconscious, through the inner music that you find there. This deepening work is one of grist, revelation, and grace. The initial experiments with your voice bring you into direct touch with the *emotional grist*—the musical moods and modes of your soul. The vocal exercises and movement practices bring *gradual revelation* through repeated practice and the commitment to a direct "gnostic" encounter with the fire and fierce wisdom that is your naked voice. This encounter will awaken a relationship with every sound you utter, from the deepest darkest vulnerability to the lightest expression of ecstasy: that is pure *grace*.

Your naked-voice practices will provide personal, interpersonal, and transpersonal opportunities to activate and restore the universal power of sound as a force that transcends old frontiers and boundaries driven by separatist thinking and instead cocreates new communication structures and a language of consciousness accessed by the inner music of the human soul.

Your naked voice, like your very breath, arises from a realm that we cannot name. Who gave us our breath, our life? From nothing we arise, and to nothing we return. This understanding is the silent ground from which your naked-voice sound appears and disappears.

Our sound brings us home to the transforming edge of who we are, where naked voice becomes naked awareness.

Transform Your Listening

Sound Awareness

Chapter 1

Your Secret Voice

1.1 Why Silence Matters

And all the while a silent laughter sings,
As wind through an open window saying
Be deeper still
Be deeper still
Sound from zero

      —"Zero," *Fierce Wisdom*

D eep unconditional listening is the foundation stone of an embodied authentic voice. In Part I of this book you discover ways to
listen to yourself from a stillness within that relaxes your rational mind
and calms your nervous system. This quality of listening will activate a
faculty of attention called the *witness,* in which you learn how to hear
and observe yourself without judgment. Witnessing opens your heart-
mind to a deeper self-inquiry as you let go of old attachments and discover your original sound, prior to social conditioning.

Silence visits our lives in so many ways. Some experience silence as "golden." Others find it austere and even frightening. There are so many silences: the silence of lovers embracing for the first time, the silence of a young child blowing dandelion clocks into the wind, the silence of the student in the examination room, the suppressed silence of the prisoner in jail, the luminous silence of the mystic in rapture, the courageous silence of the dissident, the armored silence of the victim of trafficking, the silent determination of the nonviolent activist, the austere silence of the old yogi who has been standing on one leg for the last seventy years.

There are contemplative beings all over the world right now sitting, standing, or walking in silence, dedicated to a lifetime of silence on the mountain, in the monastery, in conscious community, or wandering the world. These are silent beings we will never see, yet their silence activates a wondrous power whose life force is humming throughout humanity, streaming out across the globe and through the cosmic web of all life. This silence is a universe without words singing inside you.

> No utterance at all, no speech no sound that anyone can hear
> Yet their voice goes out through all the earth
> And their message to the ends of the world
>
> —*The Jerusalem Bible*, PSALM 19: VERSE 2

To access the silence of your contemplative heart you have to learn to listen with new ears—ears that are free of negative judgment, self-doubt, or fear. This listening establishes a lightning rod of attention within you, focused on one thing only: your naked voice, the sound of who you truly are.

Silence is not a passive blank realm. To access its depths requires first and foremost a respect for it, and more deeply a hungry longing for it and for the real sound within it, which passes all understanding.

To *be silence* we have to fully inhabit and be totally at home in our body-mind, at peace with ourselves, well-rooted like a tree or mountain. And then, from here, we begin to discover what it means to literally accept, embrace, and *be* who we are once again, sounding our truth, the original song of our spirit.

Silence is at the heart of The Naked Voice. In our retreats together, shared silence opens and closes the day. Silence is a unifying presence interconnecting all the spoken and sung practices. Breath work and meditative movement awaken the silent heart. Its presence instills our work with an inclusive awareness beyond reactive or rational thought. Silence deepens our self-awareness, dissolving separatist thinking, communications, and agendas.

This silence brings a natural mindfulness and spacious presence that interweaves its invisible music through all our practices. True silence constantly awakens the unifying presence of oneness inside every human heart. Silence is a sovereign presence, akin to the "zero point field" of quantum physics pervading the whole of life. . . . The silence I refer to here is not conditioned or unconditioned. It is not confined within the limits of time or space. This is pure and simple a dynamic silence, and in the words of quantum scientist David Bohm, an "undivided wholeness." Its invisible power is fueling the living matrix of Life. I call this silence *the unchanging note.* Life is such a great mystery, and there are many reasons why we may suddenly be struck dumb, silenced by inner-outer circumstances. Speechlessness can be another way into the dynamic silence within you.

Do you remember the last time you were stopped in your tracks, disoriented for a moment and dislodged from the meanderings of your habitual mind, struck dumb, literally silenced by the unexpected? Maybe it was an "Aha!" moment of truth in which you were shaken into the immediacy of the present moment, quickened by sheer grace or beauty in front of you. It may have been a sudden awakening to a new love, the birth of a child, a near-death experience, a shocked remembering out-of-the-blue of something very precious to you, or simply the transforming gaze of a wise being sitting opposite you in the metro. In that moment you find yourself lost for words, beyond words. Words are simply inadequate to communicate this new vibration coursing through your veins, this radical aliveness that is silence.

Meanwhile an uncontrollable smile simply keeps shifting across your radiant face, re-shaping and shape-shifting your taken-for-granted reality, as you sit in a spacious and graceful encounter with silence.

Silence is an anchor that enables me to practice *being nowhere*. Being nowhere means *doing absolutely nothing*—not thinking, not moving, not doing anything at all. Simply *being* is a way to undo old habits, and is a very enjoyable practice. It has much to offer our crazy obsession with doing, living as we do in this *doership*-identified world. Being, or nondoing, is an awareness we can develop beyond all our conceptual thinking. And that is just what we will continue to un-do in the coming pages, through my personal stories of deep listening, together with the vocal practices that will invoke a deeper listening in you.

With being there are no maps. Being still inside and self-aware means we are awake in such a way that we are no longer identified with our fleeting rational thoughts and feelings. Rather, we are simply receptive to *what is,* moment by moment. Being still inside we are at home, in harmony with a wondrous invisible power that connects every beautiful cell in our body-heart-mind. This power moves like a fine gossamer of pure being, seamlessly flowing through every in-and-out breath, every thought, every decision, and every action.

To *be-come* a conscious human *be-ing* is to fully accept, embrace, and express everything that you are. Silence can be your teacher in this self-discovery.

Sound Awareness—A Listening Exercise

What is the deep listening? A message from the secret ones inside. . . .
I would sell my tongue and buy a thousand ears when that one steps
near to the center of my chest and begins to speak.

—Rumi, Coleman Barks translation
(from *The Glance*)

The best way to begin hearing, exploring, and *being* silence is to sit, lie down, or stand in silence for, say, 3, 5 or 10 minutes. During this chosen time simply relax, watch, listen, and accept everything that is happening within and around you—all activity, thoughts, sounds arising in your inner-outer mind—with no attachment or any agenda, and no attempt to respond to or to judge what you hear, feel, or see. If it helps, simply ask yourself now and again, "Who is listening? Who is breathing? Who is thinking?" And accept whatever comes, and then let it go again.

Here begins the deep listening journey to the source of your sound.

1.2 Self Inside Self

You are nothing without me
Self inside Self, I am only you
What we are together
Will never die

—"Self Inside Self," *Sura*

Where were you most at home as a child? And what was your relationship with sound and silence then? I used to spend as much time as I could alone in Nature from a very early age. My parents called it "running away." I ran away from home as soon as I could open and close the front door of our vicarage, which was conveniently positioned beside the church and the river beyond. My mother tells me that I started these escapes around the age of four. My parents had erected a chicken-wire fence in the front drive to ensure that my three sisters and I were protected from the main road.

My mother tells of how she watched me find the place where the chicken wire began, painstakingly unhook it from top to bottom, step to the other side, reconnect the wires, and set off! The river was only a few yards away, and down a little bridge. I loved crossing the bridge and letting the waters pass under me. Then I would skip across to the other side and wander off to play with the insects and flowers along the bank. I also remember a family of lizards that I used to spend hours affectionately poking and playing with. They lived under an old flag-stone in the churchyard. My parents eventually had to employ a young woman whose specific task was to ensure that I did not disappear. She often had difficulty tracking me down. My desire to be alone was not, as far as I was aware, a deliberate attempt to be a nuisance. I just had to explore the world around me.

Once I was no longer able to explore beyond the front of the house, I focused my explorations on the back garden. Nature woke me up to the sound of silence as it appeared and disappeared between bird or animal sound, the wind in the trees, and so on. There was the sap rising up and oozing out through the brown craggy bark of the yew tree; the warmth of a nest hollowed out in tall green grasses; the soft pink furry place inside the ear of my white rabbit; the hot breath that poured from the nostrils of my sister's pony.

So it was in Nature that I first experienced the "presence," the dynamic atmosphere of silence, an experience that intoxicated my attention, connecting me with all things magical in the *now*. I have a distinct memory of diving into my favorite spinney of trees when I was five. There was a lot of undergrowth, and everything was once again new and mysterious to the touch for a novice explorer. I clambered over brambles and fallen branches. It was sheer bliss sinking myself into this wilderness world of greenness—ferns, nettles, spongy moss, earth, snails, and slippery bark. A soft morning light filtered through the leaves. Such quietness here. To the adult world, this was probably an insignificant place, but for me it was a secret space in which to be free and let my imagination flow undisturbed. I remember stopping suddenly when a sharp ray of light directed my gaze downward. Then a bright sound pierced the air. I found myself staring at a large brown bird, a song thrush, with a spotted underbelly. She blinked at me, and sang again. The sound was arresting. How was it that her eyes, her song, could evoke such a silence in me? I had never seen or heard anything like this before. We were one, hypnotized by each other in a moment of union between bird, child, sunlight, and sound.

From that moment, listening became my great love. But then, a tragedy: following a mishandled tonsillectomy, I became partially deaf. My hearing was temporarily impaired, and my listening experience turned inward. My focus shifted to my inner sound as the external world became a blurred muzak that was challenging to engage with for a few years. I became so preoccupied by my own inner world that I have little recollection of what "happened" to me in the everyday world, or how I made my way through home and school life. It was a temporary exile from my childhood adventures. I lived in a self-contained dream for much of the time, a cocoon in which the silent inner music I could hear taught me a new language of listening for which the outer world had no words. My inner voice began to take precedence over external events.

Consequently, I was constantly admonished at school for not concentrating and for dreaming too much. It was awkward to be placed at the front of the class, unnaturally close to the teacher so that I could hear her more easily, and yet her teaching content and methods failed to capture my attention. My deafness was possibly a valuable protection from the tediousness of school life and early conditioning. My form teacher was an angry old stick. I preferred the warmth and the flow of my own inner world to the exasperating staccato of her lessons. My mother eventually took me out of school until my hearing was restored. Yet my dreamy nature intensified as I grew older. I would constantly forget external time-consciousness, arriving late to school and late to lessons. I remember my French teacher laughing derisively as she made me apologize several times in French, in front of the class, for being late. My last school report from her read "too late to make up for the wasted years."

These apparently negative qualities of mine certainly impaired my success at school. But what was it all about—the rote learning and regurgitation of facts onto paper, facts about other people's lives, mainly men, who had lived, gone to war, conquered or been defeated, and died? What was all this about, this absurd process called education? Why was there no room for the natural joy of being alive that I had known from my earliest years? Why was the love of life not conveyed through the teachers' enthusiasm for their field of study? Miss Knupffer, my Russian-language teacher, came to my rescue when I was fourteen. She was an exile living in London. She had known the suffering of homelessness and rejection, the plight of the refugee. Her dark brown eyes used to pierce my questing mind as she poured the language of her Russian soul into mine with an intensity that I had never experienced before. The passion in her voice captured my attention. "You will achieve excellence in what you love," she told me. She was in love with the complex beauty of her native tongue. Her dedication to communicating its rich meanings to us absorbed the whole of her tiny high-wired body and held us all spellbound. She was a dedicated teacher of high aspirations. Her presence filled the room, and the intensity of her passion was an echo for the life I could feel in my own veins.

Throughout these years of family demands and academic expectations, a deeper voice was always calling me back to itself, the song of my soul. In the spheres of social standing such as achievement, career, and material success, this inner voice was of little significance. Yet its non-verbal presence continued to nourish and sustain me. For many years I listened to this voice in secret. It had no outer expression. I simply knew that it inhabited me, that I trusted it, that it was my lifeline, generating within my soul the longing for meaning. It was difficult to speak about it as a child. As a teenager, I tried to do so with my mother, and she likewise tried to understand this experience of an inner music circulating through my blood, which would fill me with a natural joy and leave a smile on my face. No wonder my grandfather called me "Smiler."

Did You Have a Secret Voice? A Reflective Practice

What are your memories of the first sounds of childhood?

How did your experience of your own inner sound or voice evolve through your childhood, teenage years, and adulthood?

What does your inner child have to share with you now? What is it telling you?

1.3 Be Without Leaving Yourself

Beloved source by your grace I am alive
—"Beloved Source," *Naked Heart*

As you learn to anchor your awareness more deeply in silence, you will discover a stillness within you from the source of sound itself. This stillness invokes a state of peace or presence where you can begin to hear yourself with fresh, openhearted ears. What might it be like to cross the threshold of obsessive doership and enter a more effortless way of *being*?

The great twentieth-century luminary and teacher of nonduality Ramana Maharshi inspired me with his words: *"Be without leaving yourself."* I was visiting his spiritual community in India in the late 1980s. While staying there, I made the daily pilgrimage up Arunachala Mountain to the holy cave where Ramana had been found in a transcendent state of pure being and bliss. The story goes that, as a young boy, his yearning to understand the nature of his existence and who he truly was became so intense that he finally discovered, in his mid-teens, how to literally leave his body, to physically die, and to return to his body once again. This miraculous happening compelled him to leave his family home and lead an itinerant life as an awakened being, wandering the countryside in a permanent state of pure consciousness. He was eventually found in an immobile state of profound silent meditation in Virupaksha Cave on Arunachala Mountain. Ramana was brought down the mountain, and an international spiritual community (ashram) flourished around him, dedicated to realizing Ramana's teachings on *advaita,* nondualism, and the embodiment of oneness. Ramana Maharshi became a spiritual magnet for an ever-expanding field of inquirers in search of the unifying secret art of *being without leaving yourself.* It was not long after I left Arunachala that I encountered one of Ramana Maharshi's successors, called Poonjaji, whose radical embodiment and transmission of the art of being was life-changing for me.

It is challenging in this super-noisy world of interactive technology, traffic, timetables, and everyday bustle to sustain a consistent and integrated flow of communication between one's inner and outer lives. How often do you give yourself the opportunity (or challenge) of taking some time off from your busy schedules and deadlines to let go of the noisy chatter of life—even for five, ten, or fifteen minutes—to give some attention to who you are, right now, in this moment, prior to the automatic thinking that is whirring away inside you and all around you?

The tendency is to resist this deeper connection with ourselves, assuming that to achieve it we need a peaceful or "special" place, a "sacred space," away from our home or working life. But this is not so. The danger in thinking that we need a special place or silent meditation retreat away from it all to find our true voice can mean that we ignore our deeper call for meaning, and instead we forge an ongoing disconnection between our everyday self and our innermost truth.

Yet your interaction with who you are is a 24-7 relationship, from birth to death. You are consciously or unconsciously in conversation with yourself, whether you choose to be aware of it or not. Throughout your waking and sleeping hours, the interconnected web of life ebbs and flows.

So why not lighten up your attachment to the habitual needs of your personal identity for a moment and give yourself the experience of simply being with yourself, either sitting or walking, while your everyday world buzzes on all around you. Just allow a small piece of time now to *be* without leaving yourself.

Be Without Leaving Yourself Practice

Simply stop looking outward, right now, no matter what is going on around you. Let it go and focus your attention inward. Breathe, smile, and listen to yourself, without judging who and where you are right now. Whether you are in your office, kitchen, car, a café, on a bus, or walking down the noisy street, don't separate yourself from what is around you, nor get involved either. Simply allow everything to be as it is while you are as you are.

Feel your feet connecting with the floor, close your eyes if comfortable to do so; or if you are walking keep your eyes open while lowering them so that you can focus your attention primarily on your own body field and the immediate environment.

Be aware of the connection between your feet and the ground, and also the presence of the earth beneath you, supporting your feet beneath the floor or pavement. As you extend your awareness from your body onto the presence of planet Earth beneath, become aware of the sounds of the Earth all around you. Accept everything: the sounds of people's voices, the elements, traffic, and all other noise. Let it all be there, without getting attached to it or pushing it away. Just be there with it, exactly as it is.

Now take a deep breath and smile. Say to yourself, "I am here and everything and everyone is exactly as they are right NOW." Simply watch your inflowing and outgoing breath without changing it. Notice where you are breathing from—your belly, your chest, or your head—without forcing it to change. Feel how you feel without changing it in any way. Enjoy letting go of whatever is occurring on the outside, and continue to bring your awareness inward to your own breath, its sound. Begin to investigate how your breath is faring. Is it short and fast? Is it slow and almost nonexistent; is it deep and warm or withheld and cold? Are you feeling out of breath, with a tendency toward hyperventilating? Just notice it all and enjoy listening and accepting as you strengthen your sound awareness—that is to say, an awareness of yourself and your well-being—in the midst of the sounds around you and within.

What we are beginning to build is a quality of attention called the witness, a faculty of nonjudgmental self-observation. We are not born with it, but we can learn to develop it by restoring our loving attention to our most neglected sense: hearing. Begin to strengthen your powers of nonjudgmental listening supported by the following breathing exercise.

Breathe Without Leaving Yourself Practice

This lovely little breathing meditation was introduced to me by the Vietnamese Buddhist teacher Thich Nhat Hanh at his community of Plum Village in France. Each time you breathe in or out, hear the following words inwardly. Everything is said internally to oneself.

1st cycle:	Breathe In—(inside say) "IN."	Breathe Out—say "OUT."
2nd cycle:	Breathe In—say "DEEP."	Breathe Out—say "SLOW."
3rd cycle:	Breathe In—say "CALM."	Breathe Out—say "EASE."
4th cycle:	Breathe In—say "SMILE."	Breathe Out—say "RELEASE."

After a while, this breathing practice becomes second nature. Enjoy. It's fun, simple, and highly effective in creating more of a seamless flow between your inner and outer life. Again, in brief:

IN, OUT—DEEP, SLOW—CALM, EASE—SMILE, RELEASE

Most important, on the fourth and final out-breath, "Release," let yourself breathe out as long as feels comfortable, and let your mind relax and listen. Don't rush to breathe in again. In the outward breath let the tide of your life go right out, and just silently hear the words "Present Moment." Notice what you hear, how you feel, and don't get involved—simply watch, listen, and be with whatever is occurring as you (increasingly with practice) hold a benign disinterest.

Return to everyday life. Simply notice how this breathing meditation practice begins to deepen your awareness of the sound of your voice, the space between your words, the silence that pervades all your conversations, and how you communicate with your family or partners, colleagues or friends, or even strangers in the street. The sound of the wind or rain can be a trigger to expand your awareness, releasing mental tension and restoring whole-body attention to the wider and deeper context of your life.

Whenever you have a moment, return to this simple breathing practice. It is a way to start becoming present to yourself in your body, and being at home in the world around you without the usual desire to analyze, interpret, praise, blame, or in any way separate yourself from your self or the world around you.

1.4 Wake Up Your Witness

I am not I, I am this One
standing beside me whom I do not see.

—"I Am Not I," *Naked Heart*

In my mid-thirties, while I was seeking out deeper ways to embody and express my true voice, I was introduced to a remarkable man named Salim Michael. A British-born Asian and a master of inner sound, Salim lived in Paris and had written a book called *The Way of Inner Vigilance* for the benefit of his small band of committed students and for what he described as an "agonizing humanity" who had "lost contact altogether with the sacred."

As I began to absorb his teachings I found myself in the presence of a man who had dedicated his life to a rigorous process of self-inquiry. Salim's insights were accompanied by specific practices, each revealing direct and accessible ways to live in the present moment in the midst of everyday life. Here's an example of one of his very practical yet challenging exercises:

> Pay attention to the sensation in your left elbow, at a specific time past the hour, four times a day.

His precise instructions required immense self-discipline, offering the committed practitioner the opportunity ultimately to achieve self-liberation, a state of total freedom from the tyranny of the reactive mind.

What inspired me most about Salim's approach was the priority given to the meditative art of listening and speaking, and most notably his summary presented in *The Yoga of Listening to the Sound of One's Voice*. This had direct relevance for the sound and voice-work that I had just begun with individuals and groups in my local community. In his words from *The Way of Inner Vigilance*:

> Contrary to the demands of a terrestrial existence which compels a person to remain in a constant state of movement and agitation (thus concealing his Divine nature from him) the aim of meditation and yoga . . . is gradually to arrive at an inner condition permitting a very particular inward slowing up to take place in oneself—until a state of profound immutability is reached in which the reality of one's Supreme Being is finally recognized. . . . Among various methods of meditation practiced in ancient India to this end is a very important one called NADA YOGA, YOGA OF SOUND.

I was captivated. I read on:

A most demanding and difficult exercise for a speaker is to learn constantly to listen to the sound of his/her voice when speaking to people. This is not as easy to achieve as it may seem, and calls for the utmost effort of will and inner strength if s/he wishes to succeed.

These words rang loud bells down the corridors of my childhood and upbringing, magnifying memories that I had never allowed myself to face up to before. For example, as an adolescent, I remember being accused of speaking insincerely. As the third and middle daughter, I chose the peacemaker role in our family constellation. So I was became the goofy entertainer, the one who was forever trying to make everything alright. If this didn't work, I would find myself speaking in exaggerated tones of concern and well-being for whomever was the underdog of the moment. This gushing tendency, often shored up by a rush of positive superlatives, would be prompted by anything from a disapproving glance to a helpless gesture of exasperation or a brash critical judgment. I would often go to great lengths to lift and shift the atmosphere in an attempt to lighten anything ominous, dissolving it into thin air with humor. When these tactics didn't work, I would plunge into ever-deeper concern either for, or with, whoever was in trouble, or most misunderstood at the time. While my own emotional body was internally doing its best to navigate the prevailing drama, I would be externally issuing promises of hope, encouraging positive outcomes. Reconciliatory strategies would be my most likely response in hopes of diffusing intensity and quelling my own angst as quickly as possible.

Feelings of low self-worth ran deep, and so whether or not I was the cause of the conflict I would take responsibility for it, feeling guilty and despondent for no explicable reason. If I was the actual cause of the conflict, however slight, I would respond with all the diplomacy that my reasoning could muster.

"Actions speak louder than words" was a memorable statement fired in my direction. Like all children, I was desperate for approval. With three and later four siblings to interact with, life often felt confusing and uncertain. I have no idea how my devoted mother tolerated and responded to our very different needs. We all had to somehow find our own ground, and some of us encountered more difficulty than others. Inside I felt like a loner, largely misunderstood; and on the outside, I became or perceived myself as the stubborn little girl who habitually erred from the straight and narrow. My words became self-protective weapons that shielded my more authentic feelings. This inner-outer struggle gave birth to the resulting *insincere* speak that I was accused of. I used my speech to paper over the cracks. To be ignored or rejected by my family was devastating, and to prevent this, I would often bend over backward with words of praise and admiration to counteract exclusion. This gradually forged an exile of a deeper kind: exile from myself. What could I do, inhabiting a radically different inner universe from much of my outer everyday family world?

Does any of this ring bells for you? My childhood story is no doubt a common one that probably resonates for many readers. In comparison with other more abusive or dysfunctional childhood experiences, mine is relatively harmless. Yet the impact of socio-cultural conditioning upon our own authentic voice and creative life requires for everyone a skillful listening and loving attention if we are to faithfully unravel, forgive, let go, restore, and embody the truth of who we are and how we sound.

Salim Michael's practices in unconditional listening enabled me to start engaging with the residual tension that I still held in my body. Whenever a stream of superlatives leapt from my mouth and into the lap of some unsuspecting person, I took notice.

Salim Michael's *inner vigilance* enabled me to begin letting go of the excessive and unnecessary self-conscious effort that I habitually made in communicating with others. I began to see how this achieved little more than separating myself from others. How could I redeem this verbal crisis? Clearly, speaking was more challenging for me in my early years than singing. Singing gave me a simple, effortless way to access and express my heart and soul—in choirs, at school, in church, and among the wider community. The mental machinery of the critical rational speaking voice was a far more challenging, competitive, and complex proposition. Conversations at family meal times required a sophisticated level of articulation, intellectual knowledge, and wit, none of which I felt well-equipped with. Yet I longed more than anything to express myself and to be heard, to share my love of Nature and everyday life in a simple, undistorted way.

Voice-work was clearly a key in redeeming and transforming these self-conscious, awkward early memories. I could then hand on this skill to others. Salim Michael's vocal and sound awareness offered me a way out of my own maze of self-denial. The first step was to stop judging and criticizing myself. The next was to develop a much stronger witness, a self-observing faculty of attention that could, as he put it:

> Take care . . . not to interfere in any way with the tone of (your) voice, or purposely attempt to change it simply because (you) may not like its intonation, but continue patiently and dispassionately to listen. (You) will then find that (your) voice will, of its own, take on another tone, a special tone, one which will feel astonishingly true, tranquil and natural, corresponding to (your) type and particular nature.

Was it really as simple as that? What a relief. Breathing more deeply, softening the belly, and allowing my throat and facial muscles to relax, I could begin to courageously face the deeper, rewarding impact of interacting, without judgment or manipulation, with the world around me, its light and its shadow. As Salim writes in *The Way of Inner Vigilance:*

> When (you are) with other people, (you) will—if (you are) sufficiently aware of (yourself)—begin to see in them also, simply by the sound of their voices, the same unconscious lies, concealed cunning, false friendliness, and sad inner slavery (you) had observed in yourself.

After reading these words for the first time, I began to look back over my life and remember the thousands of faces and moments, positive and negative: a dejected woman tramp by the Serpentine Lake in London; an African American bus driver singing in a tired, overcrowded bus; courageous, honest conversations with strangers in trains; the disempowering tones of one of my school teachers; cross-wires between my siblings; celebratory voices of my singing peers at school concerts; the velvet soulful sounds of close friends. I recall the empowering sound of the doctor who revived me after a life-threatening illness in my teens; the gentleness of my grandmother Gladys and grandpa Douglas; the exuberance of the women I trained for the Kenya Music Festival in 1971; the resonant wisdom voice of my mentor Archbishop Trevor Huddleston whom I used to visit in London after his return from fighting apartheid with Mandela in South Africa; the warm, welcoming New England voice of my first great love; the groundbreaking oratory of my heroes and life-changers Martin Luther King, Jr., Gandhi, Mother Teresa, Germaine Greer—radical men and women sharing the same path, diverse paths, all of them either warning or encouraging me with their story, my story, our story, all of us in search of an unconditional listening ear and a moment of rest, union, and peace.

Then, I returned closer to my present life and heard the same screams and dreams opening and closing in the voices of my students: individuals searching for something they couldn't name, a longing, a forgotten memory, an ancient voice from afar, a lost jewel that had somewhere along the way been neglected, discarded, and abandoned. Such a long and winding road.

From deep within a voice called out: "All these memories, meetings, relationships. What is it all about? Who am I? Where am I going?"

I cried out like there was no tomorrow.

"Wake up, wake up, wake up! I have to remember the forgotten sound, mine, the sound of who I am. This homesickness of the soul must end NOW." I opened my arms to embrace the widest horizon and uttered one long unfettered cry, and, sighing deeply, returned to Salim Michael's book again:

> (You) can only go by a mysterious inexplicable faith, a subtle conviction and intuitive feeling of the presence within (you) of a distant glittering light buried deep down in the innermost recesses of (your) being, ever calling (you) to turn (your) gaze inward and reach forward to it, as it has always been lovingly reaching out in vain to (you).

Every day I practiced the book's specific meditation, walking, and chanting exercises. Slowly I learned to be receptive to the Nada Yoga, the Yoga of Inner Sound. Salim Michael's sound teachings began to resonate and take effect in my life:

If (you) can be inwardly quiet enough and deeply absorbed in (your) search, (you) will, if (you are) truly persistent, suddenly become aware of an unusual, feeble sound which can be heard deep inside the ears and head, concealed from (you) before and obscured by the din of (your) incessant mental restlessness. When (you) have become aware of the mysterious presence in (you) of this sound (you) may at first be struck with surprise and awe, but no matter how weak or distant it may appear, it will be very obvious that this is no ordinary sound but a mystical one of a higher cosmic order. It could be called the Primordial Sound.

Now I was back on sure ground. Salim Michael went on to explain how it was not enough to have had the grace and privilege of hearing this inner mystical sound. What was more important was how I listened to it, and how much I could remain internally attentive to the "mysterious song of this sacred Nada." Salim described it as a sound with an unearthly sparkle about it, somewhat reminiscent of "the flickering light of a star, oscillating continuously inside one's head." Salim then assured me: "This unusual sound, with its strange vibrations, celestial twinklings and, above all, enigmatic continuity, will become a most precious support for (your) concentration in all future meditations."

As I began to listen this inner sound, I observed that it does have an extraordinarily uninterrupted continuity about it, a crystal-like vibration that resembles the noise of the ocean with many other different sounds superimposed upon it. I soon began to notice that this inner sound was most perceptible on waking in the mornings. Sometimes *it* would awaken me, beginning as a faint sound, like whispering cicadas inside my skull: a constant whispering. Sometimes it would resound as a clearer high-pitched note that would sing in my inner ear. Its volume was at times almost shocking, cutting through conversations, interrupting and literally *sounding through* my habitual thoughts. This inner sound became increasingly familiar as I continued to pay attention and became more conscious of its persistent presence within me. This process introduced a new dimension into my voice teaching.

I finally went to Paris to meet Salim and work with him directly before he died. He used to present me with challenging tasks such as standing in the middle of the room and opening my arms out like a cross. I would have to stay there, arms open for extended periods of time, until I reached a satisfactory state of inner stability. He would then suddenly exclaim: "Abandon yourself!"

The inner freedom he was encouraging me to access could not be accessed by mental thought. I simply had to free myself from all thoughts of past or future or present and abandon myself. Occasionally he would praise my inner skill to surrender everything. Other times, he would simply comment as he witnessed my depth of attention and presence, or lack of it. This practice often seemed interminable, yet it certainly strengthened my inner vigilance as I gradually learned through repeated and direct experience how to let go of imaginary things, in order to liberate a deeper listening that was sourced from an inner state of presence prior to the existence of my rational mind.

Salim's rare and precious insights into the yoga of listening awakened my own witness and harnessed my capacity to access a deeper nonjudgmental listening awareness. My vision was to open up deeper channels of listening and communicating between my body, soul, and spirit, with my spoken and sung voice. I wanted to bring the powerful impact of singing more prominently into everyday communication.

1.5 Where Silence Meets Sound

Listen to the voice inside you
She is waiting to be found
Once you've heard that sound inside you
You will always stand your ground.

—"LISTEN TO THE VOICE," *Thousand Ways of Light*

Grace can intervene in unexpected ways, especially in moments of utter helplessness. A message I received in one such moment was: "Start your own church. It doesn't have to be grand or sophisticated. It can be very simple. Just one room." This startling encouragement came from Mother Osyth Lucie-Smith, the abbess of a Benedictine community near London. The "church" she envisaged was not a religious establishment but a simple meeting place for shared sound and silence as a spiritual practice. This abbess—herself a pianist, poet, and singer—was an inspiring mentor and friend to many. She was a controversial being, a radical visionary and Christian mystic whose depth of being was so profound that she attracted an international stream of seekers from all faiths to visit her contemplative community of Saint Mary's Abbey in Kent. What I loved about this contemplative community was the adventurous, inventive, and courageous spirit in which the sisters shared their vocation. A vast, modern, oval-shaped, resonant chapel was their meeting ground for silent prayer and shared communion. Much of the music and poetic text for the communion liturgy and daily services had been composed and written by the Mother Abbess herself. So it was here that as a young adult I dared myself to explore a deeper connection between silence and my inner-outer voice.

But what did she really mean by "Start your own church"? This seemed unimaginable. I guess I couldn't have imagined that twenty years later, my conversations with this modern-day mystic would evolve not into a church but into a pioneering community of sound. She always spoke in a semi-poetic style that was mildly hypnotic. "Be silent, still, aware, for there in your own heart, the spirit is at prayer." Her low liquid voice spoke slowly and tenderly to me out of a presence that enveloped her. Her brimming aliveness bubbled up from a depth of stillness that flowed effortlessly from the source of her being.

I visited the abbey whenever I could get away from a demanding teaching job. I was still teaching in London at that time, and my retreats at the abbey restored my peace of mind. I began to write music and offer simple breath and vocal exercises for these singing contemplatives. I would meet with the whole sisterhood for an hour or so, in between their services, and they would perform my compositions amidst peals of childlike laughter and delight. The joy that pervaded this meditative community sprang from years of concentrated interior spiritual practice. As I learned to turn my attention inward, I started to listen more deeply and explore the landscape of my own soul. Gradually my heart began to open to the possibility of singing spontaneously and naturally without any intervening musical structure.

It was in their daily communion gatherings that I joined the simplest sharing of love, in a sonorous exchange that dissolved heaven and earth, unifying our spirits. Siegfried Sassoon catches it in this extract from his poem "Everyone Sang":

> Everyone suddenly burst out singing;
> And I was fill'd with such delight
> As prison'd birds must find freedom
> Winging wildly across the white
> Orchards and dark-green fields;
> on and on and out of sight.
> Everyone's voice was suddenly lifted,
> And beauty came like the setting sun . . .

Another tradition that took me further into the uncharted realms of my inner-outer voice was that of the Quakers, a spiritual community founded by Christian ecstatic George Fox, whose "quaking before the Lord" compelled him to break away from conventional religion in the seventeenth century. He rebelled against the religious and political authorities by proposing a more uncompromising "direct experience" of the Christian faith, rooted in contemplative silence. Fox was often persecuted by authorities who disapproved of his ecstatic "quaking" communications with spirit.

Quakers are not solely identified with the Christian faith anymore, although their core values of nonviolent love remain. What inspired me most was their ecumenical silent meetings for worship and their disinterest in creeds and hierarchies. The Quakers I encountered were clearly sincere about living from the wellspring of silence they shared with one another every week. Most empowering for me was the welcome they extended to everyone. And everyone was also invited to "minister," as inspired by the spirit, within the course of the meeting. This involved standing up and sharing your reflections and insights with the whole meeting. This unconditional listening community was not inviting a solo "performance" or entertainment. Nor was it a social discussion—rather, it was more of an evolving meditative dialogue, like waves arising and falling back into the great ocean of silence. The intention for the "ministry" was to punctuate and deepen the silent worship with authentic communication sourced from the soul for the spiritual welfare of all present.

At first, this context seemed an unlikely place for me to express my inner voice. However, I was surprised to discover that after several weeks of silent sitting, my inner voice wanted to join in and "minister," first with spoken words and then, as if out of nowhere, with a spontaneous song. So it was here, in this public place—a Quaker Meeting house—that I first heard, discovered, and sang the songs that started to pour from my soul, as inspired by my inner voice! For the first time I was actively encouraged to share my own inner truth, spoken or sung, naturally, freely, and publicly.

Here was a listening community that was not interested in a display of religious dogma or doctrine. Nor did they invite surface social entertainment. They were actively listening for and encouraging an authentic and in-depth conscious communication, inspired by the direct and spontaneous intervention of spirit.

1.6 Making Your Inner Life Audible

Listen to the secret sound,
Listen to the secret sound
The real sound which is inside of you
The real sound which is inside of you

—"Secret Sound," *Naked Heart*

Discovering your naked voice is like finding a treasure for life. It's as magic as that moment in *The Secret Garden* when the young girl discovers the hidden garden door that transforms her life, or when the children in *The Lion, the Witch, and the Wardrobe* happen upon the passageway that transports them into the magic world of Narnia. Your voice offers that same secret gateway into your own inner life, and from there into a whole new and unexpected dialogue with your one and only self. These communications with God are really conversations— spoken, sung, and silent—with your deep self.

Your voice is freely given at birth and knows instantly—from the moment it expresses its first unfettered cry—how to bridge your needs with your new life on Earth.

Your voice is your natural birthright, and all it asks for is loving respect and attention. Ideally, as you evolve and strengthen through childhood into the teen years and young adulthood, you learn to embody, midwife, and express the full subtlety, depth, and breadth of your feelings, resourced from the rich archives of your inner life. For the majority of people this is sadly not the case. Within the early years of conditioning, your attempts to freely express yourself are often thwarted or distorted.

When embarking upon the process of healing yourself and re-engaging consciously with your true voice, you probably do not necessarily think of using audible sound to access and express your innermost truth. Many people prefer to write their inner thoughts in a journal, and this journal is often marked "private" and rarely shared with anyone. Traditionally most people think things through silently. So you may not have been taught to consider communicating the audibility of your secret thoughts at all! Listening, expressing, really hearing, and acknowledging your sound may well feel awkward for you at first, and I appreciate that I am asking you to undergo a translating process that may feel unusual and is in itself a special enterprise.

I once carried out some market research in a shopping center and asked people how they felt about their voice. Most said they didn't like the sound of their voice. Many had disturbing self-conscious experiences with "singing," either at home or in school. They might have been told to "shut up" or simply to "mouth silently" (in the choir). That simple research with several hundred individuals over two days demonstrated that eight out of every ten people give up on their voice early in life.

But do not be discouraged. Even if, right now, you do not feel qualified for this sonic encounter with yourself, I want you to consider that by giving yourself permission to hear, accept, and enjoy your sound from the inside out, you will start to access and to express your true self and live your life with a confidence in ways that you never imagined possible.

It is also good to remember that you are not alone. For many people, especially in late childhood and teenage years, their voices, along with their self-identity and self-worth, become enslaved by the competitive pressures and mental challenges at school, where there is little outlet for authentic communication and inclusive creative expression beyond primary school age. By secondary school, the voice has become, for many, a factual regurgitator, an everyday workhorse enslaved by the pressures of learning by rote, competitive games, emotional reactivity, and seeking gratification through debate, one-upmanship, egocentric talk, fear-driven language, sarcasm, cynicism, and negative judgment.

This restrictive educational and social training procedure intensifies in adult life where corporate, political, religious, medical, scientific, and other institutional mainstream forces straitjacket our career choices in the struggle against unemployment. The voice of the human soul has meanwhile been long forgotten, left on the scrap heap of unconsciousness, or at best expressed through blurred moments of despair, buoyed up by copious amounts of alcohol at an open mic or karaoke evening.

> Listen if you can stand to
> Union with your self means
> Not being who you have been
> Being instead silence, a place, a view,
> Where language is inside seeing
>
> —RUMI, COLEMAN BARKS TRANSLATION

For many centuries now in the West, the human singing voice has been severed from its natural harmonizing role within community life. It has been made the prerogative of an elite minority group of trained musicians, solely for performance and entertainment purposes. We often hear that there are "singers" and "nonsingers." Traditionally, to be a singer, you have to undergo an audition for the school choir. There you have to be able to recognize, translate, and sing special musical symbols on a sheet of paper, both in unison and in multipart harmonies. If you can achieve this, your voice is compartmentalized into soprano, alto, tenor bass, or basso profundo. Your singing voice is then technically caught, harnessed, and refined to warble and vibrato to produce a virtuoso performance in specific styles, e.g., opera, medieval, atonal, oratorio, sprecht gesang, etc., which are then delivered on the concert stage in church or temple. If you can't achieve this daunting audition ritual, you are rejected and led to believe that you are "not musical" and certainly not "a singer."

Who decided that music-making and singing was to become such an exclusive mental affair? And at what cost for human happiness and the song of your soul? Many of the high-flying singers forget their original love of singing in their obsessive search for a technically proficient or even commercially acceptable sound that will win all the competitions leading to fame, name, and financial glory. Certainly I do not wish to diminish the illustrious world catalogue of vocal performance and recording, nor do I regret the rich years of choral singing that I experienced throughout my London teenage and Cambridge college music years. I am, however, very glad that I was spared from too much classical singing training and was thus able to maintain an authentic relationship with my true voice. For the most part, this sophisticated music production is expensive to access in more ways than one, and it claims many victims who struggle to keep pace with the competition, fame, glamor, and media madness. Others don't "make it" or are exploited by the music industry.

The Naked Voice experience shifts the focus and power of communication away from the performing minority and restores it to the truth-seeking majority of singers. And that includes YOU and everyone else interested in exploring and redeeming a healthy and conscious relationship with their true voice. As you recover the inner treasures of your soul through your sound, you will also be fast on the way to discovering the role your naked voice can play in integrating your highest aspirations with your grounded purpose on Earth. You do not have to be a trained or experienced singer-musician to access the transformative power and beauty that is the song of your soul. This way of singing is as natural as breathing, and it is for everyone.

Let's take a closer look at how you may develop this art of making your inner life audible. Be patient and gentle with yourself. Nonjudgment is the key. Let us begin with the simple skill of listening and bringing conscious attention to the sound of your voice and its well-being.

Don't hold back: enjoy the following inner-voice practice. Here begins a love affair with your inner voice.

Making Your Inner Life Audible

Practice I—Warming Up

Relax and breathe first. Start by simply letting go, taking in a deep breath and then sighing out or doodling in the air with your voice without words, whispering sweet nothings, gradually raising the volume with vowel sounds A E I O U. Move your body, and find yourself painting invisible shapes in the air with your arms. Let simple nonverbal utterance, strands of sounds, follow the shapes of your moving arms. Let simple improvisations and melodies flow out of you. Connect your inner life with outer sound, bridging your solitary or isolated inner voice with a new connectedness—interconnectedness—between your inner self and your outer everyday world. As you increase permission to express yourself, breathe in more deeply and find yourself groaning, moaning, laughing, crying, and even shrieking. Let yourself sound out as it comes *without any censorship at all.* Let the musical molecules of your emotions arise naturally, willingly, and spontaneously, kindling the fire of your being. This inner-outer communication gradually becomes a living vitality that is no longer cramped by words.

Practice 2—Conversation from the Inside Out

Procure a simple hand-held recorder or upload a recording app onto your mobile phone. You need to be able to switch it on with ease, especially as you may need it in the middle of the night. Start to open up a conversation with yourself from the inside out. I find myself exploring this practice most effortlessly in the early hours of the morning when I wake from sleep temporarily. At that time most of the world around you is still asleep, and the boundary between your conscious personality and your unconscious dreaming world is more open and reflective, as is your heart.

The aim of this practice is to listen to yourself deeply. This is not a "things to do" conversation with yourself. Nor is this preparation for a public speech. It has nothing to do with how you present yourself in the everyday world. It is about sinking into the depths of your unknown territory to find the wordless prayers hidden there in your inner world as you begin communing with the vibration of your secret voice. This inner voice carries a wealth of understanding and truth. Really trust what it has to say to you. Be patient. With your witnessing and permission it will stream forth its reflections, dreams, memories, and wise counsel about who you are and how you sound to yourself from the inside out. Remember that this practice is fundamentally *a receiving and a listening practice*.

NB: If you share a bed with someone, you might be able to share this practice with your partner, asking him or her to witness you, then alternating. It's not a social thing. So if you do share the practice, don't feel you have to get involved in interpreting each other. Simply witness. Listen. Allow the silence to cook inside you, and let the sound arise as and when, without external interference of any kind. You may prefer to rise first and find a comfortable place nearby to speak or whisper from the inside out. Whispering can be very effective because it can be a way to encourage your inner voice to come out, supporting its message without any pressure or expectation. Alternatively find a time, once you have risen, in the early morning or evening, when you can allow yourself 5 or 10 minutes to relax into this practice.

Here is a transcription of a very verbal inner voice I recorded in the early hours:

It is 6 AM on a January morning. I am in bed recording this early morning meditative conversation with myself. The sound of my voice is arising out of the silent darkness of this new dawn. No sound anywhere to be heard outside. I am presently on a writing retreat, staying in a remote part of North Devon. My words are flowing in and out of this silence without any external intervention. It's an entirely simple uncensored conversation with my inner life as it falls out of my mouth and into this tiny recorder. This voice is who I am, and the subject is silence.

Silence, what is it? Does it end when my words start? Does it remain within and between, underneath my words? Silence is my great love. I have had a love affair with silence since I was very small. My relationship with silence informs the tone and timbre of my voice. Silence inspires a sensuality in my voice, and I am always mindful to respect the silence that makes this voice and its thoughts conscious of their existence. Conscious and also grateful for my existence, this sound that I am. So the sound must seamlessly flow out of the silence and back into it without a trace, neither body nor soul, says the poet, I belong to the beloved, have seen the two worlds as one, and that one breathing human being. Breath is the bridge. Where does this breath arise from and return to? For the classical Indian musician, silence is the "unstruck" sound. Without silence there is no sound, and without sound no silence. They are inextricably linked. Silence is the inaudible music of my original or primordial self.

Infinite presence is what I understand true silence to be. Yet true silence is not just the absence of thought or the stilling of the mind. Silence can bring physical time to a stop, and yet neither timelessness nor the cessation of structured time is what silence is. True silence is a dynamic realm within, between, and beyond these words. It is a wordless emotion, a seamless beginningless, thought-free substance. Is it emptiness then? Emptiness, absence, void, darkness . . . these are all attempts to describe, perceptions of what is not there.

Yet true silence is peace beyond any understanding of it, even beyond light and dark, invisible presence, pure awareness. Christ called this awareness eternal Life, the Holy Spirit. Buddha called it the Self, pure and absolute consciousness. Ramana Maharshi called silence the deepest state of rest. It is the source of an aliveness that nourishes every atom of my being, pure consciousness, the absolute source of Life itself. There are increasing numbers of conscious people living on the planet who are radiant with this deep silence. They have journeyed to the source of silence and now they embody silence. Freed from the distraction of their busy mind, they transmit pure awareness like light pouring into the hearts of those they meet. The silence they embody is spacious, all-inclusive, openhearted, like a benign disinterestedness. It is a luminous inner peace arising freely from its source, free from all attachment; fathomless heart, unconditional love. . . . When I am silent no sound exists, so who am I now?

"Making Your Inner Life Audible" Practice Follow-Up: Enjoy encouraging this new verbal or nonverbal communication with your inner world. While practicing, pause every now and again and ask yourself: "Who is talking? From where does this sound arise?" Listen and focus on your self-inquiry. Keep listening without judging. Then ask yourself again, "Who is it that is listening?" Notice how easy or effortless it was to speak with your inner self without attempts to perform or to distract yourself. Whatever happens, don't judge, simply listen. Continue this practice whenever you feel like it—any time of the day or night, ideally when you are relaxed in body and mind. You are beginning to build a deep and nonjudgmental listening faculty of attention from the inside out. Notice how this self-inquiry process stills your reactive mind and activates your self-observing mind. In the next section I invite a deeper listening awareness supported by simple breathing meditations.

1.7 I Sing, Therefore I Am

We are conditioned and unconditioned, we are both at the same time.

—"BOTH AT THE SAME TIME," *Fierce Wisdom*

"If you are a hair dryer, you cannot be a toaster!" exclaimed Ramesh Balsekar, a radical teacher of *advaita* (nonduality) whom I used to visit in Bombay while studying classical voice with Sruti Sadolikar. Ramesh was a student of the revered master Nisargadatta Maharaj, whose teachings were transcribed in a book called *I Am That*. A Sanskrit scholar, Ramesh had made his own translations of the *Bhagavad Gita*, one of India's epic spiritual stories about the origins of love, life, and the universe. When he wasn't teaching nonduality, Ramesh earned his living as a director of the Bank of India and enjoyed a good-quality glass of scotch whiskey in the evenings. "I probably earn more money than all of you in this room!" he once announced to the amused bewilderment of his audience. I enjoyed this unusual collision of material with spiritual.

Ramesh's combination of life skills produced a formidable mental rigor combined with a wild sense of humor. Both were used as spiritual teaching weapons to great effect. He held daily *satsangs*, spiritual gatherings, in his living room for seekers from all over the world. Ramesh loved to engage one person at a time in an intense process of self-inquiry. If the conversation wasn't engaging enough, and no one was asking any substantial questions, he would simply walk out.

"A human being is just like a computer," he suddenly announced one morning, "and you are God's robot!" He drove his impassioned message home by describing how most human beings are like computers "plugged into the source at the electric socket." The personality is the computer software. It shapes each person's unique "programming." Most individuals accept that their programming is fundamentally impossible to change. They believe it is who they "are." And this illusion colors their mental and emotional state and the ways in which they will interact and sleepwalk their way through everyday life. Hence, the hair dryer–toaster analogy!

However, Ramesh's voice would sometimes turn into a whisper, and he would take us into his confidence, as if to reveal the ultimate secret of the universe, saying, "the Source of life is also de-programming some human beings to start questioning who they are!"

As human beings, we have to learn to masterfully embrace and navigate both the conditioned world of finite form and the unconditional and infinite formlessness of human nature, rooted in the awareness of "I AM." Our task is to discover how to live one hundred percent, accepting that duality is only one realm of perception that we live in, whilst knowing at a deeper level that consciousness is indivisible and that we are One.

"I am 'a somebody' is false," Ramesh would constantly remind us. "There is only one unchanging consciousness—I AM."

You are about to open your ears more deeply to the true potential and purpose of who you are behind your conditioned dualistic programming, as you investigate just how attached you are to your personal identity as "the doer." You will also begin to see and hear how you can shift your identity to being the "witness." The following sound-awareness exercises and vocal practices will help you connect who you *are* with how you authentically sound. As you begin to build an unassailable confidence in sounding your true self, your natural singing voice will start to retrieve and reveal hidden or dormant dimensions of your nature buried in the depths of your unconscious. And this doesn't require thirty years of talking therapy, either. As your self-observing witness strengthens, supported by the Naked Voice skills, your authentic voice will arise naturally from the source of your being prior to duality. Before we go any further, following are some questions for you in relation to your inner-outer vocal adventure.

SELF-INQUIRY: A QUESTIONNAIRE

Am I ready to take some risks?

Am I ready to throw my personality up in the air?

Am I ready to let go and drop all my masks of respectability?

Am I ready to surrender the entire control panel of my reactive
  mind?

Am I ready to open my heart and trust the outcome?

Am I ready to release all anxieties about what others will think?

Am I ready to slough off the cozy agonies of self-sabotage?

Am I ready to accept the praise and blame of those around me?

Am I ready to embrace all my longing for belonging?

Am I ready to navigate my vulnerability with courage?

Am I ready to play the fool with ears and eyes wide open?

Strengthening your *song of self-acceptance* is the bottom line. And
notice how different your responses to these questions will be as you
develop your sound-awareness skills throughout this book. Spontaneous sounding out is the best way to meet yourself through your voice.
Like bungee jumping, you have to throw off all the habitual chains of
restraint, constraint, and complaint, and JUMP INTO THE NOW,
abandoning yourself to the present moment and expressing yourself
like an impassioned lover. And you will benefit the most if you embark
upon this practice with the intention to trust the impact of whatever
shows up. That is where the deep nonjudgmental listening comes in.
The truth is that, in more than thirty years, I have never found anyone
who didn't find this introductory vocal practice empowering, joyous,
and liberating. So don't hold back. This is not about singing; it's about
expressing *you* in all your majesty and aliveness.

Just as you cannot fight with someone who is singing, so you won't
be able to fight with yourself once you start engaging more courageously and consciously with the volume, rhythm, and resonance of
your unique sound. Singing invites an all-inclusive awareness in which
there is no enemy, no opposition. Your attention to the sound and the
underlying question "Who is singing?" begins to dissolve the illusory
fear and separateness of your conditioned mind. Gradually the awareness "I SING therefore I AM" will begin to emerge, or more accurately
"I AM therefore I SING."

Our everyday listening capacity can easily become limited and
dulled by the superficial soap-opera communications that assail us

on all sides from the moment we are born. The media, social pressures, and the association of our voice with performance make us self-conscious even thinking about singing, let alone opening our mouth! The more conscious your intention is to journey to the very source of your sound itself, the more effortless and respectful and grateful will your relationship with your true voice become.

This is *sound awareness*, and it leads to self-acceptance. Once the social and reactive voice hooks of the personality cease to dominate your attention, you will begin to experience a clearer, more fulfilling, and relaxing creative interaction with the sound of your whole Self. The song of your soul becomes more resonant, generating a stronger field of awareness and presence all around you, sourced from within.

This deeper listening will lead you into a whole new world of experience once the appropriate conditions are created—namely the opportunity for true receptivity, relaxed self-absorption, and an understanding of the spiritual significance of sound and music through its relationship with the invisible realms.

I have heard literally thousands of stories of people who are laden with deep-seated childhood memories of being told to shut up, be quiet, leave the choir. And I have not met one whose self-awareness, confidence, self-esteem, self-acceptance, and a direct experience of loving presence was not activated by giving simple focused attention to their unique and authentic sound.

"Who Is Singing?" Practice

As you strengthen your deep nonjudgmental listening, you will soon be interacting with the real voice inside you, your natural sound, stripped of its social and mental conditioning. This is your naked voice, a primordial voice, stored in the bones of your body. Once heard, this voice awakens you to an ancient memory from deep inside. So the next step is to make a habit of the question, "Who is singing?" or with a deeper listening, "Who am I?" Once you develop this habit of asking yourself, "Who was that?" and

"Whose sound am I?" and more deeply "Who am I when the sound ceases?" your focus starts to shift from the reactive issues of your personality or ego to the quality, tone, and vibration of your unique soul sound. This will immediately start to lift the tensions of self-consciousness. Try it anytime in the day, whether you have been speaking or singing, and watch what happens as your awareness deepens, and expands.

1.8 Strengthen Your Witness: Deepening Your Sound-Awareness Skills

In section 1.4 ("Wake Up Your Witness") we began to open the door on this unique faculty of attention and its life-changing impact on your inner-outer voice. As you deepen awareness of your witness in your life, you will find yourself becoming more discerning and skillful at communicating consciously, empowered by a deeper self-inquiry that undresses your self-conscious reactive mind along with your ego or personality voice. As your authentic voice deepens your self-acceptance, you will build stronger self-worth, and with that the confidence to loosen your attachment to your reactive or negative judging mind. Your authentic voice is going to flourish, supported by your witness skills. As you enjoy an increasing pleasure in your powers of creative expression, your naked sound will become more substantial and resonant, with a far-reaching vocabulary. Your witness will certainly enable you to communicate with yourself and with others in effortless and wiser ways. "Who is singing?" remains the central question.

Three Sound-Awareness Practices

The following breathing, postural, and vocal exercises will assist you in fully embodying your authenticity and really grounding your sound as you arrive home in your body, listening to yourself with increasing self-awareness, acceptance, and presence. The following Sound Awareness exercises are divided into three groups:

1) Standing in the Presence—Vertical Practices

2) Breath of Life—Horizontal Practices

3) Silent Body Singing—Meditative Movement Practices

TIPS FOR PRACTICING MOST EFFECTIVELY:

- You may wish to record the directions first.
- You may want to ask a friend to read them while you explore.

Standing in the Presence: Vertical Practices

With your feet shoulder-width apart, stand without leaning too far to the front or back. Make sure your feet and toes are relaxed on the floor and you feel the gravitational pull of the Earth while you also feel your spine being drawn up toward the sky. Feel your body as a bridge between the earth and the sky. Even though you are standing, remember your spacious relaxed breathing exercises. Allow your abdominal muscles to relax and hang loose.

Exercise 1—Mountain Posture

With your eyes closed, stand like a mountain, arms hanging by your sides. Be aware of all the qualities of this mountain. Breathe in to the abdominal muscles. Breathe in to a greater awareness, beyond the boundaries of the skin, and breathe out into a more deeply relaxed body. Be aware of your feet, shinbones, thighbones, pelvis, upward movement of the spine, abdomen, rib cage, up into the head. Be aware of the space all around your body as if you had 360-degree vision. Breathe into that space. Let your mouth open slightly, breathing in and out.

Exercise 2—Spinal Stretch

Take your awareness to the elbows, and imagine cords from the ceiling drawing your elbows up without any support from the shoulders. Simply let the elbows be drawn up on these imaginary strings. Raise them up above the shoulders, breathing down into the abdomen, relaxing your feet. Become aware of this spinal stretch. How does it feel in the upper and lower arms, which are dangling in mid air? Now bring the wrists up higher, above the elbows and above the head, drawing the upper body toward the sky and leaving the legs behind. Feel the middle of the body continuing to breathe into the abdomen. Now feel invisible strings in the fingers and hands stretching up to the sky. Notice the sensation in the fingers as you draw them up to the sky, to such an extent that they might even float off your hands. Breathe into the belly. When you are ready, let the fingers drop, then the wrists, and finally the elbows. Notice the difference in temperature in your body. Now shake out your whole body, like a dog waking up from sleep. Shake every limb and muscle from head to toe. Shaking, sound out, exploring different vowels: A to Eee to Eyyy to Ohhhh. Keep moving and shifting the sound. Kick your legs out too.

NB: If you wish, do the Mountain Posture again.

Exercise 3—Exploring the Diaphragm as a Trampoline

Standing in this vertical posture, travel in your awareness from the crown down through the third eye, the throat, and to the center of the body and the diaphragm, a sheet of muscle that stretches across the bottom of the rib cage. It divides the upper and lower halves of the body. Visualize that diaphragm muscle as a trampoline. As you breathe in, the trampoline descends, pushing the diaphragm down as the lungs expand. As you breathe out, the diaphragm moves up into a cone shape, just inside the rib cage. Imagine invisible arrows descending from the upper torso and onto the diaphragm, and visualize yourself there. Build awareness of the descending diaphragm as you breathe in and ascending as you breathe out. Your mouth is slightly open. Start to explore sounding out on the sound Errrrrrrrrrrrrrrrrr on the next breath. Errrrrrrrrrrrrrrrrrrrr. Be aware of thousands of molecules bouncing onto the diaphragm as you sound out on Errrrrrrrrrrrrrr.

Repeat this on different pitches without trying to sound beautiful. Just sigh out on pitch, Errrrrrrrrrrrrrr.

The main thing is that you are aware of the vibrations in your body, especially at that central point on your diaphragm. Visualize the sensation, and the sound itself, coming from the body the whole time.

Exercise 4—Open Hums

With your mouth still slightly open and your awareness in the belly, look for a sound that really helps you to find a vibration in the belly. Imagine yourself humming with your mouth slightly open.

Extend your awareness up from the belly to teeth and lips as the breath leaves. Yield to the incoming breath as it goes down into the belly, and then simply sound out with your awareness. The sound you make will have a FFph sound to it. But don't try to make it. It is simply a result of the reflexive breathing. Phpherrrrrrrrrrrr.

Exercise 5—Rocking the Foundations of Your Body

Lightly close your lips and be aware of how the vibrations build in the belly and then dance up to the front of the mouth, gathering on the inside of the lips. You will be aware of a tickling sensation there as you breathe in and sound out on a light humming sound. Again, access a sound in your belly that connects you from belly to mouth. Sustain your awareness from the belly to the mouth.

Once you can feel that tingling sensation, explore how it would be to breathe in and then to drop the lower jaw onto an UmmmAaaah. Start with Ummmmmmmmmmmmmm then move to Aaaaaaaaaaaaaah. The voice will naturally and effortlessly project itself out of the mouth. Practice this several times until it feels quite natural. Then, having opened into the Aaaaaaaaaaaaah sound, close the mouth into an Ummmmmmmmmmmmmm sound again. Explore the same practice at different pitches.

Breath of Life: Horizontal Practices

Exercise 1—The Gratitude Breath

Begin by lying down on the floor. Lie on your back and let yourself relax totally. Make sure your arms are by your sides and that
your palms face upward in a gesture of receiving. Feeling the gravitational pull of the Earth beneath you, simply let every cell and
muscle in your body relax. Let any tension in the body go. Sigh it
out and let go. As you become aware of the thoughts in your mind,
the sounds around you in the room, and the wider environment,
breathe more deeply, let yourself smile, begin to focus more on
your breathing, let go of all thoughts, and begin to relax into this
time which is entirely for you. Who are you? Bring this question
into the center of your chest, your heart center.

Remind yourself: Singing is fundamentally a listening activity.
The source of this listening is silence before thought. Out of silence springs the singing heart—natural, spontaneous, and free.

Beginning in the horizontal position is important because it
helps you to relax and to align the spine. A substantial voice depends upon a strong and relaxed spine. Simply continue to listen
and to breathe, observing your breath more and more closely. Let
the feeling of gratitude enter and flow through your body. It may
be helpful to visualize a loving presence in your life—a child, lover,
elderly person, animal, or friend—and let yourself sigh with relief
and gratitude for their presence in your life. As you focus on this
feeling of gratitude, let it deepen. Extend your exhaling and inhal-
ing breath gradually and naturally, without any strain. Don't change
your breath—simply relax deeper and deeper into it.

Sighing with relief is the most natural way to breathe. Gratitude is a sure way to open the singing heart. It can be easily overlooked. Now begin to observe your breath more closely.

Let yourself breathe in to the count of four—one, two, three,
four—and then breathe out to the count of four or more—one,
two, three, four, five, six—and sigh the rest away. At this point let
yourself breathe in and out through the nose. Notice that as you

breathe in, your awareness expands beyond the boundaries of the skin, and as you breathe out, you relax your body more and more deeply. Let this breathing process continue through the forthcoming relaxation exercise. The essence of a powerful, substantial voice that sings with resonance and clarity is a deeply relaxed body and mind. Now begin to let all thoughts of past, present, and future dissolve. Be here, now, in this moment.

Exercise 2—Muscular Relaxation from Toes to Head

Take your attention down to your toes, and say to them, "Relax, toes and feet." Then relax ankles, calves, and thighs. Relax pelvis, relax hips, relax abdomen, relax spine, relax all the inner organs. Relax rib cage and chest. As your chest relaxes, so do the shoulders, falling upon the floor very happily. Relax upper arms, elbows, wrists, hands, fingers, and thumbs. From the shoulders to the fingertips, all the muscles are relaxing happily.

Continue to notice yourself breathing in as awareness expands beyond the boundaries of the skin. Move your head gently from side to side. Relax ears, and all the muscles of the face. Relax eyes, forehead, nostrils, lower and upper jaw, to the hinge between upper and lower, in the middle of the ear to the sides of your head, tongue, lips, and all the muscles in the cheeks and face—relax totally.

Visualize your face from the inside. Let all attempts at putting on a good face dissolve completely. Now relax the whole body. Let the gratitude inside you free the breath.

Singing is a receiving activity. It is more often portrayed as a giving process, and with that perception arise questions about projecting our voices. You will find your own answers to these questions once your deep listening faculty is awake and you have begun to hear the real voice inside you: the voice of your singing heart. But first the body-mind has to prepare itself to return the vocal awareness from the throat to the belly, to strengthen the vocal muscles in the belly, and to develop skillful means such as self-acceptance and nonjudgment. If your inner resources are strong your voice will contain a penetrating presence impossible to ignore, and all concerns about successful voice projection will disappear.

Exercise 3—Facial Massage, Body Stretch, and Yawn

Lying on your back, simply lift your hands up to your face, and give the point between the upper and lower jaw a good massage. Massage any points in the face that feel tense. When you are ready, have a good stretch on the floor and roll about like a puppy or a tiger cub. Find ways of moving in which you feel the muscles of your body stretching and opening. Finally, return to lying on your back. Drop your jaw. Now feel the need to yawn. Open and receive the breath; open and close. That yawn extends from sighing with relief. It's a great release for the body. Enjoy it as it opens up the whole of your face.

Exercise 4—Skeletal Relaxation

We have spoken of how the primordial voice is older and deeper than the social or mental voice. Information about the vibrational frequency of your voice is stored in the marrow of your bones. This information is released when your primordial voice sings. So, as you lie on the floor for this exercise, picture the bones of your body from feet to skull and relax and release any tension in the bones. This tension may be blocking the true vibration of your voice. Now become aware of the space between one bone and the next: the bones of the ankle joints, the shinbones and how they connect through the knees to the thighbones, connecting in with the hip joints, the pelvic girdle. Continue to be aware, as you breathe in, of the space between one bone and the next: the tailbone as it unfolds into the spine itself, the vertebrae along the spine and the space between each one, the rib cage as it expands and contracts with your breath, the shoulder girdle on top of the rib cage, the shoulder blades and the shoulder sockets. Be aware of the connection between the shoulder sockets and the upper arm bones, the forearms, wrists, and hands; rising up the arms to the vertebrae of the neck, then the seven little vertebrae that rise up into the skull itself. Between the bottom of the skull and the top of the spine there is a space. Be aware of it as you breathe in and out. Be aware of the bones in the skull and of all its orifices: the eye sockets, the nostrils, the ears, and the jaw. There are spaces within and between all the bones in your body. Breathing in and out, become aware of the total skeletal structure of your body, and of the spaciousness that flows throughout the whole body.

Exercise 5—Moving from Your Throat to Your Belly

Bring your arms and legs off the floor and give them a good shake. Take a good breath in and sound out as you shake your arms and legs, massaging your spine along the floor and calling out as you do so. Call out separately A E I O U. Release your sound spontaneously, without a care in the world. Don't try to sound beautiful, and really let go with your sound for the sheer love of it. It is now time to shift the vocal awareness from the throat to the belly if we are to develop a full-blooded, resonant, openhearted sound. First of all, raise your knees and place your feet on the ground, feeling your back lengthening and widening, and notice what happens to the base of your spine as you do so. Feel your spine relaxed along the floor and, continuing your breathing awareness, focus now on your breath in the center of your belly. Place your hands on your belly, at the muscles at the bottom of the rib cage, where the ribs jut out the most. It is crucial that these vocal muscles become strong. Picture a magnet in the center of your belly, and travel with your breath inside the belly. Be aware of the breath filling the whole torso. Notice what happens to your hands as you inhale, and as you yield to the exhaling breath. Breathe slowly into your hands and let yourself yield to the exhaling breath and the incoming breath. Do not control the breath. Let the breath be reflexive. You want breathing awareness not breathing control.

NB: I use the term "belly" to refer to the lower abdomen, not just the stomach.

Exercise 6—Energize Your Laughing Muscles

Laughing is a very important practice in the strengthening of your sound. So let's explore the belly breathing more closely and deeply. The belly is the home of your instinctual sound. Your life force or "chi" energy is generated and strengthened from the belly. All your "gut" instinctual emotions, all your laughter and tears, re-side in the belly. A clear and healthy relationship with your belly is therefore essential for a true and naked expression of your sound.

Place your hands gently on your belly, with the longest fingers lightly touching at their tips. As you breathe in, become aware of the belly filling and your fingers moving away from each other, then coming back to touch at the tips as you breathe out. Once again, slowly inhale through the nose—in, two, three, four; hold, two, three, four—then drop your mouth open as you sigh on the exhaling breath—out, two, three, four, five, six, seven, eight. Repeat: in two, three, four; hold, two, three, four; and out, two, three, four, five, six, seven, eight. Inwardly visualize your breath and your sound arising from and returning to the belly. Focusing your attention on the belly muscles beneath your hands, allow a feeling of joyful en-ergy to come into your body. Let the feelings increase and develop into laughter. Feel the laughter filling you up with positive energy from deep inside your belly. Explore this laughter a while, follow it, feel how it engages and energizes you, exercising all your belly muscles in one go. Let go more and let rip as the laughter builds further, like the bursting of raw sound from the source of your life.

Now generate a longer cycle of laughter, as if you have just pressed a replay button. Be aware of the laughter/vocal muscles beneath your hands. Breathing into your hands, watch how the laughter muscles contract and expand as you empty and fill up with energy each time, increasing the laughing. Breathe in and take another cycle of laughter, and watch more closely what happens with your belly muscles.

Keep exploring your laughter as you make the connection between laughter and your sound awareness or singing energy. Let your laughter increase again as you keep your attention on the vocal muscles at the center of your body. The more laughter you bring to your vocal practice, the more you will strengthen the vo-cal muscles in your belly.

Silent Body Singing: Meditative Movement Practices

Start by listening to the silence around you. Close your eyes. Take in a breath and sigh out deeply several times. Relax. Arrive. Give your attention to the silence within and around you. Don't get involved or distracted by external sound or noise. Focus on the silence within, between, or beyond the sounds or thoughts you hear in the space.

I have found this practice to be an effective way of connecting with your naked voice, especially if you have never before considered sounding out as a serious practice in your life. The beauty of Silent Body Singing is that it offers a silent movement practice, which gives you and your body time to adjust to this new and courageous relationship with your emerging naked voice.

Stage 1: Warm Up Your Body

Rag Doll Shake-Out—Starting by shaking out your wrists and extend the shaking to your shoulders, head, and neck, your whole torso, pelvis, thighs, knees, ankles, and feet, until you are shaking your whole body like a rag doll, then shaking out. First do this silently, then sound freely while you continue shaking out, using different vowel sounds A E I O U.

- Shoulder rotations—back and forth.
- Arm swings—to the right and left of the body, tapping your back.
- Breathing in sync with arms—breathe in, raise arms up. Breathe out, lower arms.
- Rag Doll Shake-Out—Repeat the shake-out at the opening of this exercise.
- Mindful reflective walking and breathing in the space.
- Slow jogging, running, slow jogging, etc. (alternating).
- Standing meditation—witnessing the space inside/outside.
- Deeper relaxation and formlessly moving.

Stage 2: Focusing on Silent Body Singing

- Wakame (seaweed): With your feet well rooted on the ground, close your eyes and imagine that you are a piece of seaweed standing (or sitting) on the ocean floor. Let your body relax and flow in the imaginary ocean waters, side to side, forward, backward, spiraling, folding over, up and back, arms splaying outward effortlessly, face reaching upward toward the light where the ocean's surface interfaces with the dry land and open sky. Continue this gentle meditative movement for 3–4 minutes, increasing as and when it becomes more familiar. Smile, enjoy, as your breath automatically deepens, filling your lungs with new life. Come to a close. Let yourself stand (or sit) in silence a while longer, relaxed, aligned, and at one with yourself. Now start to move your body freely. Silently ask yourself, "How are you feeling today?" Let your body move freely as you sound out freely in response to how you feel, for 5–10 minutes.

- Deepening the practice: Let your body silently express and reveal how it feels right now, 5–10 minutes.
- Relax. Come to a standstill, eyes closed. Standing meditation.
- Place your crossed, overlapping hands over your heart center.
- Breathe into your heart, receive, accept, let go.
- Bowing to yourself, without judgment, say "Thank you."
- Come to a close.

NB: Practice without music to begin with. If preferred, add music later.

1.9 Spontaneous Utterance: A Morning Wake-Up

I once heard the musician Bruce Springsteen say, "Don't die with the singing inside you." This powerful statement really brought home to me the urgent call to express who you are, what really matters to you. "Go out on your rooftops and sing!" Rumi proclaims.

In section 1.6, "Making Your Inner Life Audible," you dared to open the door on the extremely private communications you have with yourself. They are so private that you may not want to admit you are having them, or you bar them from conscious remembering. Certainly these *courageous conversations* don't always make their way into our private journals. They can be so significant and yet we may dismiss them as being insignificant, like doodling with a paintbrush or humming a tune under your breath. These fleeting yet soulful pastimes are regarded at best as "daydreaming" and are therefore not worth taking seriously.

The threshold between your dreaming and your waking voice can be a crucial turning point in building a deeper self-awareness through sound. It is a transitional bridge where unexpected visions and new decisions can come hurtling into your conscious world out of nowhere—yet in ways that can be profoundly disorienting, and shocking, but most often *life-changing*. So, I ask you, at what cost do you keep that magical swing door shut tight between unconscious-conscious awareness?

The essential practice of *spontaneous utterance* assists you with opening wide the door between your dreaming and waking worlds, allowing your unconscious voice the opportunity to infuse and integrate with your everyday voice without compromise.

Spontaneous Utterance, a Morning Practice

What sounds might fall from your mouth, effortlessly, organically, with no desire to impress, no performance, no separation between your self and this moment? Enjoy playing with your sound and bridging unconscious with conscious realities. We began to explore a related practice in section 1.6, "Making Your Inner Life Audible." Now you have a new sound task, which is to effortlessly transit with awareness from sleeping into your waking day. Allow 5 or 10 minutes or more for this process, so as to provide maximum opportunity to access the messages, dreams, and reflections emerging from your sleeping world.

When I wake I relax in bed, eyes open or closed, and adjust to the transition from sleeping to waking. I don't stumble halfheartedly out of bed and stagger about cursing myself that I didn't go to bed earlier. Well, sometimes I do. But on a good day I simply listen to the silence and the sounds around me, then try out the tone of my vocal sound as I awaken from sleep into a new day.

As soon as I begin to waken fully, I slowly open and close my eyes a few times. I most likely wrestle a little with "Shall I or shan't I get up?" I listen to my reflective mind, remembering and letting go of early morning dreams. I gently navigate this intervention of morning light with the four walls of my bedroom, the fixtures, fittings, the sounds of birds, wind and weather from outside, doors opening and closing somewhere nearby. Other human beings are rising somewhere else in the building.

Allow questions to arise: Where have I come from? Who am I now? What messages am I still reaching out to remember and catch from my dreams before they disappear? I am letting go attachment to the dark warmth of the night.

You are now in transition between worlds. You can feel the warmth of your breath around your mouth, and you smile as it flows in and out; you flex your body, stretch your hands and arms, feel the strength of your whole back spiraling around, easing itself onto one side, and then over onto the other side, arching your back as if swimming. Explore breathing in for longer, sighing out more deeply, noticing the mood you are in as the sound intensifies and releases. Draw in the next breath more willingly; abandon yourself to a much longer, deeper outbreath. Receive more air in through your open mouth, then sigh out and connect with the sound more consciously without judgment or attachment to storyline. Open your mouth wider, receive more breath, stretch your wing bones, press your neck into the pillow. Give thanks that you are breathing. You are alive, you are here.

Silence, bird song, traffic outside—I become aware of the world outside waking up more loudly now—sounds of car engines firing, voices calling out, goodbyes between parents and children, lovers, friends. At this moment I am so grateful to be self-employed and for the good fortune of being able to choose at what time I will rise today. I consciously delay the attempts of my business mind to get cracking and dive into the 101 things awaiting me at my writing desk, and I extend the luxury of this in-between world a little longer.

Open and stretch your legs wide, breathing more deeply, pressing your feet down toward the end of the bed; then like the tide coming in, draw your toes up against the sheet as your knees follow, bending up toward your smiling (or grimacing!) face. The rest of the day can wait just a little while longer. This is a unique moment. Relax and breathe even deeper. You are simply here, happy to be so and grateful for this relaxing transition from night into day. Hear your breath rising and falling, sigh out a longer sigh, and, with gratitude, breathe in more deeply. Allow more sounds to arrive—gentle laughter maybe, groans, mumbling moans, gibberish, sweeping sighs from low to high, swooping down deep, vowel sounds A E I O, humming, Ommm. . . . Experiment, explore, let come what comes as you breathe deeper, receive more life into your body, give more away. Now allow stronger energy sound to pour out of your mouth.

Let yourself experiment in as many ways as you are inspired, following the direction of your body-mind.

I love to wiggle my toes and scrunch my feet, as my waking consciousness increases and my whole body is spiraling right to left, as my splayed-out arms dance in slow strong widening arcs across the bed, and I paint invisible shapes in the air with my hands. I am opening and closing my eyes, hands, genital muscles, and feet, receiving the light of the day into my eyes, as I bid farewell to my dwindling dreams, and the darkness of the night world dissolves into this new day.

Be aware that you will have to rise soon. Can you rise effortlessly, without resistance?

Connecting with your breath more consciously, breathe in—two, three, four—and out—two, three, four—letting your belly muscles flex and flow as your chest and back open, hips soften and spin slowly this way and that as your yielding heart finally lets go all the stories of the night.

Then let a random nonverbal song find its dreamy way out of your mouth, gently bridging the connection between unconscious and conscious mind. Let it invite you up and out of bed, into the bathroom, to wash and sing in the shower, then sound in harmony with the bee-like drone of your electric toothbrush. If you don't have an electric toothbrush, simply enjoy the sounds you can make from all sides of your moving mouth and jaws while you brush. Be aware of the rhythm and speed of your body movement as you dress and your sound leads you to breakfast. You might become the beat with the staccato sounds of chopping fruit and pouring of cereals into a bowl. As the volume intensifies you might find yourself dancing around the room, moving to the lyrics of your favorite wake-up music.

My voice sometimes streams out across the room uncensored, as I start engaging full-throttle with my everyday world. There is no time for self-doubt, regret, or melancholic ruminations to disperse or drain my energy, or take me somewhere I don't need or want to go.

This sonic fanfare transition from horizontal into vertical life is an empowering and encouraging way to live in the present moment, without either resisting the activities to come, or rushing into them in a chaotic frenzy.

Explore Spontaneous Utterance for yourself. Discover what unexpected new sounds, spoken songs, and nonverbal moody messages may emerge from your shift from night into day.

1.10 Voices That Change Our Lives

Dear soul dear soul
What is my life consecrated to?
            —"WHAT IS MY LIFE?" *Naked Heart*

I didn't realize until my late twenties that my solo singing voice—as opposed to my choral voice—was going to play an essential role in forging my spiritual path. Before this could occur I had to undergo a paradigm shift from a traditional, professional Western path of a classical singer to a way of singing that is inspired by a mystical devotional relationship with the singing voice as a mouthpiece for spirit. This involved really waking up to the reality that my voice—and especially my singing voice—was to serve this evolving journey.

Whose voices have influenced and inspired your life so far? The signals or triggers for my vocational singing path started increasing in my early twenties when I first heard the extraordinary singing voice of a remarkable French woman named Chanterelle. She was a concert violinist, singer, and the wife of the Gandhian nonviolent activist Lanzo del Vasto. They founded the Communauté de L'Arche, a nonviolent community in southern France.

I had already found myself captivated by the voices of other nonviolent visionary leaders such as Martin Luther King, Jr. and Gandhi. I was also taken by the penetrating voice of Edith Piaf and the eccentric, mesmerizing voice of the Egyptian singer Oum Khoultum. It was said that when she sang, the whole of Egypt stopped. Her funeral magnetized millions to mourn and honor her passing. There were also the impassioned erotic voices of singers such as Nina Simone, Aretha Franklin, Joni Mitchell, Carole King, and Annie Lennox, alongside the great operatic divas such as Maria Callas and Elizabeth Schwarzkopf.

Yet there was something in Chanterelle's sound that was clearly free of all attachment to ego, everyday needs, demands, and longings. Hers was a voice that soared and transcended the dramas of everyday life.

"Si j'étais une colombe, j'irais voler dans le désert."
If I were a dove, I would fly in the desert.

It wasn't so much the words as her vibration and tone of voice that pointed to a world and a way of being that was liberated, self-contained, at home with itself, and completely free of fear. Her sound was full of a healing light. She was a guiding star pointing me toward the voices of other spiritual teachers and devotional vocalists, most significantly the great luminary of India, Anandamayi Ma (Blissful Mother), whose voice was her very Self.

The voice of Anandamayi (1896–1982) was the primordial sound of an awakened Being, direct from source, the effortless mouthpiece of spirit. Whether she was singing with the homeless, a group of Western spiritual seekers, with world leaders such as Nehru or Mahatma Gandhi, or to vast thousands at the national Kumbh Mela gathering of saints from across India, Anandamayi sang consistently. Her voice covered a vast range of human-divine feeling—from the luminous

Anandamayi (Mother of Bliss, India. 1896–1982).
Photo by Richard Lannoy

darkness of the warrior goddess Durga to the heavenly decibels of Krishna, the god of Light and Love. Wherever she went she galvanized thousands to join with her in ecstatic chant and song.

It was my encounter with Anandamayi that enabled me to really *hear* for the first time how the naked human voice has the power to transform all suffering, however great, dissolving the veil that hides our true Self.

"Destroy the veil that hides your own Self" was her eternal refrain.

While exploring Anandamayi's teachings I had a vision in which I heard and saw the sound of humanity as forming an exquisite vessel, like a cosmic singing bowl, whose sacred presence had been forgotten. I also visualized the peoples of the world in the disorienting throes of a rebirth in consciousness while seemingly having lost all connection—individually and collectively—with their true voice and purpose as stewards of the planetary mind and beings of Light. This vision inspired me to dedicate my life to creating opportunities for the recovery of humanity's authentic voice, the original song of creation.

I established voice workshops, retreats, and gatherings to help people to experience their own naked voices. I found myself passionately dedicated to facilitating others to experience what I could see and hear as the authentic spirit within every living being.

It soon became clear that these gatherings were offering something unique, something that school had overlooked: the opportunity for individuals to reconnect their spoken with their sung voices, which simultaneously catalyzed a direct experience of their true path or calling. This calling didn't have to be some huge spiritual act or mission. It didn't even really matter how the human life then played itself out. Simply sounding one's true self and connecting directly with every cell of one's being as the true self was what I knew—from hearing Chanterelle and Anandamayi especially—the naked voice could ignite.

To support the evolution of the Naked Voice work I started collecting and sometimes composing my own healing songs, chants, and spoken or sung poems. I also began to find that any questions I had could turn themselves into musical melodies. Key questions started to inspire and direct my decision-making. Somehow singing my questions gave them greater clarity and inspired a clearer, more effortless response—for example:

Dear soul, what is my life consecrated to?

I started singing this question many years ago, at the beginning of a Naked Voice workshop in a beautiful Irish retreat center called Dunderry Park, deep in the countryside close to Navan, not far from Dublin city. This song I dedicated to the remarkable Dunderry Park team and kitchen staff, who provided hundreds of Naked Voice practitioners with the perfect sanctuary to find and transform their voices through the 1990s and new millennium. (See section 6.6, "A Wisdom Older and Deeper.")

Singing the question over and over anchors the voice of your soul in the body. Your voice and the intensity of your inquiry or intention fuel the energy of the sound, connecting it with the aliveness in your heart. In this way your voice soon becomes like a rudder or a compass that strengthens your soul's song-line and simultaneously helps you navigate the deeper course or direction of your own inner question or search.

Dear Soul, Dear Soul, What Is My Life Consecrated To?

Who am I?
How can I transform my sadness?
How can I integrate the conflicting dimensions of my life?
How can I step into this new cycle of life?

I allowed these and other questions to sing from my soul too. Once new songs were cooking, I started to compose more healing songs and chants inspired by new melodies and musical modes. These new songs started to teach me how close the connection is between our emotions and our musical expression of those emotions. The diatonic and chromatic musical scales came in to assist me in creating and developing more consciously the actual musical tools with which I could help others find their true voice as metaphor, and as music as well as a metaphysics, of being.

The musical scale—or *octave of consciousness*—that we know from school as *doh re mi fah soh lah ti doh* provides a vibrational template for exploring the architecture of the human spirit through specific sounds and musical intervals. These sounds and musical intervals translate into melodic shapes, the ever-changing moods and musical modes of the soul. Your body gradually becomes a temple of sound, a vibrational field within which your voice can be heard, witnessed, tracked, and honored through the songs that your soul sings.

Some human beings have many songs to sing. Others have just one song. Through the discovery of the Eastern and classical Indian music spiritual philosophy about the voice as a vehicle of spirit, I was able to start working directly with the musical energy systems of the human body, notably the musical chakras, key energy points related to your central spine from the root to the crown. We'll start to explore these very soon. But right now, let's take a closer look at the story of *your* voice, and the voices that have changed your life and awakened a more conscious relationship with your authentic voice.

1.11 Vocal Self-Portrait

The wanderer, the exile, home,
Coming home
One Self is all there is
Home coming home

—"ONE SELF," *Fierce Wisdom*

Your relationship with your own inner-outer voice is one of the most intimate you will ever have. As your witness and sound-awareness skills strengthen, you will discover how to listen to your voice with deepening acceptance and respect. In this chapter I invite you to begin unraveling the story of your very own voice more deeply with an exercise called "Vocal Self-Portrait."

Although I have worked with thousands of individuals, I have never heard the same vocal story or vocal self-portrait twice. Every human being is born with a unique sound. And that song carries a unique vibration encoded within your body from conception. This sound is available to you like a guiding star, whenever you choose to listen and tune in. This unique voice gives you an essential understanding of who you are, as well as how and why your life is unfolding the way it is.

As soon as you slide down the birth canal and out into this world, your natural voice bursts out. From thereon begins a long winding road of learning how to best express your truth and to be truly heard. The stability of the environment into which you were born, your waking and sleeping patterns, your opportunity to suck breast milk, to be nurtured and loved in the early days of this unpredictable and vulnerable shift from womb into life on Earth—all these events and more impact your voice and freedom to express yourself. As you explore your environment, the sound of your voice is constantly on call, issuing a range of emotional demands from alarm to deep satisfaction, shock to sweet utterance, laughter and tears, to whispers of tenderness and delight. As your limbs discover themselves, your primal sounds reach out nonverbally, stretching your tiny lungs with a startling array of vowel sounds spiraling around—"aaaah," "uuuu," "mumum," and "dadada"— one sound waving into the next. Your awkward and miraculous arrival into this new unknown world gradually lets go.

According to the melody and vibration of your song, you will start communicating with the world around you, with shifts reflecting what you experience: the quality of attention, creative support, and loving presence received, or perhaps indifference, neglect, abandonment, or abuse. There is no knowing how the song of your soul will be enhanced or inhibited by your early childhood years.

From the hundreds of vocal self-portraits I have been privileged to read and process, it has been evident that the apparently negative conditions of early childhood did actually provide, for some, the essential grist and resistance required to inspire their unswerving drive to stay true to their authentic voice, or to access it once again in later years. For others, it was the positive nurturing environment and the prosperous conditions that provided exactly the appropriate setting to flourish and harness the expression of their true voice once more.

This practice offers you an opportunity to build a balanced life, a healthy conscience, and the creative will to inspire an authentic presence on Earth. Its revelations may well motivate you to deepen your self-inquiry through the voice and written word.

Vocal Self-Portrait Practice: Reflection

Note: This reflective writing practice will require at least an hour of your time to really benefit from it. Its aim is to deepen your adventurous intention to explore and bond with the original sound that is your true voice.

When you look back to your childhood years, how did you most easily communicate, both with yourself and with others? Were you more at home alone, in communion with your inner voice of silence, or was it through your speaking voice that your true authority emerged? What part did singing play throughout your life in revealing your essence to others?

Imagine writing a vocal self-portrait that describes your relationship, from the inside out, with your voice as you experienced it in all its forms, e.g. hidden, reserved, vulnerable, dull, frightened, alienated, empowering, true, passionate, charismatic, overwhelming, transformative. As you journeyed from childhood into adolescence and adulthood, what enabled you to communicate yourself most authentically, in your raw naked truth, without censorship or self-consciousness? Which situations made your blood run cold, causing you to retreat into yourself?

This reflection encourages you to turn over every stone of your life: significant others, parents, siblings, elders, friends, strangers, animals, ceremonial events, accidental disasters, initiations, achievements, obstacles, and challenges. Were there passive voices of contempt and disempowerment, imagined voices, neglected voices left behind, unfulfilled dreams, voices of self-protection and denial, as well as wise voices, courageous and fulfilling, that instilled hope and possibility?

You are now invited to write your vocal self-portrait, the story of your voice—silent, spoken, and sung—in no more than four pages. The aim of this vocal exercise is to build a clear, courageous, and openhearted relationship with your life and with the voice that has brought you to this moment. The practice will enable you to let go and forgive old stories and to build the courage and honesty to restore honor where required to your family and your community. The practice invites you to remember the true voice of your soul, your naked voice, the authentic voice of your life.

Vocal Self-Portrait: Preparation

Be sure to approach this practice with the same nonjudging mind and loving presence you have developed thus far through a direct experience of your witness consciousness.

You will need a pen, some paper, and a quiet space and time to relax into this process with no distractions.

Choose any of these approaches to kick off your writing process:

- **Brainstorm:** Hand-write in an uncensored stream of words, using word association to trigger the significant moments in life and activate your historical imagination.
- **Recording:** Start remembering your vocal journey by speaking your story into a recorder so as to catalyze your memory.
- **Body movement:** Start by moving, letting your body remember and express the highs and lows, weaknesses and strengths, from birth to present day.
- **Singing:** Begin by improvising and sparking your memory of the highs and lows, along with specific memories of how your voice blossomed, contracted, and evolved throughout your life.
- **A combination of 1–4:** You may want to integrate some or all of the above approaches to access and arouse the story of your voice.

Vocal Self-Portrait: Completion

Once you have brainstormed, made notes, and recorded the story in as much detail as you can remember, set aside a relaxing space and time to sit down and write your unique vocal self-portrait.

Chapter 2

Your Instinctual Voice

2.1 An Instinctual Leap:
The Dance of the Jumping Goat

Freedom Freedom
Living laughing crying
Meeting parting dying
All for the love of you
Freedom Freedom

　　　—"FREEDOM," *Contemporary Devotion*

Black was my favorite color as a child. Black: the deep dark unknown, unfathomable space, the womb of the primordial Mother, the belly of the whale, an echoing empty chamber where water drips, where the original sound of creation heaves, groans, and resounds. These are sounds that tear your heart open, throw you down on your hands and knees, sounds from the black well of silence.

Black is that luminous dark unknown world I sink into when I am alone. Throughout childhood, I always had some deep-down intuition about the power of the dark: the unknown way, the *via negativa,* the dark side of the moon. Something in my sunlight-loving nature was drawn to its opposing pole: the void. So I brought black into my life. In adolescence I painted abstract pictures in black—elemental forces, wizened faces, mythological creatures, labyrinthine patterns—which brought into my daylight world the expressions of invisible underworld places and unanswered questions left unattended by my Christian, pristine, white middle-class environment.

> You do not have to be good
> You do not have to walk a hundred miles on your knees repenting
> You just have to let the soft animal of your body
> Love what it loves . . .
>
> —MARY OLIVER (EXCERPT)

As soon as my formal schooling was over, I decided to defer my Cambridge college plans for a year to travel into the unknown. I secured voluntary work for seven months as a village schoolteacher in the Akamba Mountains of Kenya.

The journey to Africa was a must. I had to go as far away as I could, to a culture whose grounding in the physical and instinctual would help me to anchor mine. Africa took me away from the sophisticated constraints of British life and opened the door to the wild.

Put to the test I was! I was eighteen. My soft princess feet kicked off their glass slippers and touched the raw earth for the first time. The air was dusty, dry, and hot. It took a few moments to adjust to the new texture and temperature of the ground. The heat penetrated my tired flesh and rose up my legs. I found my balance and looked around: black faces everywhere I turned. The pungent smell of the flowers intermingled with the musty smell of ammonia. Open sewage systems ran in thin channels beside the curb where I walked. There were people of every age, height, width, strength, and weakness imaginable. There were barely-clad beggars with no legs, only a wizened old torso, transporting themselves along the pavement on their hands. There were resigned old men, squatting on the ground outside hotels, shining the shoes of rich businessmen. Long corridors of stalls lined the streets with busy vendors with wares of every kind. The whole game of living and dying was played out with painstaking resignation here.

I had to make my way to my destination by bus. It was a precarious route riven with potholes and sharp bends up into the mountains. Two little black babies were thrown onto my lap. I was suddenly part of the scene, no longer a tentative observer. The midday sun burned through the window beside me, scorching my left shoulder.

The school where I was to teach was an educational experiment. Its aim was to bring together girls from different tribal backgrounds to generate more harmonious inter-tribal relationships. It was a secondary school, yet the girls were the same age or older than I was.

When I walked into my first lesson, I was stunned to see a roomful of vibrant black women, all sitting awaiting instruction. What could I possibly teach them? Their faces gazed at me quietly and unconditionally. I gazed back in awe. There was silence as thirty pairs of eyes met mine. Words felt inadequate. Suddenly a peal of laughter cracked through the air, cutting the tension and uniting us all.

"This is a PE lesson, isn't it?" I called out.

"Yes, Miss Goodchild!" they roared back.

"What do you do in PE?" I asked.

"Come with us!" they shouted. "We'll show you!" Suddenly everyone was piling out of the classroom and onto the netball pitch, which was a bald rectangular stretch of ground.

My first ordeal was the Dance of the Jumping Goat. The women gathered in a circle and placed me in the center. They proceeded to move in swaying rhythmic shuffles around me. One woman called out a refrain, and the rest of the circle echoed back her call in spontaneous harmony. As the dance rhythm became more animated, the refrain increased in volume. I stood at the center of this circle of women singing wildly for all they were worth. This was an initiation that I would never have imagined possible in my squeaky-clean British homeland. Was this dream or reality?

"Dance!" they called out to me.

I was the jumping goat. The women sang with exuberance and

Dance of the Jumping Goat (Ukia, Kenya 1971)

boundless delight. As the singing increased, our cultural differences fell away. We were of one blood, one voice. The goat had been accepted into the community.

Music was central to the rhythm of their life. I shall always remember the sound of the women's voices, together with the percussive rhythms that drove each song along. Their voices came from the belly. They were forceful, abrasive, impassioned, searing. The sounds the women made were devoid of all self-consciousness. They arose from the gut, from the raw material of Earth: they were the sounds of rain worship, the sun dance, the heartbeat, the sounds of storms. Such sounds can be dangerous. These sounds were their gift to me. They took the lid off the boiling pot of my cultural conditioning, enabling me to see and hear the neuroses of my own upbringing. It instilled in me the confidence to follow my own way in life. I returned to England seven months later triumphant, singing the song of a woman who had come through the trials of life and was returning to tell the tale. My experience in East Africa opened and strengthened my capacity to see, to face, and to navigate the instinctual voice of my own personal challenges and longing.

2.2 Sounding Your Name

Are you looking for me I am in the next seat
My shoulder against yours!

—"Breath," *Naked Heart*

"This has come upon me through repeating my own name to
myself silently till all at once, as it were out of the intensity of
the consciousness of individuality, individuality itself seemed
to dissolve and fade away into boundless being, and this not
a confused state, but the clearest, the surest of the surest,
utterly beyond words—where death was an almost laughable
impossibility—the loss of personality (if so it were) seeming no
extinction but only the true life."

—Tennyson from "Effortless Being," Alistair
Shearer and Richard Lannoy

I started experimenting with the practice of sounding my own name in the early 1980s when I first began to facilitate voice workshops. I would find myself in a circle of strangers, and introducing ourselves to each other was often an awkward task. I would invite each person to simply say their name, and maybe where they were from. Sometimes we would echo their name back to them, so they could feel that they had been heard. It then became obvious that speaking your name was helpful, but it still didn't achieve much for relaxing the mental constraint. So one day I decided to experiment with transferring the spoken-name practice into the sung version. What a difference! The terror that people had walked into the room with relaxed into deep relief at having taken the lid off inhibitions. Sounding Your Name became an integral and ongoing practice within the protocol.

Sounding Your Name can be a disorienting experience when you hear your natural authentic voice for the first time. As you begin to express the sound of your name, the vibration in your sound immediately begins to dismantle the tight shoe of your mind. Once your inner song begins to sound out, your reactive mind has no power to resist it. Your personality begins to surrender and melt in its presence. It's like a love affair that requires no outer or separate object of love. For the purposes of this practice, both the object and the subject of attention are YOU.

For a moment in time you find that you are free of all habitual tensions as the frozen history of your upbringing starts to thaw, melt, and dissolve. Once your authentic voice is heard, everything starts to change.

Simplicity is the key of this exercise. And it is a highly effective practice that doesn't require years of psychotherapy, interpretation, or analysis of any kind to access and express this name of yours. It's a stand-alone, self-healing, and empowering practice in which your spontaneous utterance itself is listener, guide, and friend, singing back at you and revealing everything you are calling for in the moment.

In ancient cultures, ceremonial or archetypal names are often sung as a way to invoke a heightened or sacred state of being. Sounding your own name brings the practice home and carries an intimacy and accessibility that shine the light on you and your ordinary-extraordinary self.

Sounding Your Name Practice

This practice can be experienced alone or in a group context. If you are in a group it can be relaxing to ask the other members to hold a humming or instrumental drone sound for you to sing over. If you are alone it can be empowering to sing your name to yourself in the mirror.

- Choose a time and place where you know you will be undisturbed for 15 minutes or so.
- Sitting or standing, close your eyes, breathe in and sigh out several times, and arrive in this present moment, relaxing your shoulders, head, and neck.
- Scan your body from feet to crown, ensuring that your vertical axis is strong. Close your eyes and feel gratitude for your name.
- Visualize someone you love and the endearment with which they call you. See your name in your mind's eye. Begin to develop a sense of the melodic shape and rhythmic feel of your name. Hear it internally. Bring your awareness to the center of the chest, activating a loving respect for your name.
- Begin to whisper your name like a secret, hearing its presence and feeling the sensation of the vowel sounds within your name moving through your mouth and into the space in front of you.
- Deepen your breath in and sigh out your name with a sense of relief and acceptance of who you are. Increase your inhaling-exhaling breath and the sound of your voice, and invite your hands and arms to encourage the sound as the melody of your name begins to find its shape.
- Explore as many ways as your voice wants to express and share the changing sounds of your name.
- Give it away. Receive it back again. Let the sound of your name ebb and flow as your heart connects with it and you express your feelings for it from the center of your chest. No need to be polite or try to sound nice or beautiful. Let laughter, tears, or whatever emotions present color your sound.
- When you are ready to finish, close your eyes, cross your hands over your heart, bow, and say thank you. Reflect on your name and the direct experience you have just had. If possible, don't just stand up and rush back into automatic mode.

- You may want to write about the experience in your journal.
- Once you are familiar with this practice you can integrate it into your daily life in less formal ways, like in the shower or the car, or while making a meal. You may want to share it with a colleague, friend, child, or lover, back and forth, singing each other's name.

NB: Always remember this is not a performance, it's a simple and unforgettable way to begin connecting with the unique song of your soul.

2.3 Whose Voice Was That?

I have a feeling that my boat
has struck, down there in the depths,
against a great thing.
And nothing happens! . . . Is it that nothing happens, . . . or are we
standing now, quietly, in the new life?

—FROM THE POEM "OCEANS" BY JUAN RAMON JIMINEZ,
TRANSLATED BY ROBERT BLY; SUNG WITH THE TITLE
"MY BOAT HAS STRUCK," *Contemporary Devotion*

And a new cycle of life it was for a woman attending my Tuesday morning voice workshop. Her desperate human cry suddenly exploded unpredictably and triumphantly out of nowhere. And she was really serious too:

I'm struggling with my monster, struggling with my monster, struggling, struggling, struggling with my MONSTER!

She shrieked this out over and over. . . . Her primal screams penetrated the walls of the building, pouring out and away across the city. I have never forgotten it. This was not merely a display of dramatics—it marked an important turning point for this highly gifted human being who had lived most of her life in a deep depression. For several weeks, since the beginning of this voice course, she had barely opened her mouth beyond a few resigned mutterings. Then, suddenly, everything changed. Through the vehicle of her voice, this victim of chronic inertia shifted her condition into a tower of strength and an unstoppable determination to face the dark aspects of her nature. Now she was radiant.

After her chant had finished, she stared at us in amazement. "Where did that come from? Whose voice was that?" From that moment on, it was impossible to stop her desire to express herself. She looked magnificent and proud, having caught the first glimpse of her true authority. She then proceeded to tell us that her only motivation to get out of bed at all was for these Tuesday voice workshops. They had given her the challenge that she had been looking for to sing her way back to life. Her voice was her lifeline, a crucial thread between unconscious and conscious worlds. And so it was for us all.

What always astonishes me with these vocal insights is the total unpredictability with which they emerge from each soul. They arise with such authenticity and substance from the lips of the singer. After the emotional expression come the words for new songs, fresh gardens of discovery, imaginal territory, sonic landscapes interpreted through sound and rhythm. The natural voice, freely expressed, is a sound-seer, the soul's messenger. With lightning speed it dives deep, returning with a poignant message or question. My task, as with my own voice, is to help people hear themselves, without the obstruction of judgment or paralyzing self-consciousness.

What a teacher the voice is! Out of my own suffering, self-inquiry, and subsequent vocal insights, I created a job helping others undertake the same process of exploration. At that time (the early 1980s), none of the traditional institutions offered any form of vocal training quite like this. It was crucial to start encouraging singers to respond to their own voice with sincerity and pleasure. As this therapeutic singing continued, I discovered how, with permission and purpose, each voice could tell its own story. The work was as varied as the individuals undergoing it. My multicultural students brought me the music from their own cultures: the ecstatic Qawwali singers from Pakistan; the dissonant raw beauty of Les Voix Bulgares; the iconic devotionalism of the Greek Orthodox liturgy; the passionate peasantry of Norwegian cattle calls; the Islamic call to prayer; Spanish love songs; the civil rights movement songs; the ethereal Celtic Christian and folk songs of Ireland.

There was no end to the sounds that began to fill my life. Meanwhile the opportunities to witness the revitalizing power of voice work increased. My students were discovering the art of sounding out spontaneously with the authenticity and power of their own voices. They would know when their singing was beginning to really resonate in their bones and sound true—for the voice would suddenly have a penetrating edge to it, awakening every cell in the body. Its vibration and presence gave us goosebumps. Always a sure sign.

Anyone Can Sing *(an excerpt)*

Anyone can sing. You just open your mouth,
and give shape to a sound. Anyone can sing.
What is harder, is to proclaim the soul,
to initiate a wild and necessary deepening:
to give the voice broad, sonorous wings
of solitude, grief, and celebration,
to fill the body with the echoes of voices
lost long ago to bravery, and silence,
to prise the reluctant heart wide open,
to witness defeat, to suffer contempt,
to shrink, lose face, go down in ignominy,
to retreat to the last dark hiding-place
where the tattered remnants of your pride
still gather themselves around your nakedness,
to know these rags as your only protection
and yet still open—to face the possibility
that your innermost core may hold nothing at all,
and to sing from that—to fill the void
with every hurt, every harm, every hard-won joy. . . .

—William Ayot (from *Small Things That Matter*)

Much of my time was spent releasing what I call the "metal grip around the throat" syndrome. As throat after throat opened like flowers to the sun, I would stand back to hear unique songs arising from the belly with an increasing and unstoppable force and freedom. The sound would continue rising and falling in an expanding stream of quarter tones and whole tones, sliding and soaring, sometimes jumping in jets of sound, spilling out of the body with surprised abandonment, aliveness, and uncontrollable laughter or tears.

I encouraged everyone to remember the songs from all realms of their lives: nursery rhymes, folk tunes, arias, jazz, and musicals. This nonthreatening connection with both the familiar and ancestral sounds dissolved barriers and encouraged a deep primordial connection with each person's core self from source.

2.4 One Breath, One Voice

You who are my earth my anchor
You the one who shines the sword
You with eyes as flames of thunder
Singing search lights sounding board
      —"You," *Thousand Ways of Light*

"Don't think—sing!"

I say this to myself when I am hovering on the brink of communicating something essential, something that must be expressed and heard right now without social airs or graces of any kind, without any censorship at all. Singing your own song reveals what you don't yet know about yourself, and it requires a courage that comes running to support you once sound is pouring out of your mouth. Choirs are wonderful, but singing your own song requires a will all of its own. The great dare is to open your mouth and let whatever wants to come out of you come out.

Fearful always moving mind
The one who has no beginning is
thinking of how hunger may
fall away from you
No ritual, no religion is needed
Just cry out one unobstructed cry

—RUMI, COLEMAN BARKS TRANSLATION

One Breath, One Voice is one of the core practices of The Naked Voice because it's one of the most accessible and fastest ways I know to retrieve the raw truth about yourself and your life.

And you don't have to be a "singer." Just a risk-taker. The good news is there is everything to gain and nothing to lose. Once you get used to letting your voice out, the self-consciousness starts to disappear and your listening attention becomes more focused and fascinated by this new vehicle of expression. As your confidence in your own voice strengthens, you will start to build a more resonant and robust voice, extending the breath, energizing the sound, and expanding your vocal range.

One Breath, One Voice reveals what you don't yet know about yourself. The unexpected nature of this vocal practice has you sounding out in ways you never imagined possible. Questions such as "Who was that?" and "Where does it come from?" captivate your imagination and deepen your self-inquiry as you begin to evolve an intimate and inventive collaboration with the mouthpiece of your soul. This capacity to express yourself spontaneously signals the beginning of a new way of being and communicating. As you undress the voice of your upbringing, your sound begins to relax, loosening the layers of armoring and self-consciousness that previously prevented you from expressing yourself.

As your confidence grows you will encounter a greater willingness within yourself to meet the unexpected, unpredictable, and unknown parts of yourself. What you don't know about yourself is fascinating and empowering.

Ask yourself, "Who am I, and who is this unknown voice within me? What is it telling or expressing through me?" and "Do I want to live my life solely in the safe harbor and comfort of my social conditioning, or am I ready to take a voyage into the uncharted ocean of my soul?"

Without taking this journey we may be in danger of missing that essential encounter with our life as yet unlived. Your life force is governed by your heart, the headquarters of your body field, an unstoppable center of operations, a mighty muscle, responsible for coordinating your physical existence with your psycho-physical and spiritual evolution, with the support of the brain. As well as pumping seven thousand liters of blood around the body every day, your heart assists in stimulating and awakening specific energy-wheels of awareness, also known as *chakras*. They are located in the etheric or subtle body from the root (anus and perineum) to the crown (top of the head), and run through the pelvis, solar plexus, heart, throat, third eye, and back of the head. These energy resource points are resonating chambers that can be activated with the support of breath and sound awareness. When these energy points are firing and spinning well within, you will feel radically alive, embodied, and balanced.

We live in such a self-conscious culture, dominated by the rational left brain. One Breath, One Voice enables you to launch and move beyond the self-consciousness and false perceptions about your voice, empowering you to step into an entirely new cycle of life with your voice. I have been privileged to facilitate this simple practice with thousands of individuals. Here's an excerpt of a wonderful Mary Oliver poem ("The Journey," *Dream Work*) to inspire your practice:

One day you finally knew
what you had to do,
and began,
though the voices around you
kept shouting
their bad advice—though the whole house
began to tremble

and you felt the old tug
at your ankles
"Mend your life!"
each voice cried.
You knew what you had to do

One Breath, One Voice Practice

This practice was inspired by a unique moment that I shared with my father just before he died. The privilege of being present with him as he breathed his last breaths brought me face to face with the precious fleeting gift of life. The exercise practice is exactly as it sounds. You simply take in one huge breath and sound out for all you are worth, as if you are about to utter the last or first breath of your life. As you surrender your whole self to this spontaneous utterance, you will enter an immediacy with the present moment. "Ahhhhh" is a good sound to start with because you will naturally relax and drop the jaw, opening your mouth wide.

As soon as sound is spilling from your mouth, the breath, heart, mind, and body unify, vibrating and resonating together. An alignment takes place; you will integrate previously disparate or fragmented parts of yourself. What is most important about the practice is that you absolutely let go. Give it all away. When the sound comes to an end, don't rush to breathe in again. Let yourself dwell in the silence that meets you there before the next breath naturally draws in again.

Here begins a deeper relationship with yourself, and a creative interaction with your life. Practice for 3–5 minutes to begin with. Don't judge, simply document what you hear. Describe it, begin to communicate with it as you might an intimate friend. Enjoy the surprises that arise from your One Breath, One Voice practice, songs of an unexpected life. When 5 minutes feels too short, extend the practice to 10, 20, 30 minutes and more. And don't feel you have to wait for a special time or place.

Explore One Breath, One Voice as you walk to work, down the high street, whilst shopping. Enjoy!

2.5 Initiation Song: Madison Square Garden

Stroke my songbird strike my flame
Juicy Lucy's alive she's insane
For the lightness your touch brings

    —"RED WET SONG," *V Day*

I was in conversation with Eve Ensler, world peace activist and author of the acclaimed performance and script *The Vagina Monologues*. She had asked me to collaborate with her team as musical co-director for her forthcoming musical premiere of *The Vagina Monologues,* to be performed in New York City's Madison Square Garden in February 2001.

"Chloë, I want you to create a grief wail that embraces the suffering of the world then redeems and transforms it in about three minutes. Can you do that?" It was for a key point in the show, just before Oprah Winfrey's monologue called "Under the Burka."

Eve and I had first met the year before in a west London restaurant to discuss my musical involvement in her New York performance for V Day, the front face of her campaign to bring an end to violence toward women. Eve and I sat together, getting to know each other, when she suddenly stopped short after speaking about my album *Devi* that she had been listening to.

"I want that sound in the Garden," she said, meaning Madison Square Garden, the V Day venue.

Months later, in New York, and only weeks away from the Madison Square Garden performance, Eve was honing in with a focused gravity on what vocal sound and music would be the most poignant and penetrating to accompany the new "Under the Burka" monologue.

"One Breath, One Voice!" I exclaimed.

"What's that?" she asked.

"Well, you take a huge breath in, then you let go, sounding out whilst abandoning yourself completely, expressing absolutely everything you

Chloë singing in Madison Square Garden, NYC (2001). Photo by
Aliki Sapountzi

can, in just one breath. You sing with fierce intention as if this breath is
the first or last breath of your life!"

"What does it sound like?" Eve asked me tentatively, all ears.

The only way I could describe the sound was to demonstrate it.
So I let out a long rip-roaring primal sound on "Aaaah," which blasted
through the room.

Eve responded like a wild cat pouncing on its prey. "That's it—I
love it!" she shouted. "And remember, there mustn't be any recognition of or affiliation anywhere in your music to one religious language
or another. The sound simply has to be universal."

I had my work cut out for me.

When the moment came, my grief wail resounded across the infinite space of the "Garden," enveloping me in the longest breath imaginable. Its intention was to fulfill Eve's original wish—to embrace suffering, and to redeem it, in three minutes. I laid my life on the line. There were in total three long breaths and sounds, accompanied by the pounding rhythms on drums played by three ground-shaking Native American women singer-sound healers.

And as one spotlighted young woman in a wedding burka processed slowly and ceremonially down through the audience toward the center stage, the rest of the Garden darkened. One singular stream of light followed her to her meeting point with Oprah Winfrey, who slowly and quietly lifted the burka from the young woman's body, as twenty thousand people applauded triumphantly. My initiation song had served its purpose.

2.6 The Sword and the Flower: Meetings with an Energy Movement Master

The sword and the flower
The sword and the flower
Is all that I bring
My soul's offering

—"Sword and Flower," *Laughing Heart*

I first met Masashi Minagawa in 1995. He is now a master of an energy movement form called Shintaido, which means "new-body-way."

I was living on the northern slopes of the Roman spa town of Bath in the UK. My neighbor called to say that I absolutely had to have a massage with a remarkable Japanese shiatsu practitioner she had encountered. Masashi had moved from Japan to Bristol with his English wife and three young children in 1990. I phoned Masashi immediately and arranged for him to come over and give me an Amma Shiatsu massage. The bell rang, and I opened the door: an unassuming young Japanese man in his forties was standing on the step. Masashi Minagawa introduced himself, bowed, and stepped lightly over the threshold into our house. The shiatsu consisted of a fully clothed bodywork session. Unlike other massages I had experienced, this was a precise and enlivening method of bodywork, based on the activation of specific meridian points throughout the body, from head to toe. Rather than spacing out, I felt alert. At the end of the session I arose to find Masashi standing, eyes closed in a meditative mood, at a respectful distance away from the table. As I sat up to get off the massage table, he looked up smiling and bowed discreetly once again.

"This is not all you do, is it?" I asked curiously. There was a pause as he reflected quietly on this unexpected question. "What else do you do?" I continued. He laughed, opening up and relaxing into a more informal mode. "Would you like some tea? I would love to hear more about your life and work," I said.

He graciously accepted the invitation while maintaining a certain formality—a Japanese cultural trait, perhaps. Little did I realize that I was about to be initiated into a whole new cycle of life, and with it, a refreshingly new perspective on ways to embody and communicate my voice work.

We drank tea beside the crackling fire in my sitting room overlooking the rolling English countryside. Masashi began to tell me about the great vocation of his life: Shintaido, an energy-movement practice inspired and created by Masashi's master Aoki Hiroyuki in Japan, several decades previously. Masashi was part of the original community of Shintaido students who lived, breathed, and researched this pioneering energy art. The more Masashi told me about Shintaido, the more fascinated I became. Our teatime came to a close, but not without Masashi agreeing to bring one of his students to my house to demonstrate this movement.

Some days later Masashi returned with a young female student. They both changed into white outfits called *gi* in Japanese. We cleared the furniture to the side of the room so that they could move with as much ease as possible. After bowing to each other, they proceeded to engage in a series of spontaneous movements together that were clearly extremely energizing and enjoyable for them both. I was fascinated by this dynamic dance of giving and receiving. The movements gracefully integrated tension and release in ways that challenged and transformed the limitations of my mind. Shintaido provided a stable ground for a whole spectrum of expression that required no words. Such a relief! The clear boundaries allowed for an intimacy and a freedom of communication that was liberating for both practitioners. When their movement came to an end, I was speechless. I felt energized by simply witnessing this spectacle of aliveness. I knew that this practice was something I had to explore more deeply for myself.

Masashi then came to a concert that I was giving in Bath. He offered to open the evening with some movement to clear the energy of the performance space before I sang. I was very happy. The simplicity of his movement as he entered was breathtaking. Dressed once again in white, he simply walked very slowly onto the stage with his arms and hands leading in a spirit of offering. Once on stage, he faced the audience in silence, looking into the far distance, opening his stance and his whole energy field to embrace everyone present. This took place in total silence, without any self-consciousness or pretentious avant-garde performance. His presence was simple, genuine, calming. He closed his stance, bowed, and walked slowly off the stage, leaving a field of silence and deep listening everywhere.

I then entered the space, improvising freely, nonverbal ribbons of sound issuing from my open mouth and expanding into the space further. The evening unfolded into a program of East-West sacred chant, sound, and naked song as, together, my percussionist and I explored the musical language of the soul through sound and rhythm.

At the end of the evening Masashi came up to me and said, "I think I can see what you are doing." He was referring to the energetic impact of the vocal sound on the audience. Pointing toward the sky he said, "You are sending your sound too far away! People are listening to you and yet asking themselves, 'Where has she gone?'"

We both burst out laughing. I was intrigued by this new way of seeing the energy of my sound as a vibrational force-field, capable of building or diminishing the energy-field of the audience. As a singer it was essential that I become more aware of how to consciously energize and nourish the audience through my sound.

Masashi Minagawa, a portrait (2002).

A couple of weeks later, Masashi returned with his student, and
this time we went to the local village hall. The aim was to give me the
opportunity to have a more direct experience of this magical energy-
movement work. What I loved most about Shintaido was its poetic

flow. To a novice, Shintaido could be seen as a combination of T'ai Chi and Aikido, two practices that I had explored earlier in my life. Yet added to this was the innocent, joyous unpredictability and spontaneity of two free spirits playing like children. As I looked more deeply, I realized that Shintaido offered an extremely radical and challenging encounter with one's true self through movements that sought to transform rather than overthrow, to empower rather than diminish or kill.

A deep nonjudgmental listening was the shared ground for our work. Such a listening requires a precision and fearless attention that is often challenging. Certainly no one had taught us about this in school. It required the ability to both objectively observe and subjectively engage with, simultaneously, whatever was happening. This listening had to be of such an unconditional depth as to be able to:

- Fully engage the trust of the practitioner.
- Empower them to interact fully with all presenting emotions.
- Integrate this new experience of sound with energy movement.
- Let go, accept, and step into a new depth of practice and self-awareness.

The aim of our work together was to shift from a "me-centered" to an inclusive "we-centered" awareness in which everyone is accepted, respected, and honored.

What I enjoyed most about working with Masashi was his humility and choiceless dedication to the practices. He certainly didn't teach by fear. He taught through joy and a simple delivery of this transformative energy movement, from the warm-ups to the meditations and more rigorous stick and sword work. It was the essential ordinariness of our evolving collaboration that made it empowering and profound. We actually spent most of our first "Shintaido lesson" cleaning the floor of the village hall before practicing together.

Masashi agreed to come and demonstrate Shintaido energy movement in one of my workshops called "Wild Prayer." I will never forget the sheer élan with which Masashi demonstrated his wild prayer by leaping like a giant frog down the full length of the workshop hall—to the stunned amazement and delight of all participants—demonstrating how free human energy can be when the body simply lets go of holding onto fear and abandons itself into free expression. He was the naked voice in action.

I was blessed to find myself in the company of a vocationally driven artist, and the "driver" was not Masashi's personality. It was the source of life itself.

The three pillars of Shintaido energy movement are as follows:

TENSHINGOSO, *The Cycle of Life, Five Phases of Heavenly Truth,* expressed through the vowel sounds, A (Ah) E (Eh) I (Ee) O (Oh) UM (Um).

EIKO, *The Glory*—An exhilarating sword-like movement that integrates Heaven and Earth, through the sounding of Um to Eh, or Um to Ah.

TAIMYO, *Symphony of Love*—A three-part series of movements that challenge, empower, and ultimately lead practitioners into a direct encounter with themselves.

As our shared voice, sound, and energy movement research developed, Masashi began to introduce movements that were directly supportive and expressive of the Naked Voice vocal practices—for example, some special meditative hand movements to accompany the journey I came to call "The Seven Sounds of Love." (Section 5.2 in Chapter Five will take you deeper.) These seven sounds offer a dynamic vocalizing of the musical chakra sounds inspired by the East Indian classical vocal scale, with its Sanskrit-based sounds that are *mantras* (spiritual words of power).

Masashi introduced other meditative martial-art movements, with special hand gestures called *mudras* (another Sanskrit word). These have a radical impact on the flow of energy and sound through the body, inspiring the vocalist to express and embody sound more deeply. The more I witnessed Masashi's movement, the more at home I felt in his presence and the fierce lightness of his approach and teaching way. He was and is a great mirror and friend.

When time has allowed, Masashi travels with me for work. Our respective disciplines complement each other. Masashi focuses mainly on the meditative dimension of Shintaido in our workshops, always choosing the most appropriate movements to empower the vocalist to connect their inner, deeper human feeling and authentic expression. Shintaido offers a visible expression of the sacred architecture of the human soul through energy movement, creating a grounded framework for the invisible music that is the naked voice.

We soon came to respect and understand most deeply the importance of our shared work through a recognition of our respective lineage holders. For Masashi it was his master Aoki Hiroyuki. For me it was my master Anandamayi, one of India's greatest female saints of the twentieth century. It was our encounters with these luminaries that had confirmed our life's calling. We have often enjoyed sharing our personal stories about our respective traditions, encouraging others to do the same within the field of our work together.

As the years have passed and our work together has matured, Masashi and I have begun to explore more deeply the interface of sound with energy movement in structured ("sei" in Japanese) and totally abandoned ("dai") ways.

Synchronistically, the Heart Sutra was a mantra central to us both, and we have spent many hours over the years sounding and moving with this mantra, whose essential words are: *Om Gate Gate Paragate Parasamgate Bodhi Svaha!* (meaning) *GO, GO Far Beyond, Far Beyond the Wisdom Is!*

Before we chant the mantra, we always begin with silence. Then as the sound of the mantra enters my voice, I focus my attention inwardly while simultaneously witnessing the impact of the sacred syllables on Masashi's movement. As our shared attention to the sound and the energy movement has evolved, it now effortlessly accesses a peaceful presence generated between sound, movement, and the space between the two. The boundaries between us disappear as our shared devotion becomes an invisible vessel, spacious and empty.

It is our recognition of this interconnected field, or presence, that we are privileged to share with others. And the concept of *the field*—inspired by the Rumi poem of the same name—confirmed and consolidated our future collaborative research with what came to be called the Singing Field, which is the subject of Part III.

In 2000 we named our collaborative work "The Sword and the Flower" following a meditation practice together that gave birth to a simple chant of the same name.

The sword and the flower is all that I bring, my soul's offering.

The Sword and the Flower, a caliograph by Masashi Minagawa

2.7 Where Sound Meets Energy

Thousand arms of compassion
Thousand wings so bright
Thousand blessings for our children
Thousand ways of Light

—TITLE TRACK, *Thousand Ways of Light*

The energy movement practices in this chapter will unfold and reveal the multifaceted nature of the naked voice within you. You will discover through the energy movements of Tenshingoso, or the Five Phases of Life, a more in-depth experience of the primordial OM through the five vowel sounds A E I O U. Each sound is accompanied by a specific energy movement that unlocks the vital healing power of sound energy within you.

These five sounds—when sung consecutively—create the unifying sound of OM. Whether we hear it or not, the unchanging OM is ever-present. Even scientists agree that this all-pervading sound exists in the universe. As you learn to restore this sound within, you reconnect with your core self. Remembering this one sound enables you to listen to yourself and others, once again, with unconditional ears. The more attention you give to accessing the source of your own sound, the more you will become aware of a great stillness within you. Singing these five sounds calms your nervous system and emotional body and is the fastest and most efficient way I know to dissolve the tyranny of the reactive mind.

The sound SA is another name for this unchanging note. SA is the root sound of the ascending-descending scale of classical Indian music. SA is the equivalent of the first note—the tonic or home note—in our Western musical scale. Unlike our Western music, which loves to change its harmonic ground or musical center, modulating many times within one musical piece, the SA, or home note, of Indian music always remains in the same place. SA calls us into the timeless unmanifested part of ourselves from where all the sounds of the universe appear and disappear. SA inspires all the other vibrations and sounds to blossom and flourish.

SA is what you might call a magic key, like a "sonic code" that has the power to give birth, energy, and life to all the other musical notes of your singing soul. The sound of SA calms the singer's mood and vibration. SA is an anchoring seed sound that contains, envelops, protects, and ultimately empowers the vast range of your emotional and musical expression. It also awakens and frees your spirit, and liberates your heart-mind from outworn patterns of thinking and believing. SA *reveals* your singing voice as a transformative agent capable of harnessing the whole musical spectrum of human feeling. Later in Part II we will discover more of the musical role that SA plays, as the source of all sound, within the Seven Sounds of Love.

The following energy movements focus on the cyclical movement practice of Tenshingoso, or Cycle of Life, one of three pillars of Shintaido. This magical movement is made up of five phases that begin and end in the same place, with the same sound, UM. This universal movement is accessible to everyone and restores inner-outer harmony while simultaneously embodying your voice in a way that is extremely grounding.

> If you want to awaken all of humanity then awake all of yourself. If you want to eliminate suffering in the world, then eliminate all that is dark and negative in yourself. Truly the greatest gift you have to give is that of your own self-transformation.
>
> —Lao Tzu

Sound-Energy Movement Practice

Since Masashi Minagawa first demonstrated this profound way to access inner stillness and presence through energy movement, I have found Tenshingoso to be the most complementary partner for the naked-voice practices.

Tenshingoso is a journey of self-discovery. It is also called the "Hymn or Cycle of Life" and is one of the fundamental movements of Shintaido. *Tenshin* means "heaven" or "universal truth" in Japanese. It also refers to the shape of your unadorned true self and the perfect freedom. *Goso* literally means "five phenomena" or "stages." It is derived from esoteric Buddhism and represents five ways of embodying the universal creator. Before we approach each stage we must first develop a strong awareness or witness consciousness. We can then begin to absorb and embody the meaning of the five stages. Each stage-movement is accompanied by a mantric sound in Sanskrit: UM-A-E-I-O-M. Even though we sometimes practice one stage independently, it is important to remember that the five stages are essentially interdependent and flow together as one cycle or hymn of life.

TENSHINGOSO—*The Five Stages in More Detail*

1) UM: Emptiness, Darkness

Stand with your feet and big toes touching. Your right hand rests lightly inside your left hand. Place your left thumb lightly in your right hand and hold your right four fingers with your left fingers. Drop both your arms. Face forward with your eyes half or completely closed.

Sounding Um we enter a place of emptiness, darkness, humility, and a time before birth. We must not underestimate the profound depth of Um. Close your eyes and let yourself become smaller and smaller until you bring all your concentration into one single point where everything disappears. Sink down inside yourself as you sound the Um until you disappear into emptiness. Release all tension from the top of your head down to your feet, and let your attention drop deeper, down into the center of the Earth. It may be helpful to imagine that you are a pebble descending slowly to the bottom of the ocean. Travel on down beneath the ocean floor to the Earth's core. Everything comes from here; it is the source of our life. It is a vast place of emptiness and total humility. There are so many layers of Um, and the more concentration you bring to it, the more effortlessly you return to your original nature.

2) A: Expansion, Acceptance, the Ideal

From Um to A the pure energy rises like a flower opening, giving birth to your life. As you sound Ah open your hands out and spread your feet a little more than the width of your shoulders. At the same time, let your arms continue moving backward, relaxing your shoulders, and let your fingers and palms open and stretch back. Bend back and reach behind you, pushing your hips out, and look toward the sky. As your hands open and you reach upward, you expand out and rise up into your highest aspiration. Increase your awareness and open gradually, following your hands as the energy ascends up the center of your body, from the Earth to the sky. Push the palms of your hands upward into the sky, concentrating the energy through the heels of your hands. Slowly bring your wrists up until they are facing each other over your head. Reach up as high as you possibly can. You are reaching toward your highest ideal. Don't worry if you feel ungrounded. Reach up as far as the energy will take you. Let it take you. Expand beyond your limitations and receive grace by opening your whole self. Trust your body. Follow your ideal.

3) E (Eh): Integration, Actualizing the Ideal

This shift can sometimes be very challenging as we learn to integrate the ideal A into the reality of E. Don't compromise your ideal, yet be willing to accept the present conditions of your everyday life.

At the outset of A, with your arms and hands stretched skyward, make the sound E and start to bring your little fingers together while looking to the far distance. Your arms are like two swords. Let them cut open what is blocking the way in front of you. It may be more helpful to imagine you are cutting through mist or opening curtains in front of you. Twist your arms and hands, bringing your little fingers together and the back of your hands near to each other. Let your arms stretch upward a little. Now—as if you are opening a curtain or outlining Mount Fuji in front of you (from its summit) with your hands—start turning your palms outward, leading with the elbows and little fingers. This is the movement of integration, as you bring your dream into reality and carve out your future, sounding E. Bring your arms down and out, shoulder-width apart. Move your elbows out to the side and bring your thumbs to the front. Your palms are now facing forward and your elbows pointing outward. Make sure your hands are not too far apart. If they are too open, the experience will be too shallow, and the energy will dissipate. Standing in this posture, penetrate your inner frontiers.

4) I (EE): Management Control and Development

Sounding I (Ee) you discover your capacity to manage, control, and develop your original hopes and dreams effectively in the world. I (Ee) brings self-confidence and grounded engagement with your daily life. Imagine you are sounding I (Ee) from the top of a mountain with the whole world at your feet. There are two movements here. First, from the wide position of E, bring your arms and hands down toward the pelvis. Let your index fingers close together as you push the hands out in front of the lower abdomen. This is management. Second, development: stretch your arms forward and gradually push your hands up, and bring together your index fingers and thumbs to create a triangle in space. Set your visual focus on the infinite.

5) O (Oh): Reconciliation, Completion, Offering

Sounding O, embrace and reconcile yourself with everything in your life and the world as you feel the presence of universal love in every cell of the body. Sounding O, make a big circle, spreading your arms wide open and back a little. Envelop everything in front of you. Your hands move down and forward at waist level. Bring them together and push forward and up as far as possible with the palm facing forward and the fingers pulled back and downward. This is a gesture of offering and completion. Standing in this posture, offer everything back to the center of the great universe.

From here, let yourself relax and return to the original stage of Um where your mind is free from all ideas and thoughts. Bring your little fingers together and overlap your hands, like two resting wings, right hand over left, and then down to the Um position.

Return to nothingness in preparation for the next Cycle of Life.

UM (begins again)

Continue for as many times as is appropriate. A maximum of three cycles is enough to begin with.

Chapter 3

Your Still Voice

3.1 Mantra: A Direct Experience

Sink deeper down
in
ever widening circles
of
Being

   —"Deeper Down," *Naked Heart*

A mantra is a sacred sound or simple collection of sounds that constellate to form a holy prayer bringing you home to your deepest self, a still point within, prior to ego and duality. There are ancient mantras that date back thousands of years, many of which are associated with a specific religious faith. In more recent times, we are witnesssing an emerging contemporary interest in sounding and chanting mantras that have a more universalist or "pathless" orientation. They have no attachment to one religious tradition or another. Whether the sacred mantra is ancient or modern, the intention is always to inspire a state of oneness. "All these religions, one song," says Rumi (Coleman Barks translation).

Mantras are essentially magical sound codes or words of spiritual power invoked from the heart. They are traditionally sung in ancient languages such as Aramaic, Latin, or Sanskrit. They also inspire divine utterance within the primordial music of aboriginal and shamanic cultures, where the spirit of oneness or the presence of "great mystery" is revealed as a portal of transformation and renewal, collapsing the old dimensions of duality to unify the visible and invisible worlds. The great mantras are thousands of years old, handed down orally from master to disciple, student, or apprentice. In essence they are golden vibrations of light, transmitting the deepest communion within subatomic particles, molecules, and cells of our body-minds, awakening the energies of Love. The sound of a mantra usually revolves around one *unchanging note*. This singular note is a pivotal point of dynamic stasis. I love to call it the zero point of consciousness, a liberating emptiness, pure presence. "Mantra" means "word of spiritual power" or "wisdom sound."

When I once inquired of Anandamayi what a mantra is, she replied as follows:

> While one is bound by the idea of "I" and "You" and identifies with the ego, the mantra represents the Supreme Being in the guise of sound. Do you not see how beautifully certain syllables have been joined together to awaken you? True knowledge can enter you at the very utterance of a word of power, which is composed merely of a few ordinary letters joined together. How mysterious and intimate is the relation between these sacred words and the One Self! A mantra is a combination of sounds that has the power to free you from the notion of separateness by which your mind has been held captive all along. It is through this sound that one penetrates into Silence.

Unlike secular singing for social entertainment, where the melody and harmonies are constantly stimulating and changing the emotional life of the singer or listener, the magic of mantra is in its simple repetitive and unchanging nature, usually focused on just one phrase or sound. Mantras are often accompanied by a drone sound, such as a rattle or drum, a one-stringed instrument such as the African *birembau,* or a four-stringed Indian gourd instrument called a *tampura,* or a portable keyboard known as a *sruti* box or harmonium.

The beauty of this repetitive mantric chanting is that anyone and everyone can do it and derive immense benefits from it.

In the UK alone, millions of working days are lost every year due to stress-related illness. Mantric sound, song, and chanting offer an efficient and radical response to the needs of a struggling humanity facing ever-dwindling energy resources. A mantra does not depend on outside resources, special equipment, or technology. It is an inner resource. Mantra is our spiritual inheritance. It is not the exclusive possession of any one single religion.

Sounding AUM (OM): A Direct Experience of Mantra

One sound is recognized by humanity everywhere as the source of all mantra: AUM. We began to explore the powerful interface of sound and energy through the movement practice of Tenshingoso (section 2.7), which provides a solid way to fully embody the sacred mantra AUM through the sounding of A E I O M with the associated body movements. The AUM (or OM) mantra is described in a 4,000-year-old Sanskrit wisdom text called the Mandukya Upanishad. It reveals the four levels of consciousness contained within the sound of AUM, as follows:

1. WAKING—*Vaishvanara*
   Sounding **A** focuses your attention on the external manifesting world.
2. DREAMING—*Taijasa*
   Sounding **U** focuses your attention inward.
3. INNER PEACE—*Prajna*
   Sounding **M** focuses your attention on stillness before thought.

When these three indivisible sounds are sung over an extended period with full attention, devotion, and loving presence, AUM has the power to catalyze a fourth state, awakening.

4. AWAKENING—*Turiya*
    Sounding **AUM** as one unified sound.

AUM as an Energy Movement Practice

Enjoy sounding the AUM with the following energy movement practices. It requires considerable focus and visualization. AUM will open your heart and bring you HOME.

- Standing in Mountain Posture (upright, relaxed, arms hanging) or sitting, focus your awareness of AUM into the center of your body, breathing into your belly and sounding out OMMMMMMMMMM over and over.
- Stand or sit in a relaxed position, feet hip-width apart, hands by your sides. Breathe in and as you sound out on Aaaa, open your arms to embrace the whole universe, raising them up above your head, reaching to the sky. As you sound Ummm, bring your hands together, palms facing inward, closing them like two folding wings down the center of your body, moving your folded hands down until you are holding them at your root chakra as the sound Ummm comes to an end in silence. Bring your feet together simultaneously at that point of completion. Then breathe in again and repeat this exercise. Enjoy these energy movement practices focusing on the sound of the AUM in your own natural timing and breathing rhythm. If you feel dizzy at all, it's because you are generating more oxygen through your blood circulatory system. This is a good sign! Simply stop and relax. Breathe normally until you are ready to start again.

3.2 AUM: Singing from Source

The essence of all beings is earth,
The essence of earth is water,
The essence of water is plants,
The essence of plants is man,
The essence of man is speech,
The essence of speech is sacred knowledge,
The essence of sacred knowledge is word and sound,
The essence of word and sound is AUM

— FROM THE UPANISHADS, IN JOACHIM-ERNST BERENDT,
The World Is Sound: Nada Brahma

In the beginning was sound. Sound is the interconnective tissue of the universe. Having begun to embody the sound AUM, you are now going to travel back in time to reconnect even more deeply with your ancient origins through the primordial sound AUM (commonly known as OM). For the ancients of the East the sacred AUM was the manifestation of the supreme word and will of God. And of course we hear this same sound resonating through other universal sounds such as the *Amen.*

Ancient teachings and modern science now agree: you, I, all living things in existence are made up at their most essential level of vibrating, pulsing energy. Scientists have detected an unchanging and all-pervading hum resounding across the universe. For millennia, mystics have recounted their experience of this energy sound, which is felt as an all-pervasive humming vibration, similar to the inner sound (also known as the *nada brahma*) that we practiced in section 1.5, "Where Silence Meets Sound." In the Sanskrit tradition, this background hum is called *anahata nada,* the "unstruck sound," meaning "the sound that is not made by two things striking together." The point of this particular distinction is that ordinary audible sounds are made by at least two elements: bow and string; drum and stick; two vocal cords; two lips against the mouthpiece of the trumpet; the double reed of the oboe; waves against the shore; wind against the leaves. All sounds within our range of hearing are created by things, visible or invisible, striking each other or vibrating together, creating pulsing waves of air molecules that our ears and brain interpret as sound.

Sound that is not made of two things striking together is the sound of primordial energy, the sound of the universe itself. Mythologist Joseph Campbell likens this unstruck vibration to the humming of an electrical transformer, or the unheard humming of atoms and molecules. The ancients have described the audible sound most resembling this unstruck sound as the syllable AUM or OM.

Three indivisible sounds, A-U-M, were handed down through the ages in the form of this holy mantra, a sound of spiritual power. The sacred sound AUM was regarded by the ancient yogis, sages, and saints of the East as the mother of all mantras. These three seed sounds A-U-M unify the external, internal, and transpersonal realms of our consciousness into one indivisible wholeness, or "undivided wholeness" as quantum physicist David Bohm described it. When sounded together, these three sounds, A-U-M, can catalyze a fourth state of pure consciousness called "Turiya." This silent sound is said to liberate the singer from the suffering of separateness, awakening a state of oneness, or what the saints have called the "second birth," meaning freedom from the suffering of duality. This state of consciousness is referred to in esoteric Christianity as "second heaven."

Over the course of civilization, however, humanity began to forget, disregard, and abuse the primordial sound. We misused our powers of communication and ceased to hear the original sound of our true nature. In losing touch with source we began to regard our communication generally as a slave or warhorse to serve our needy desires, driven by individual free will at the expense of the universal will. The more dissociated we became from our true nature, the more fragmented our relationship with our body-mind integration became. The head brain dominated the heart brain, and rational intellectual speaking assumed priority over intuitive song.

This unheard sound was thus forgotten and banished to the monastic realms, rarely visited by anyone except contemplatives in search of peace through isolation and the sublimation of love through celibacy. As the primordial sound became separated and secreted away from our everyday consciousness, so too our communications became increasingly compartmentalized into speech for everyday purposes, relegating song to "other," more special occasions.

Fortunately, thanks to relatively recent developments within quantum science—including its acknowledgment of the interconnected web of the universe—and an evolutionary consciousness shifting toward a planetary mind aided by the worldwide internet, a renaissance is taking place at the ever-expanding frontiers of spirituality, with *the remembrance of sound as a spiritual force and a sacred language of wisdom and oneness, older and deeper than the polarity of all conflict.* A whole new language of listening and conscious communication is being reawakened. Also, an increasing number of contemporary devotional singers, sound healers, and yoga practitioners have been acknowledging A-U-M as the great universal sound. AUM or OM can be heard resounding through the many yoga and meditation studios in our cities.

However, the centuries of apathy, neglect, and ignorant misuse of sound have rendered everyday communication more and more dysfunctional, imbalanced, and distorted. Communication is largely used to emphasize the polarities of our nature, our duality, rather than our commonality and oneness. The noble heartfelt practice of sacred sound and song has for the most part been replaced by heady combative speech. Humanity has hypnotized itself into creating communication systems and languages dominated by competition and fundamentalism that have further estranged us from our core values. This unconscious ego-driven process has veiled our true interconnectedness with Mother Earth and the cosmos. The reverence for the sacred laws of life has been neglected in favor of the glamorous seductions of consumerism.

As I sit here writing amidst the ancient moors and stone circles of Dartmoor in the Celtic Isles, this tiny island called the United Kingdom is being battered by hurricane-force winds and the most severe floods in several hundred years. The United States is meanwhile experiencing unprecedented snows in the East and heat waves in the West. Despite all the hurdles that humanity faces, a fierce wisdom catalyzed by Mother Nature herself is waking us up to the environmental conditions and climate change that human ignorance has created through excessive pollution, greed, and war. All of these have been accentuated by millennia of disconnectedness from the source of our true sound.

However, despite the dark propaganda of the media, changes are occurring. . . . Many of us have begun to access and research ways to transform our disconnected relationship with sound and voice, restoring its true purpose once again as a catalyst of authentic expression, sustained by self-acceptance, gratitude, forgiveness, and loving presence.

And this sound direction is supported by scientists such as Ani Patel of the Neurosciences Institute in San Diego, who says, "The idea that the origin of language came from song just feels right to a lot of people" and "We feel music just taps into this kind of pre-cognitive archaic part of ourselves." For Ani Patel it makes sense that music and the melodic mind came "before we had this complicated articulate language" that we now use to do abstract and analytical thinking. According to Patel, Charles Darwin wrote about our ancestors singing love songs to each other before we could speak articulate language, a hundred thousand years ago, when language as we know it today was first emerging. Then singing was the primary source of communication. So it is time to restore its sovereign role again NOW. (Patel quotes are from a Jon Hamilton interview on NPR called "Singing, Signing, and Speaking: How Language Evolved.")

I see three major resources of sound awareness emerging and evolving today:

Sound Medicine: an understanding of the restorative and healing power of sound for health and well-being through vibrational healing, contemplative voice work, sacred chant, and mantra.

Sound Energy: helps us recover awareness of how our energy system, the chakra system, and the human body-field as a whole can rebalance and restore healthy conscious relationships and communication.

Sound Love: the process by which we rediscover how to awaken the musical energies of love and thus to integrate our instinctual, intuitive, and insightful language of love. This language of love is informed by a direct experience of our elemental, emotional, and ethereal music languages, all rooted in an auditory consciousness sourced from the dynamic sound of silence, or *sound before sound.*

Sounding the AUM enables you to open up your heart and mind, so that you may surrender totally into your one true Self. So let's return now to the sacred sound of the AUM to discover its capacity to facilitate and to deepen your evolving sound-awareness skills.

Singing from Source: AUMKAR Practice

If chanting the AUM is the source and ground of all sound, then you are about to discover its transformative benefits through a more detailed investigation of the traditional AUMKAR practice. Here we go.

Let yourself sit in silence for a while, relaxed, aligned, and at one with yourself. Make sure you are sitting comfortably. Let your tongue lie relaxed on the floor of your mouth. Take a deep in-breath and while holding your teeth and lips slightly apart, permit an "A" sound to formulate and vibrate in your throat. Feel the vibrations there. Let the sound rise up spontaneously and, as it enters the space behind your tongue, the "A" sound changes imperceptibly into an "O" sound.

Stretch your breath as much as possible, and ensure you reach the very end of it. Make full use of the cavity in your mouth by allowing the lips to come gently forward in an "O" shape. As the sound rolls over your tongue, you feel the vibrations in your mouth. Your lips should very gradually begin to close. As the space between your lips becomes narrower and narrower, the sound changes imperceptibly from an "O" to a "U" sound. Finally, with the meeting of your lips, the sound vibrates as "M," and the vibrations can also be felt in the nose, around the eyes, and throughout the skull.

With the meeting of your lips and the merging of the "U" into the "M" sound, the AUMKAR reaches its highest peak of volume. The descent gradually begins with the "M" sound, which progressively tapers off and merges into silence. Let the silence coincide with the pause between two breathing cycles and prolong it as long as possible without discomfort. With the cessation of the breath there is a cessation of thought, and a calm fills the body-mind. Enjoy it; bathe in its peace. Let the next cycle of the AUM-KAR be chanted within this pool of tranquility until the mind is completely immersed in it.

3.3 The Seven-Chakra Mantra: Vibrational Building Blocks

Lam (Root), Vam (Pelvis), Ram (Solar Plexus), Yam (Heart), Ham (Throat), Om (Third Eye), So Ham (Crown)

This mantra is another great anchor for your sound-awareness practice. It is one of our most popular naked-voice mantras. This is a tantric mantra and derives from the Shakti yoga tradition. Its aim is to strengthen your self-awareness through sound awareness, awakening the eight wheels of energy from the root to the crown of our human consciousness. Each sound is a *bija* or "seed" syllable that activates a specific level of consciousness when sung with single-minded focus, intention, and commitment. This mantra strengthens the vertical axis of our being and ultimately shifts our attention from a limited state of self-consciousness to a deeper sound consciousness. The repetitive sounding of this mantra's vibrational building blocks gradually gives birth to a faculty of attention called the witness consciousness, a self-observing inquiry that is able to witness everything going on inside and outside yourself with great dispassion and without reactivity or attachment.

The mantra is profoundly calming and grounding. You can practice it internally without movement, or you can sound it externally with movement. It builds an inner sound awareness, and still presence, as you travel in your awareness from the root chakra at the source of your consciousness, through all the musical chakras from the belly (my will) into the heart (thy will) and up into the crown of the head (that will). Breathe deep. No rush. Allow one breath at a time for each mantric seed sound. Enjoy the silence that deepens between each chakra sound. When practicing alone, you may prefer to focus on one seed syllable for a longer time, repeating it several times to establish a clear presence in that level of consciousness before traveling on to the next chakra.

Some Personal Background: I was first introduced to this tantric mantra when I was staying on the Island of Crete in the late 1980s. This is where I began to have the dreams of my spiritual mentor Anandamayi Ma. I did not know at this time what a profound impact she was going to have in forging and shaping the methodology and spiritual philosophy of the Naked Voice. I was alternating between sleeping on the seashore there and a nearby chapel. Crete is known as one of the great sacred realms of the Goddess.

The Seven-Chakra Mantra was a lifesaver for me when I first returned from India in 1990. The lid had been blown off my mind there, and so for a period of several months I was walking around in an all-pervading blissful awareness without any presence of my previous habitual ego or reactive mind. As my detached state yielded to ordinary consciousness over time, the Seven-Chakra Mantra sustained and anchored the stormy interface between the "enlightened" self and the as-yet unpurified persona called "Chloë." This nonseparate state inspired many of the vocal and self-inquiry practices that are now integral to the Naked Voice teachings. The naked human voice is the most effective and direct way that I have found to help individuals access this nonseparate state of oneness for themselves. The singing voice can dissolve the rational mind.

By grace, during this turbulent time I met the Sufi master Irina Tweedie, author of *The Chasm of Fire,* whose awakening in the hands of a Sufi Baul spiritual master enabled her to track what was going on inside me. Irina listened to my story and encouraged me to let sound and voice be my teachers. She told me that they would create a strong container to balance and ground this new awareness. Following our meeting I began chanting the AUM, the Seven-Chakra Mantra, and the Heart Sutra (which follows) together. These three mantras were the pillars of sound awareness that anchored and stabilized my emotions. They enabled me to sustain a spacious awareness of the vast presence my life had become.

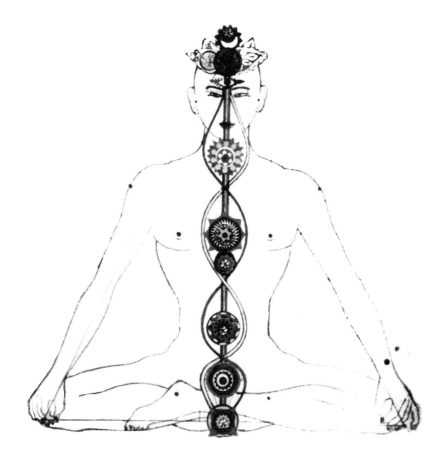

The Seven-Chakra Mantra, a visual human map

The Seven-Chakra Mantra Practice

First of all, have a good shake-out: swing your shoulders, jog on the spot, run around the room. Jump, sounding down into the feet as you jump up and down.

Let the sound arrive down in your feet as you call out A–E–I–O–M.

Stand in Mountain Posture. Internally visualize the chakras from the root to the crown. Each chakra point is accompanied by a sound that cleanses and energizes that realm of consciousness as follows:

LAM: at the root
VAM: above the pubic bone
RAM: the solar plexus center
YAM: the heart
HAM: the throat
AUM: the third eye
SO HAM: the crown.
Explore each sound then thread them together.
LAMmmmmmmmmmmmmmmmmm
VAMmmmmmmmmmmmmmmmmm
RAMmmmmmmmmmmmmmmmmm
YAMmmmmmmmmmmmmmmmmm
HAMmmmmmmmmmmmmmmmmm
AUMmmmmmmmmmmmmmmmmm
SO HAMmmmmmmmmmmmmmmmm

3.4 The Gayatri Mantra:
Invocation of the Ten Thousand Suns

This ancient mantra is sung all over India at sunrise, noon, and sunset. It is known as the Maha (Great) Mother of Mantras, and the Mantra of Purification. It is said that the chanting of the Gayatri mantra has the effect of liberating one from the fruits of karma, the natural law of cause and effect that many believe controls the cycle of birth and death. The one who chants the Gayatri mantra is also thought to be blessed with attributes such as longevity, courage, physical strength, awareness, psychic healing of ailments, sweetness of speech, and the facility of celibacy (if required) for the purpose of spiritual practices. Gayatri the deity is the personification of the triadic divinity composed of Gayatri, Savitri, and Saraswati. Gayatri is also considered the Mother of the ancient wisdom texts known as the Vedas. It is said that chanting the Gayatri mantra brings about the "second birth," which is freedom from attachment to suffering.

The Gayatri mantra is made up of the following five phrases corresponding to realms of awareness:

> The first phrase is *AUM,* in which one inwardly welcomes the whole cosmos.
>
> The second phrase, *Om bhur bhuvah svah,* praises Earth, Heaven, and Beyond.
>
> The third phrase, *Tat savitur varenyam,* welcomes the goddess Savitri, "daughter of the sun," whose energy is equated with the power of the sun.
>
> The fourth phrase, *Bhargo devasya dimahi,* refers to the radiance, luster, and illuminating power of divinity, which facilitates our transition from the world of darkness into light, separateness into union.
>
> The fifth phrase, *Diyo yo nah(ah) prachodayat,* welcomes the compelling power of this mantric prayer, building our intention to transform through the recitation of these sacred sounds.

A simplified summary of the Gayatri Mantra: When you have chosen the way and the brilliant sun has begun to shine in you, and you have sustained it and maintained it, it purifies that subtlest, most *sattvic* (unified) part of you called the *buddhi* (wisdom) within which Atman, your human soul, reflects your pure Self.

Om
bhur bhuvah svah(a)
om tat savitur varenyam
bhargo devasya dimahi
diyo yo nah(ah) prachodayat
Om

As you chant the mantra, visualize the light of ten thousand suns rising through your whole body, linking the earth, the heavens, and beyond. Feel gratitude for sounding this mantra and for the invisible blessings it bestows. Consciously intend that all your fear be transformed into the great burning splendor of the ten thousand suns, as the mantra proclaims. *Bhargo* means both "fear" and "splendor." As you sound this mantra, consciously release all attachment to any negative thoughts or personal suffering of any kind.

3.5 The Heart Sutra: A Sound Dream

Om gate gate paragate parasamgate bodhi svaha
Om Go Go far beyond, far far beyond the wisdom is

The Heart Sutra is the third of the three mantras central to the naked-voice sound-awareness chanting practices; the first two are AUM and the Seven-Chakra Mantra. The contemplative quality of the Heart Sutra draws you into a stillness within that is lasting and beneficial in stabilizing your emotional and nervous system. It is effective in strengthening your vertical axis, your relationship between earth and sky, and your spatial awareness, as well as deepening your witness consciousness and inner stillness. The Heart Sutra will firmly anchor your spirit in the body, heart, and mind. It will bring peace to every level of your life. Enjoy chanting this mantra alone or with others.

The instruction to learn the Heart Sutra came to me in a dream more than twenty-five years ago. I was on a silent meditation retreat for a few days, staying in a guesthouse on the grounds of a contemplative abbey in Wales. On the third day, in the early hours of the morning, I had a dream that shocked me awake. In it, a huge crimson Buddha was sitting in front of me, icon-like, gazing upon me in silence. Slowly he raised his finger and began to repeat the words, "Know the heart sutra, know the heart sutra" several times, like a mantra. What was the meaning behind these words? Why a Buddhist apparition? His presence had been so potent and realistic in the dream that I awoke expecting him still to be sitting there in front of me.

The Heart Sutra, or "the Heart of Understanding," is part of a collection of spiritual teachings called Prajnaparamita or "Perfection of Wisdom." These sutras—which include the Diamond Sutra—are central to the teachings of Mahayana Buddhism. "Mahayana" or "Great Path" refers to the path of the Bodhisattva, a being seeking complete enlightenment for the benefit of all sentient beings. These texts are the subject of worship in Mahayana Buddhism, in much the same way that devotional figures were. Prajnaparamita eventually became personified as a goddess, but this is not her mantra. This one is associated with the Perfection of Wisdom texts themselves. The content of this wisdom is the realization of the illusory nature of all phenomena—not only of this world, as in earlier Buddhism, but of transcendental realms as well. Its essential message is that form is emptiness and emptiness is form.

At the time of my dream I had little knowledge of these Buddhist texts and their spiritual verses, or sutras, which form part of the ancient teachings on perennial wisdom. It was not until I heard the American mythologist Joseph Campbell speak on the meaning of sutra and its connection with the French word *suture* (seam, a line of stitching which unites or binds together) that I made some connections. A sutra links the numerous spiritual teachings of ancient Buddhism.

Thich Nhat Hanh and the Red Buddha

My understanding was immediately deepened when I attended a meditation retreat on the theme of "Being Peace" with one of the greatest exponents of the Prajnaparamita Heart Sutra, the Vietnamese Zen Buddhist monk Thich Nhat Hanh. "Thay," as he is called, is without doubt a living embodiment of the formless in form.

The translated text of the full Heart Sutra begins as follows:

Form is emptiness, emptiness is form. Form does not differ from emptiness, emptiness does not differ from form. The same is true of feelings, perceptions, mental formations, and consciousness.

Thay explained this riddle to us in the following way: "In order to understand the nature of our own emptiness, we first have to realize our interconnectedness with all forms of life." He spoke in simple everyday terms, in ways that revealed the inextricable link between the worlds of matter (form) and spirit (emptiness). Then he lifted an imaginary glass into the air and laughingly invited a response to the question, "If this glass is empty, what is it empty of?" He singled out a child in the front row, and in all seriousness and humility whispered to her, "Can you please help me answer this question?" She stood up and replied in a shy voice, "It is empty of everything and nothing." The audience laughed with approval. Thay smiled serenely at her with a satisfaction and a sincerity that acknowledged her childhood wisdom and continued from where she had left off. "Yes," he agreed, "and so to be everything and nothing at once, this cup has to be empty of a separate self. That is to say, empty of all attachment to being a glass forever, or any other notion of permanence and predictability that might feed the experience of separateness. All beings, feelings, perceptions, mental formations, indeed consciousness itself are imbued with this emptiness, which is at the heart of our awareness of our interbeing, the invisible dance of infinity within the visible fullness of creation."

Upon hearing this, a thousand fragmented jigsaw pieces suddenly fell into place for me. Simultaneously, my eyes were alerted to a flock of birds outside, who suddenly flew all at once off an old oak tree. As the branches of the tree sprang back into place they showered raindrops to the ground in the refreshing breeze. I became the tree, the wetness of the raindrops, the cool breeze, the solid trunk rooted in the warm earth, the new leaves and the old, this crowd of listeners, all of us sitting within the giant ear of the universe, our globe, a speck of sand spiraling with unstoppable force through space.

My body began to laugh all over. Others joined me.

I can't know, only You can,
What makes my heart laugh,
This branch of flowers,
Shaking in Your wind.

—ANDREW HARVEY, *Love's Fire*

Heart Sutra 1, a caliograph by Masashi Minagawa

3.6 Transmission by Sound:
Singing for the Dalai Lama

The Heart Sutra is linked to one of my most transformative—as well as comical—singing/chanting encounters. It took place in Northern Ireland in the presence of His Holiness the Dalai Lama.

I had been asked to coproduce the music for a world event in 2002 called "The Way of Peace," an initiative established by the Christian monk Lawrence Freeman and Simon Keyes, founder of the St. Ethelburga's Centre for Reconciliation and Peace in London. The Dalai Lama attended this peace gathering during his visit to support the Peace Talks in Northern Ireland. Many more world religious leaders and representatives were present at The Way of Peace event, which extended over several days and took place at many different venues and gatherings throughout the Belfast area.

At one of the events I was asked to chant for His Holiness at Queens University in Belfast, where he was to receive an honorary doctorate. As soon as I arrived, I was assailed by one of the event managers who asked me earnestly, "What are you going to sing that would be appropriate to accompany the Dalai Lama as he processes into the ceremony room to receive his doctoral award?" He had a nervous animation in his voice, as it was not long before the Dalai Lama was to arrive with his entourage, secret police, and the press.

The Heart Sutra was the most appropriate music for this occasion. The event manager replied, "Fine—I'm sure that would be just grand, but can you give me a bash on your harmonium first behind the stage so I can hear if what you are imagining will work well."

"Sure!" I exclaimed as he whisked me at great speed behind curtains and into a back room. I opened up my harmonium and began to play and chant this holy mantra, sung for millennia in the Buddhist tradition. There was something incongruous about having to produce the goods in this way; however, there was no alternative, so I trusted the situation. I had hardly begun to chant when he interrupted me: "That will be just grand, Chloë, thank you. Now you must take your place for the ceremony."

I walked out in front of the stage, looking around somewhat furtively for direction. I was soon ushered by one of my students into my sitting position facing the audience, on the ground level with them, in front of the raised stage. The row in front of me was almost empty so I assumed that some members of the arriving procession would be sitting there. A table was awaiting my harmonium, and I took up position, waiting for the sign to start chanting.

The hall was already filling fast, and in no time it was full to bursting. Then a sudden silence fell upon the gathering, and an usher signaled me to begin chanting.

As I was accustomed, I collected myself and began:

Om gate gate paragate parasamgate bodhi swaha

Om gate paragate parasamgate bodhi swaha

I entered a timeless realm, focusing on the meaning of the chant and inspired by the intensity and awesome nature of the situation. How had I gotten here? How had I come to be singing for this "holy man of compassion from the East" as I had heard him described by a local Irish fruit seller? In seconds all thoughts fell away as I continued singing, abandoning myself into the silent depths of this beloved mantra that I had sung for years.

At the beginning of the chanting I visualized all the Buddhist practitioners and monks all over the world chanting with me. I closed my eyes, but I could see nothing at all. All I knew was that the Dalai Lama was slowly processing down the center of the room, flanked on all sides, before and behind, by the university chancellor and other academic scholars, dignitaries, and members of the noble establishment and security guards. The Dalai Lama must have been nearing the front of the great hall when I suddenly became aware of an unexpected sensation in my throat that immediately affected the quality and resonance of my voice. My voice was changing in ways that were out of my control. I began to sound much lower and fuller altogether. My voice took on a richer, darker, and deeper resonance. I simultaneously felt awakened and energized throughout my body. As the muscles in my throat began expanding and opening up inside, I became aware of the central vertical column of my body and spine like a huge mine shaft, stretching from my throat vertically down into the center of my body and on down into the Earth's core.

Although disoriented by this experience, I continued the chanting that had taken on a momentum of its own, no longer requiring effort from me. I had no choice but to continue chanting until the Dalai Lama was sitting in his place. Time seemed to stop, and I was now sounding and resounding within this ever-expanding spacious awareness. What was most evident was that my voice felt as if it had extended itself down this empty vertical column, causing the whole quality of the sound to assume a much stronger, vibrant, sensuous, and earthy quality. It felt much more substantial and embodied than ever.

I had never experienced the inner authority of my voice so intensely before. Somehow I returned to the present moment. It was all I could do to bring my awareness back into the room. As I slowly completed singing and opened my eyes out of the dark interiority of the sounding I found myself staring into the direct gaze of the Dalai Lama, whose smiling face filled every cell in my body with an electric childlike joy.

There he was standing in the front row, only a few feet away to my right. He looked utterly delighted and seemed deeply accepting of everything that was going on around him too. He was dressed in full Western academic regalia, complete with mortarboard. It communicated a cosmic absurdity which he was—in all humility—willing to play along with. What struck me most was the simple patient obedience and radiance with which he waited for the ceremony to unfold while transmitting an astounding compassion, his depth of stillness sending waves of unconditional love in all directions. He bowed at us continuously, his eyes like two fiery radar echolocation beams cleansing the whole space. His essence was joyous innocence. His presence was at once electric and radiant, yet he was entirely ordinary. As ordinary as a child playing at ceremony games can be!

His Holiness eventually climbed up onto the stage to give his honorary doctorate speech of gratitude. He was initially preoccupied with the tassel on his mortarboard cap, making it dance and bob about, much to the amusement of the audience. Then he composed himself into a more serious mood and brought the gathering of several hundred into his confidence by communicating in a low hushed voice, thanking the university for bestowing this doctorate upon him. He especially thanked them for dressing him in these important academic clothes.

"Very beautiful clothes!" he softly roared. "But not very comfortable!"

This brought the house down in an instant as, suddenly, this elite and somber audience of intellectuals and dignitaries disintegrated into hoots of laughter.

Such is the simple ordinary grace of the one who has travelled beyond all the forms, seen through the veil of illusion, and returned to reveal the cosmic joke.

The Heart Sutra took on a new significance for me from that day.

Heart Sutra 2, a caliograph by Masashi Minagawa

PART II

TRANSFORM
YOUR COMMUNICATION

Sound Intelligence

Chapter 4

Your Heart Voice

4.1 A Sound Language for Love

We are conditioned and unconditioned
We are both at the same time.

—"BOTH AT THE SAME TIME," *Fierce Wisdom*

For many years I have sung and shared my love of silence through sound—spoken and sung—inspired by my European classical music upbringing and later by my travels in Africa, Asia, and (more recently) North and South America. Speaking and singing is the vocal clothing of silence, and it has always been my task to express and undress all the vibrational veils, emotional colors, and costumes that the voice uses to touch the transformative secret of sound, which in essence is unconditional love. I love exploring the vast spectrum of human feeling inspired by the East-West, left-right sides of our brains. This singing definitely changes the way my brain operates, depending on whether I am influenced by indigenous African and Native American roots, a more devotional Asian-inspired incantation, or the more ethereal heights of polyphonic European music.

The human voice has an infinite capacity to express the full spectrum of consciousness, from its earthy primordial origins to its sublime celestial realms. Yet why, if it offers us so much inspiration, radical impact, and empowerment to communicate the wisdom of the human spirit, is it given so little opportunity to demonstrate its power as a catalyst for change, team-building, conscious relationships, leadership, and decision-making at all levels of society?

The head rather than the heart perpetuates the old paradigm, but change is on the horizon. The naked voice is definitely a product of the new heart-mind orientation as we forge ahead with our motto, "I sing therefore I am." And we are not alone. It is heartening that millions of people across the planet are shifting consciousness from a talking-head to an intuitive-heart paradigm. In the sound realm this is largely being led by the choral movement, which—thanks to the power of the worldwide web—is building awareness of the existence of an all-inclusive *planetary mind*. It is inspired by such remarkable webinar choral initiatives as Eric Whitacre's *Virtual Choir,* Gareth Malone's TV series *The Choir,* as well as mainstream TV singing competitions such as the *X Factor, Pop Idol,* and the national talent shows. This evolving movement is also inspiring a significant increase in neurochemical research that is demonstrating the many ways in which singing impacts the brain while also improving social cohesion, releasing stress, and mitigating depression, dementia, and Alzheimer's.

As wonderful as these choral-singing social movements are, time will tell to what degree the positive energy that thrives within the concert programs and competitions will generate the depth of consciousness and compassion required to unplug the old model of communication dominated by win and lose.

As much as the naked voice enjoys the profound well-being created by its own choral gatherings, it is less interested in this performative impact on the collective soul. It is more focused on the transformative potential of the human voice to awaken consciousness at a deeper level of the human heart from a depth of auditory consciousness, prior to duality. This doesn't require quantitative change; rather it focuses on qualitative change. For if we can transform the ways we listen to ourselves and each other at a depth of listening that is "older and deeper than the polarity of all conflict," we can begin to radically restore singing and soundmaking more efficiently in our everyday lives, beyond the confines of the music-theatre stage. This in-depth focus and sound-led orientation will by its nature innately and effortlessly spread like wildfire.

As you are already discovering, soundmaking and singing open up a multidimensional relationship with yourself and others, inspired by your feelings and a willing open heart, in a way that no other form of communication can. And it's free!

In the following sections we are going to explore what it takes for each of us to evolve and embody a language for love. What would that sound like? You are about to find out. The following poem gives you a clearer sense of the world you are entering.

THE FLUTE OF INTERIOR TIME

The flute of interior time
Is played whether we hear it or not
What we mean by "love" is
its sound coming in
When love hits the farthest edge of excess
It reaches a wisdom
. . .
It penetrates our thick bodies
Goes through walls
Its network of notes has a structure
as if a million suns were arranged inside.
This tune has truth in it
Where else have you heard a sound like this?

—A KABIR POEM FROM *The Kabir Book*, ROBERT BLY

"Music" and "love" are essentially two words for the same thing. The most beautiful music is love in disguise. Love is at best a music of the soul. Music and love are invisible art forms. Yet they both know how to spontaneously express or transmit the vibration and tone of a feeling, deeper than thought. You probably have experienced that urge to sing or sound out whenever you feel inspired by a friendship or love affair. Witness the thousands of songs that have been written to express great love. Shakespeare's famous phrase "if music be the food of love, play on" heralds the multitude of poets, singers, and composers across the centuries who dedicated their lives to composing or communicating the ultimate love song in a myriad of styles and musical forms.

Contrary to what your academic education system would have you believe, your emotions offer a direct line to your soul. They energize and empower you to anchor yourself in a depth of listening and a chemistry of being, from where you will discover your own authentic language of love, spoken and sung. Your emotions play a key role in these vocal practices because they provide you with a new understanding and information about your singing soul and *the sound of love coming in*. Courage, discernment, and a deeper witnessing of your feelings are going to be essential from now on.

Your naked sound is so powerful that whatever you "think" or "believe" your emotional state to be, when you start singing, your actual mood will reveal itself through your sound. So often individuals have said to me, "I feel really depressed," but when I ask them to sound that feeling, the energy and tone of their sound is anything but depressed. What we learn from this is that the ego-mind or personality has a story about being depressed, while their soul is actually joyous and free. The practice of nonjudgmental listening continues to be an essential ally in your forthcoming revelation of how alive and open your heart and soul can actually be. And "revelation" is an essential word here. Revealing your naked voice is a terrifying prospect for some.

As the poet David Whyte reminds us in his book *The House of Belonging*: "Revelation must be terrible knowing you can never hide your voice again. It orphans you from your old home." There are parts of us that are afraid of accessing and expressing the true depths of who we are, "and want to have nothing to do with the revelation that's at the heart of (our) gift. . . ." Love moves immensities inside us beyond the comprehension of the ordinary mind. There is a wonderful Rumi line that reveals this too: "Oh Lord my boat is so small, how can this great Love be inside me?" (Coleman Barks's version in *The Essential Rumi*).

The big question now is what part will your voice play in transforming your capacity to feel and express love more authentically? How effective can your vocal sound be in navigating and embracing conflicting emotions such as depression, sadness, grief, anger, longing, unrequited love, overwhelm, rage, and passion in all their forms? Your naked voice can empower you to face and ultimately to embody these inner-outer frontiers and questions. It will initially be through the simple sounding of devotional chant that you can discover how to establish a sound foundation from where the emotional launching pad of your soul can express itself safely and freely while you begin to access your more complex and in-depth feelings.

"The Seven Sounds of Love" will then follow to strengthen your "house of song." These seven sounds are located at energy points in your body, between the base of the spine and the crown of the head. They will energize and catalyze a more fulfilling relationship with your emotional body.

These and other easily accessible vocal practices will continue to strengthen your *sound awareness.* The seven sounds provide the stable musical container required to allow your emotions to come out and play with ease, enjoyment, and as much passion as you like. The seven sounds will assist you in embodying your voice more deeply, as well as feel your whole self—body, mind, heart, and spirit—as one.

Later we will explore more closely the journey from what I call *sound into soul communication* via the medium of poetry. Poetry was the inspiration for my first recording experiences in the early 1990s. The translations of Robert Bly, Andrew Harvey, and later Coleman Barks of poets like Rumi and Kabir illuminated my singing path at that time.

Next I invite you to engage in a new vocal exploration—a *vocation*—beginning with devotional chant, which provides a simple bridge between our sacred and secular dimensions. With commitment, courage, and creative intention, you will start to heal within yourself the previously divided realms of silence, spoken voice, and sung voice.

It is the integration of these three sound realms that awakens the full joy of consciousness that is the naked voice.

True singing requires a mastery of our emotions that often seem too complex or overwhelming to navigate, let alone befriend and transform. We live in a culture that still sees singing as merely a performative expression of a song. The performance—if it is to be well-delivered—is done by a "professional singer," who has to be able to convey the emotional message of the song with everything it takes to impact and inspire their audience. The professional singer may well have spent many months, possibly years, training in the technical art and emotional expression of the voice, supported by breath practices to strengthen the diaphragm, postural programming, and a correct awareness of the vocal sound and how it is emitted from the various resonant chambers in the body.

Moving our attention away from the technical proficiency of the professional singer, let us ask the rest of humanity, the so-called "non-professional" emitters of emotion, how we may masterfully engage with and navigate the music of our emotions, especially if we haven't had all that intensive and specialist vocal training? First, we have to open our minds to this new understanding that our emotions are dynamic phenomena, to be engaged with consciously and *sonically,* rather than reactively, psychotherapeutically, or even spiritually.

If you have enjoyed the auditory and vocal practices of Part I, you will have experienced enough of your sound potential by now to realize and agree that there is indeed a very close correlation between your emotional energy and your vocal expression. You do not have to be a trained "professional singer" to be able to breathe in, sigh out, breathe in again, sound out for longer in order to instantly hear what kind of emotional state you are in. And the more nonjudgmental attention you can give to that sound practice, the more quickly the unique melodic nature of your voice will start—with loving attention—to express itself.

In all simplicity, vocal melodies are musical shapes arising directly from the density or levity of your moods or thoughts that—given a safe and supportive environment—will start showing up spontaneously. The sounds arising are the raw material of the songs in your heart. So, if you are feeling low, the sound coming out of your mouth will give off a kind of minor or sad shape. If you are feeling positive and motivated, your sound will be more upbeat/joyous/passionate, even spacious. The spaces between one note and the next—otherwise known as musical intervals—will be more or less contracted or expansive depending on your emotional state. Regardless of the mood or state you are in, your voice knows—without thinking—how to express itself directly. Whether you are conscious of it or not, there are hundreds of tunes and songs stored inside you that have been longing to express themselves since your birth. Unfortunately, Western education and social conditioning have compelled us all to compromise our natural musical awareness, and to prioritize our rational mind at the expense of our heart-mind.

In this chapter, I present a diverse range of characters who have each been instrumental in influencing my understanding, such as Darnell and Smokey, my medicine elder friends living in the East Glacier Mountains of northern Montana. Theirs is a wisdom culture and it is literally *sound-led*. The pure values embodied in these elders have sadly fallen victim to Western domination, having been severely oppressed, to the detriment of their sons and daughters. Nevertheless, despite the tortuous conditions that have been inflicted upon them by "the white grandfather in Washington," their sharing of specific sound, song, and dance remains a high priority as a force for peace, cooperative decision-making, and leadership. Their wisdom tradition has been steeped for centuries in a lineage of healing songs sourced from a direct engagement with Mother Nature and a reverence for the elemental and animal kingdom.

As you begin to give priority to singing your heart song in your life, you will find how your emotions are the sonic energy of your soul seeking to be expressed, heard, and acknowledged. Given loving attention, this emotional energy cannot help but blossom into melodies, rhythmic patterns, and ever-changing vibrational colors—the myriad moods of consciousness that have been buried in your unconscious, awaiting expression.

Let us be clear: these moods matter. Left to their own reactive devices, they can become self-destructive moods, the music of low self-esteem, isolation, and separateness. Once honored and respected for what they really are, however, these moods can transform themselves from the songs of depression into an awareness of an unrequited longing, and further into heart songs inspired by deeper states of positive feeling.

Just as plants and flowers prosper and grow with regular watering and the appropriate weather conditions, the musical messages of your heart will start to bubble up and flow into your family and working life, quenching a long-held thirst to be heard and acknowledged. Once heard there is no turning back. An urgency kicks in, bypassing the rational mind, as your singing voice starts to take on a life of its own, galvanized by the call of your emotions, and of life itself.

A wondrous power can be generated by the sound sourced from the core of your being. Its vibration quickens your mind, heats up your body, awakens intention, and opens your ears, your eyes, and all your senses to the energies of love inside you.

While your witnessing mind continues to observe that all is well, it is time to face the unexpected. With the support of the inner practices from Part I, you are now equipped with a range of simple resources to explore a deeper level of sound and singing. Singing in this new way begins to unify the creative and compassionate voices inside you. Meanwhile, that unique naked voice of yours continues to embrace and unify them all.

For many people the resistance to opening the mouth and letting the sound flow out with total abandonment can be immense. When you hear the true sound of who you *are*—your *naked voice,* that is—there is often the accompanying experience of wondering "Who was that?" along with a strange sensation of sloughing off an outworn identity. This can be terrifying to let go of.

However, you have started to build your "house of song" with the support of the Seven-Chakra Mantra practice in Chapter 3. You are now ready to expand your tool kit of sonic skills to constellate and form a new intelligence of sound. This is the evolving intelligence, the essential component of your new sound-led life. Your *sound intelligence* will bridge an understanding of sound as both metaphor (spoken everyday-life sound) and musicianship (consciously created or sung sound). Your new naked-voice skills will strengthen your emerging sound intelligence with the support of your nonjudging mind, deep listening, loving presence, creative intention, and courageous and conscious communication. As you further embrace and strengthen your sound-intelligence skills, you will begin to appreciate the significant role that your voice can play, not only in transforming the music of your emotions, but in the emotional struggles of those around you.

As you gradually learn to access and respect the true authority of your sound power, everything changes. A new energy arises from within, an aliveness that is empowering beyond belief. It's like taking the lid off the tight jar of your reactive mind and unblocking a long-held dam of trauma, abandonment, and neglect inside you. This wounding is the raw sound material of that wild river of music in your soul. As it finally bursts through the restraints of your rational mind, it will gradually find expression in your musical emotions as you bravely and mindfully hone new ways to flow effortlessly once again. You may well find yourself sounding a whole new perceptual field of awareness into being.

As the frozen music of your conditioning and ancestral history begins to melt, new energies of love awaken within you. This is a falling in love without the need for an outer lover. As the cloudy sky of your mind begins to clear, old wounds are acknowledged and released and old stories forgiven. You enter a new depth of listening, and previous fears subside as you hear yourself as you truly are. This is a homecoming like no other, bringing the liberation of a more spacious awareness, and with it the inner resilience and capacity to engage with the full-sound spectrum of who you *are*, whatever the consequences.

As you continue the courageous sonic voyage for a *sound-conscious* life, you will start to discover your whole life as music and thus begin to recognize just how important your naked singing voice is—its sheer power and range of expression, its eloquence, and most importantly, its humility.

Your sound awareness and listening skills are giving you formidable nonviolent creative weapons to let go your attachment to the illusory constraints and struggles of daily life. They will bring you home to yourself and to what it means to be truly a *sound human being*. Your unfolding relationship with the polarities of your nature through the corresponding forces of sound and silence also wakes you up to all the other corresponding forces of your life on Earth—as between your invisibility and your visibility, your being and your becoming, your stillness and your activity, your conditioned personality and unconditional being.

Heart Meditation Practice

First and foremost, enjoy relaxing into the following Heart Meditation. Use it as a way to relax, breathe, and open the doorway of your heart ever wider and deeper. You may prefer to create your own Heart Meditation, possibly using this one as a springboard.

HEART MEDITATION

I am relaxing
breathing in and breathing out into the center of my chest
opening my heart
feeling the beauty of the world around me
opening my heart
breathing into this moment
opening my heart
hearing the sound of wind, birds, people's voices
opening my heart
opening my heart to you my soul
to my children, my siblings, my mother, father, relations, friends
opening my heart
opening my heart to all my positive and negative feelings
opening my heart to my life as it is right now
opening my heart
opening my heart to the music of my life
opening my heart
opening my heart to what is and what will be

opening my heart
opening my heart with gratitude and forgiveness
opening my heart
opening my heart to who I am
opening my heart

4.2 Where Emotion Meets Devotion

Self inside Self you are nothing without me
Self inside Self I am only you
What we are together, what we are together
Will never ever die

—"SELF INSIDE SELF," *Sura*

Since my early years of self-discovery through Asian-inspired chanting in the late 1980s and '90s, I have had to ask and answer questions about the nature of freedom and spirituality in musical expression, as well as questions about the future role and direction of music in the twenty-first century. Once I had discovered the sacred power of inner sound and voice (following a transformative "no mind" experience in India), I then had to inquire what it really meant to *surrender* to myself through my vocal art. And I am not just talking here about the content of the music but the *awareness of the singer*. Meanwhile the simple recurring nature of devotional chanting continued to tear my heart open, inspiring a new language for love, within and beyond name and form.

Devotional or sacred chanting and personalized or secular singing have always been indispensible traveling companions, serving different yet complementary roles in revealing the multifaceted power of sound. Together they fuel and enhance the journey of self-discovery. Chanting and singing are like two musical tributaries of a much larger river that, when they meet, can create a resonant alchemy of rhythmic texture, recurring melody lines, and original improvisation, generating a vocal experience that uplifts the soul of both singer(s) and listener(s).

Devotional chanting is a more personalized version of mantra chanting. Like mantra, its intention is prayerful and meditative. It is often a shared practice. Whereas mantra is usually sounded on one unchanging note that may possibly be supplemented with the musical tone above or below it, devotional chants—sometimes called *bhajans* or *kirtans* in Asian music—may be made up of more intricate melodies with simple modulations and harmonies while always returning to the original home or "tonic" note. In devotional chanting a simple recurring melody is sung, often as a call and refrain that is shared between a lead vocalist and a group of singers. In Asia sacred mantras and devotional chants are traditionally sung in unison. More recently, Western devotional singers have chosen to embellish the mantra or the chant with multipart harmonies, often modulating into other musical keys before returning once again to the original home or SA note.

The purpose of the one unchanging note that underlies the sacred mantra or chant is to tether the melody to its source. As the melody is repeated your mind relaxes, generating a deep sense of calm. The sacred melody is often accompanied by spiritual words of power that always arise from and return to the one unchanging note of the mantra. Such devotional sound activates a wondrous power inside you as your ordinary mind subsides and the heart opens. Gradually your listening awareness shifts from a mental analytical mode of being to a deeper heartfelt connection with your self and the world around you.

Devotional chants are very easy and nonthreatening for everyone, from children to seniors, to access and remember. The chant melody is as innocent and simple as a nursery rhyme or lullaby. Yet rather than sending you to sleep, its intention is to awaken your soul and inspire a spirit of inclusiveness that transports everyone into more expansive realms of consciousness.

Personal songs—while sometimes delivered in a devotional way—are generally more akin to storytelling, focusing less on the meditative and more on down-to-earth human issues that highlight everyday conflict, resolution, and possibility. The aim of such singing is to communicate the highs and lows of the human story in a more harmonic and diverse way. The singer may sing a cappella, or be accompanied by anything from a solo instrument such as a piano or guitar, to an instrumental ensemble or big band orchestra. Such singing tends to cover a wider canvas of emotional and experimental vocal expression in any one of a range of styles.

Chloë Goodchild, devotional chanting (1988)

So how on earth can something as seemingly inconsequential as devotional chanting have any relevance for your life and the issues facing you in the world today? How can an activity that is more commonly associated with rowdy football crowds at one end of the spectrum and contemplative monasteries on the other have any place in a serious discussion about improving your life?

The practice of devotional chanting was until recently considered an esoteric, alternative, or New Age activity. However, as the chaos and uncertainty of our world intensify, shared sound, singing, and chanting are becoming increasingly essential, and therefore popular, in all walks of life, both as a solo and shared recreational activity. Chanting is turning up in the most unlikely places, such as "away" days for senior managers and company directors and in-service days for head teachers. I was even asked to introduce it as a "special musical surprise" to a group of international policy-makers during a weekend conference on the global crisis. (See sections 6.1 and 6.6 about the Singing Field in Part III.)

Chanting has the power to awaken and guide humanity through one of our greatest spiritual crises. Who would have believed that shared chant and song would have the power to unlock and release core emotions buried inside for centuries? Yet the recovery of this healing sound invokes a depth of intuition and insight capable of transforming the language of separateness and fear, inspiring a new harmonic resonance for our time.

We face grave challenges. In the words of Thomas Berry in *The Great Work*:

> We are facing a defining moment, one in which the Earth calls out to us to embark upon a re-sacralisation of nature, a new ecological and spiritual beginning where we must consciously move from being a disrupting force on the Earth to a benign presence.

This benign presence can be accessed and expressed most effectively through simple chanting, accessible to everyone.

I love to create unique meeting places where that presence can be accessed and shared by everyone through the repetition of simple melodies, handed down through the generations, and chanted with specific mantras. These mantras are sonic formulae drawn from the ancient religious alphabets of the last five thousand years. They have the capacity to awaken consciousness through the experience of intuitive flashes that open the heart, bypass the rational mind, and bring us into a state of presence beyond separateness. Chanting together in this way creates a context within which a deep nonjudgmental listening can be sustained.

Chanting, unlike social-entertainment singing, offers a way of sounding out that is so simple that anyone can do it and no one is left out. Its impact is so immediate, accessible, and unthreatening that it literally *en-chants* even the most defended or diverse groups of people to let go of their opinions, relax, and discover new coherent ways to communicate with each other without judgment or fear.

Singing for social entertainment has a different purpose. It romances our imagination, stimulates the emotions, and draws our attention out in the external world of relationship and drama. It calls us out to play, to invent, to build stories in our minds, to lament, to generate longing, to yearn for some unreachable person or dream. Chanting takes us the other way. It draws our attention inward, encourages us to let go of our outer preoccupations as we open to being touched at deeper levels from the inside out. As previously mentioned, both these forms are complementary and bring great value into our lives.

Chanting can be associated with loud collective activity too. However, whether you are singing for all you are worth in a football match, on your knees in prayer in a church, or patiently biding your time in a traffic jam, chanting can come to your aid. It enables you to reach deeper inside yourself to a place where your longing heart bursts wide open to sheer joy—naked, spontaneous, and free.

4.3 Sounding Your Instinctual Heart

Om tare tutare ture so ham, Om tare tutare ture so ham
Woman of the wisdom tree, Goddess of humanity
Singing of the unity we long for
—"Om Tara," *Fierce Wisdom*

Devotional chanting as a complementary practice with sacred mantra is an essential ground of the Naked Voice. In Chapter 3, I introduced you to three of our key mantras: AUM, the Seven-Chakra Mantra, and the Heart Sutra. They create the sound foundations for all the other Naked Voice practices and vocal skills to build upon. Sounding these mantras on a regular basis, even for five to ten minutes each day, can make a powerful impact in stabilizing the nervous system, balancing the emotional body, and replacing stress and insecurity with a deeper state of calm and inner security.

The simple act of chanting provides the sound foundations essential to generating a deeper confidence and intention to explore the full spectrum of your singing soul. You will soon be building your very own "house of song" with more creative vocal maps assisting you to integrate the elemental and emotional language of your voice. I love this image of the human body as a "house of song." As mentioned earlier, I came across it when exploring the love songs of a group of Indian Sufi singers called the Bauls of Bengal. For these ecstatic lovers of God, the human body itself is a sacred vessel of the human voice. And the sole purpose of the human body is to transmit the mystical language of love in rousing rhythms and sung stories communicated directly to listeners.

Without your body of course there is no song. Devotional chant bridges the impersonal, interior focus of sacred mantra practice with a freer, more personalized way of expressing your soul. But before we venture more deeply into the music of your emotions, I invite you first to come with me and explore an empowering and uplifting way to sing your heart out with the support of a selection of my favorite devotional chants, inspired by some of the world's chanting traditions, primarily Judeo-Christian, Hindu, and Buddhist.

A devotional chant is usually a sung invocation or prayer in offering to a specific deity, sacred quality, or attribute. The following chants provide user-friendly, heart-warming melodies to bridge all the elements of your being—earth, water, fire, air, and ethereal—in recurring refrains that always return to the one unchanging note. However, where they depart from sacred mantras is that they allow you more emotional freedom to express yourself as inspired. As the melody becomes second nature, you may soon find yourself improvising with it as your devotional heart opens and surrenders into deeper states of self-acceptance and gratitude. Soon you find yourself letting go while empowered by the spirit of the chant and the all-inclusive atmosphere of singing with others too.

I have collected and sung these chants over the years with diverse groups of people and cultural backgrounds, some of whom appear in other chapters: The Blackfeet medicine elders, the Dalai Lama and religious leaders in Northern Ireland, my father on his death bed, victims of 9/11, and inmates of a high-security women's prison in New York. Traditionally these devotional chants would have been sung in specific ceremonies and religious communities. The music was handed down orally over the centuries from generation to generation, or the songs might have been transmitted from master to disciple through what is sometimes called a *diksha* or initiation ceremony. As my lineage is universal and pathless, I have not identified with the religious tradition that the chants derive from but am simply inspired by the pure and transforming nature of their *inner message*. I received my favorite devotional chants either in dreams (the Heart Sutra) or via encounters with other singers or spiritual teachers who have been inspired by specific mystical sounds, sacred mantras, or devotional chants.

It was America's great East-West folk hero, Ram Dass, who first introduced me in the 1980s to the transformative power of devotional Hindu chants, sometimes called *kirtans* or *bhajans*. Prior to that time, Ram Dass (originally Richard Alpert) had been researching the transformative use of consciousness-altering drugs such as LSD, for which he was fired from Harvard University as a psychology professor in the '60s. He subsequently travelled to India with a group of friends. There he met several powerful spiritual masters—notably Neem Karoli Baba—who inspired the name Ram Dass (Servant of God) and a pioneering new (to the West) language of consciousness that has influenced countless spiritual seekers for decades.

It was also Ram Dass who decided one evening to give a slide show of his favorite Indian saints and masters. And it was the photograph of the revered Indian woman saint Anandamayi Ma—one of twentieth-century India's great luminaries—that changed my life forever. She was an ecstatic singer whose devotional chanting alone transformed thousands across India. Her radiant and unconditional presence was a lightning rod and a firebrand of consciousness.

In the 1980s my then-partner Roger Housden (author of *Ten Poems to Change Your Life*) and I, along with a wonderful group of friends, used to bring Ram Dass to Europe, where he would lead meditation talks. We would feed more than a hundred people at a time during the five- and ten-day meditation retreats in UK, France, and Italy. Ram Dass's teachings always included electrifying chanting sessions for the many people there. Ram Dass was accompanied by a wonderful "chant wallah" named Jai Lakshman who soon inspired me to chant with him in that way. This was my first exposure to public devotional singing as a soloist. I was thirty-three years old.

The first devotional chant Jai taught me was "Radhe-Krishna" in praise of Krishna, Hindu God of Light, and his consort Radhe, queen of the universe. Its mesmerizing anthemic melody is a celebration of the sacred union of masculine and feminine. This empowering chant entered me like medicine. I have sung it for over three decades in various ways. Its melody finally evolved into a world anthem that I named "Gaia" and is one of my favorites on my *Fierce Wisdom* collection of world chants.

My chanting journey subsequently took me from Europe to the USA and Canada, where I collected and reinvented many new chants along the way. The simple melodic architecture of each chant had a magical way of creating a secure sanctuary within which I could express my unique heart's longing. This nonthreatening musical form was a far reach from the more sophisticated choral music of my "Cambridge University Singer" days. Yet, paradoxically, it provided a much deeper container within which I could release long-held tension and reach deep into my soul, accessing a forgotten depth of joy there.

You will find chanting to be a refreshingly accessible and powerful way to dissolve outworn stories, facilitating your navigation beyond the self-conscious restraint of your personal history. It can double as an effective complement to talking therapy. Enjoy immersing yourself in this new relationship with the power of sound through chant. It will

Chloë Goodchild chanting with Jai Lakshman (1987)

anchor your heart in your body, helping you to embody your sound in new and unexpected ways.

Singing in this way enables you to embrace and surrender your heart to new modes of listening and, most importantly, of *being heard*. Not being heard by someone outside you, but by your very own self. The world is so full of noise, angst, and doership, with little interest given to strengthening the self-awareness that arises from simply being present, being nobody, just being. Rather than needing to express all the usual kinds of dramatic stories of frustration, unrequited love, blame, shame, and separation, you can simply engage, receive, and open to the energy of sound flowing through you from deep inside like an endless and unstoppable wave arising from the source of your being.

4.4 Sound Medicine:
Meeting the Piegan Wisdom Elders

Om Anandamayi (Blissful mother)
Chaitanya mayi (Awakened mother)
Satya mayi (Mother of Being)
Parameshwari (Supreme goddess—she who is beyond all form)

—"Laughing Anandamayi," *Thousand Ways of Light*

The simple secret power of chanting can awaken a wondrous power inside you. Once this power is touched, life is never the same again. A few years ago I was given a rare opportunity to chant for two medicine elders called "Riders at the Door," otherwise known as Darnell and Smokey. Their lineage is the Piegan Nation, and their vast lands once extended from the Rocky Mountains of northern Montana up into Canada and beyond. Piegan is pronounced "bee-gun-knee." (Many Westerners know the Piegan Nation as "The Blackfeet." They were given this name by the British.) Chanting for these remarkable wisdom elders was an unforgettable gift that I will treasure for the rest of my life. Singing for them showed me how chanting can bridge worlds in unexpected ways.

It was the summer of 2006 in Missoula, Montana. I had been invited to give a weekend voice workshop there by one of my Naked Voice students, Cris Mulvey, a fiery Irish woman in her forties. She had moved to northern Montana following a strong call from the land that was sacred for the Piegan Nation. Cris had been passionate about Native American culture and spirituality from a young age. She began working as a teacher and development worker in the local Piegan school.

Cris had always been keen to introduce me to her Native American friends. So following my Naked Voice weekend workshop in Missoula with a diverse group of health workers, business professionals, artists, musicians, and environmentalists, we took the road north toward the Rockies. Our destination was East Glacier, the heart of Piegan country. After several hours the great mountains of Glacier National Park became visible, rising up thousands of feet into the sky, welcoming us from across the plains. I was speechless at the vast scale of Mother Nature as she embraced us in all her glorious summer colors.

Cris and I share a fascination with the power of language to express the wisdom of an individual or culture. We had both spent extended periods of time living in indigenous communities. It was thanks to the strong links that Cris had already forged with the Piegan people that I was privileged to enter the inner sanctum of their community. Cris really wanted to see what kind of alchemy might take place between our respective ways of giving voice as a vehicle for spirit. I, meanwhile, was eager to learn from their skills of interconnectedness and how they instilled and disseminated their core values. I was used to coordinating and co-creating cohesive group-listening practices that enabled diverse individuals with different backgrounds and beliefs to listen, accept, and honor each other without prejudice or fear. I wondered how this would compare with the Piegan ceremonial structures and wisdom councils.

Cris was especially excited for me to meet her two closest friends, Darnell and Smokey, Medicine Bundle carriers. They were a handsome husband-and-wife team and the highly respected elders of their people. Before meeting them we booked ourselves into a motel near Glacier National Park, a few miles from the restaurant in the center of East Glacier, where we were all to have dinner together.

During our journey from Missoula to East Glacier, Cris told me one of the great medicine creation myths of the Piegan Nation: the ancient tale of Scarface, who brings the healing medicine of the sweat lodge and the sun dance to his people from the Sun. It is a story similar to that of Christ, in which the male hero has to undergo a journey of death and resurrection to redeem the feminine and bring harmony to the world. Scarface is the archetypal medicine healer. His presence was imprinted in my mind as we approached our two Native American friends in the restaurant queue.

Cris, Darnell, and Smokey fell into each other's arms, laughing and hugging. Darnell had been a close female friend and ally for Cris during the years that she worked in the school in East Glacier. There was clearly a strong mutual respect among the three of them as they chatted and caught up on local news and stories, all of which was carried out with animation and laughter.

I was initially aware of a certain polite reserve toward me. Was I perhaps just another of those white western spiritual shoppers that they had tolerated for years? I certainly looked the part, yet I was Cris's friend. So Darnell and Smokey graciously accepted my presence and gradually warmed toward me as the evening unfolded.

Darnell and Smokey, the Piegan Wisdom Elders (2014). Photo by Wesley G Hannon of Remember Forever Studio

The remarkable stories they shared with us that evening were all infused with a profound reverence for and connection with Mother Earth. Gradually, our conversation focused on the ways in which Darnell and Smokey's intimate harmony with Great Nature had inspired and supported rites of passage and rituals—ceremony, dance, music, and healing songs all sustaining a balance between heaven and earth. Their rare connection with "great mystery" led into a deeper discussion about the meditative practices that informed and resourced their spiritual way of life. Then, suddenly, something strange started to happen—I noticed that my two new friends were becoming more guarded about what they would share with me, until finally they refused to communicate with me at all. The conversation came to an abrupt halt, followed by a long pregnant pause. What on Earth could have provoked this? Darnell and Smokey started to talk earnestly with each other in their own language. Then they both turned to us.

Smokey was looking at me with his penetrating eyes and then spoke emphatically: "We can go no further with this conversation until we have heard your sound!"

"Ah!" I responded. "Yes, and I would love to hear yours!"

"Very well!" exclaimed Smokey. "We cannot do that here, so we will take you somewhere else."

Soon we were driving at some speed through the reservation, up and down dark streets until we arrived at a small cottage, the home of one of Darnell's siblings. We entered.

Then something quite unexpected occurred. Speaking with each other in their own tongue, Darnell and Smokey started to rearrange the furniture so that I had to sit in a chair in the middle of the room, while Darnell and Smokey sat together behind a table, facing me. What was this extreme formality all about? It felt surreal. Darnell and Smokey sat rigid and upright, like two characters preparing themselves for a photo shoot and bracing themselves for the flash. They continued staring at me. Silence descended. I was now expected to hold forth like a student at some traditional singing audition. Was this some kind of strange payback for all the years that I had told my students, "Don't think—sing now"?

What was I to do? I closed my eyes, took a deep breath, and waited for an impulse from within. Finally it came, and someone called "Chloë" opened her eyes saying, "I am going to sing a sacred chant for you. It's a hymn in praise of the Great Mother."

The atmosphere remained awkwardly stiff and somber. Yet I could feel that the sincere quality of their listening was empowering me to proceed with their request.

I waited a few seconds, just gazing back at them.

Then I closed my eyes and disappeared inside the sanctuary of my heart. Silence inside, silence outside, all around me. Silence. I was listening and waiting, listening for a vibration from deep inside my soul, somewhere I had never been, a place beyond this world calling me. I fell into a warm darkness inside. Soon I was falling down deeper inside myself, falling, falling, falling, deeper down, spiraling down and further on down beneath the polarities of my ordinary nature, beyond the limitations of time and place, beyond the confines of the everyday world, into a secret place . . . ah yes this place again, I remembered it, I was home inside myself again, deep inside the most interior cavern of my singing soul, trusting and peaceful.

No one said anything. Two medicine elders, somber-faced, simply waited patiently for the white woman to share her sound.

"I will sing in Sanskrit," someone inside me muttered. "It's a universal language most associated with India. But it does not belong to India. It is free of all cultural or religious associations."

More silence, then I took in a deep breath, closed my eyes, sighed out, centered myself, and the sound finally started to emerge.

Who was singing? I didn't know or care anymore. More silence, then, slowly, I breathed in, drawing energy up through my body, inviting the sound to ride out on the energy from the root up to the crown. "Chloë" disappeared and a singing soul with an authority all her own began to fill the room.

"Om Anandamayi, Chaitanyamayi, Satyamayi, Paramayi."

The voice sang of all the qualities of the universal mother, the blissful mother, the unconditional mother, the mother of truth, mother of compassion, the mother who relieves all suffering, the mother beyond all her forms. And the singing praised her in all her glory, from the valleys of her dark origin into the high mountain pastures of her supreme celestial and cosmic presence, on and on she sang until at last she reined herself in and disappeared into nothing again. Silence returned. I was once again inwardly still and peaceful.

A timeless moment passed. We all sat together in silence. Slowly my eyes opened, saw nothing, and then closed again. The room was so silent that my slowly emerging mind wondered if perhaps I might have been left alone in the middle of nowhere, with no knowledge of how to find my way back to my guest house!

When I opened my eyes a second time, I became aware of the environment, a dim kitchen somewhere in East Glacier, northern Montana. Here, a white woman had been singing her soul, singing of her past lives with her ancestral brothers and sisters. I remembered the strange formality in which I had been asked to sing and closed my eyes once more, enjoying the vibration and presence that enveloped us all.

When I finally focused my eyes more clearly to witness my Native American friends' response, I was startled by what I saw. This time the energy of the room changed, and we were all changed. As I looked toward Darnell and Smokey, I beheld my two "Riders at the Door" lurching forward in their seats with their eyes fixed upon me, staring at me in total disbelief, their disoriented faces straining, mouths agape, to absorb what had just happened. They were looking at me as if I were some kind of alien or a bizarre scientific specimen. Who was I? Where had that sound come from? How could it possibly have arisen from this white female form? I stared back at them without concern, patiently awaiting their response.

Whatever had happened, there were no barriers now, no frontiers.

The atmosphere was strangely relaxed and peaceful. Darnell and Smokey's eyes softened as they relaxed back into their chairs. Then they turned toward one another, speaking in their native tongue again, this time in earnest tones, words jarring and sparring between them, trying to decide how much they would, or would not, reveal of what they had heard.

I waited. I was relaxed, fulfilled, and nourished, entirely at home in my skin. Finally they turned to me again.

"Where did you find that melody?" asked Smokey.

I smiled and then explained that I had been singing it for fifteen years, having received it during my travels along the west coast, in San Francisco from another singer of Indian devotional songs. Somehow, no words could really express for Darnell and Smokey what had just occurred, and whoever it was that had just sung.

"Well," Smokey said, "your melody and the vibration and rhythm of your song are just like the songs in our most sacred ceremonies!" I was stunned. We gazed upon each other with the innocence of three children who had just discovered a beautiful secret. We continued to stare at each other in amazement, like ancient friends who belong to no man's territory. Before we knew it, we were free and laughing loud and strong.

"It's no accident you came here!" Darnell exclaimed.

"We have work to do together!"

4.5 Awakening Sound Intelligence

There is some kiss we want with our whole lives
The touch of spirit
On the body

—RUMI, COLEMAN BARKS'S TRANSLATION,
"THERE IS SOME KISS," *Fierce Wisdom*

The day I discovered that my sound could transform my tears was a day like no other. From that moment on, everything in my life changed. I began to uncover the "secret" power of sound to transform my negative emotions into deeper positive human feelings, one by one. I have already mentioned "sound intelligence." Your sound intelligence has the power to switch on the whole light bulb of your brain. Sound intelligence is music, new science, and philosophy rolled into one. It's a quality of "knowing" derived from an integration of right-left brain, particle and wave at once. It's not overtly intellectual or intuitive. It doesn't depend on specific techniques or rituals. It catalyzes a direct access to who you are as a sound beam of light, an embodied intelligence no longer bound by reactive thought nor identified with the duality of daily life. Your sound intelligence enables you to discover your self and your whole life as a symphony of love. Why? Because your true sound is fueled by the universal life-force, which fuels your spirit, which fuels the vibration pulsing in every cell of your body, mind, and soul, the chemistry of your being.

This sound intelligence is essential because it melts down the old, outworn circuits dominated by your thinking mind and rewires the energies of love within you from your head to your toes, providing an effortless access to the original song of your soul. Your sound intelligence enables you to unify your objective, self-observing mind—your wise witness—with your subjective, intuitive heart—your emotional wisdom. Your authentic sound provides a flowing stream between the two. As it dissolves the old boundaries between your talking head and your singing heart, your old small-minded voice is replaced by your "whole" voice. This wholeness of sound awakens your whole self.

"One self is all there is homecoming home" (*Fierce Wisdom*).

This is your naked voice as you have never known it. This naked voice is the mouthpiece of your naked self, meaning there is nowhere to hide anymore—neither your self from your voice, nor your voice from your self, nor your self from the world. Your sound intelligence enables you to masterfully navigate and transform your negative emotions into positive human feeling. For one thing, what you once judged as "negative" or "positive" is in truth just the play of dark and light energies seeking recognition and authentic expression.

You may ask how this understanding came about. The following two stories of epiphany were pivotal in the activation of my own sound intelligence. The first story, "Surrender," took place in the mid 1980s in a singing session with my first classical Indian voice teacher, Gilles Petit from France. The second story, "Homecoming," happened in 1990 in Lucknow, India.

Surrender

It was in the presence of Gilles Petit that I first experienced an inner abandonment through singing. Gilles Petit was an East-West vocalist and composer from Paris who had spent many years imbibing the music of north Indian vocal raga and instrumental sound. He introduced me to the far-reaching possibilities of the voice as a vehicle for true self-expression. The voice was Gilles's life passion and study, and he had mastered many Western vocal styles: medieval music, opera, oratorio, and *sprecht-gesang*, together with folk, jazz, and ethnic vocal styles. He could also play many instruments and had invented his own to create sounds that conventional instruments were not capable of making. There was no limit to his research, and his vocal range stretched from *basso profundo* to the ethereal high-pitched *musique cosmique*. But Gilles Petit was not only a unique virtuoso vocalist and remarkable performer; he lived and breathed his art. The world of sound was his life. It was a spiritual, philosophical, and psychological exercise, experienced by means of rigorous physical practice and an intensive exploration of the space around the body, of balance, and of rhythm. Indian vocal music was his ground, and he slowly initiated me into it. His work provided a crucial training for me, bridging the worlds of body, spirit, and psyche through the vehicle of my own voice. In Indian vocal music, the authenticity of the voice is central to the music. It is a fully embodied expression of the human spirit through sound.

Gilles taught by means of a musical drone instrument, a small portable harmonium that provided an unchanging backcloth of sound on one note, out of which the vocalist could sing freely, returning to that home note on completion of improvisation. I subsequently bought myself a harmonium. This way of singing was for me a meditation, the drone representing the unchanging sound of silence, and the improvised melody symbolizing the phenomenon of thoughts and ideas that arise from the mind but that must always return to a state of silence. Before improvising, we first had to learn how to make a substantial sound, from the belly. This took many months to develop and sustain. I could not believe my good fortune in meeting this unique voice teacher. His way of sounding-out seemed tailor-made for me.

One evening something remarkable happened. I was sitting with Gilles and a group of his students in my home toward the end of a course. The course had been physically and vocally rigorous, and everyone in the group was euphoric. The atmosphere was celebratory. Following a feast of Indian food and wine, individuals began to sing songs from their own culture, songs from childhood, songs of labor, love, and longing, devotional and folk songs, humorous songs, Gaelic,

Celtic, country and western, the blues and gospel songs, together with their own compositions. The scene became increasingly animated, finally reaching a climax that heralded the call for a new direction. There was a pause, and I took this opportunity to ask Gilles if I might improvise with him alone, either on a specific raga or in free improvisatory style, accompanied by tambours, harmonium, or guitar. There was another pause, then he responded quietly, "We shall sing Malkauns, the raga for the midnight hour, when twelve o'clock strikes." The party resumed in original gaiety once more as new songs were sung.

As midnight approached, Gilles suggested that we all retire into the more spacious room next door. As we all resettled, Gilles began to sing songs of a more melancholic nature, in Spanish and Italian, which lulled most of the group into a horizontal posture. Fatigue was setting in. I could barely keep my eyes open. The energy was surely spent. Had Gilles forgotten about our midnight duet? At two minutes to midnight, he turned to me with a smile on his face, saying that it was time to introduce the Malkauns raga. He began with a song in French that he had composed using the notes of the Malkauns scale. "This is the raga of fearlessness," Gilles explained. "It is about stepping out into the dark alone, without fear." I was caught. There was a poignant sorrow in the sounds he sang. My memory shot back to all the painful goodbyes and unfinished business of my past, dragging behind me in an invisible dark sack.

Then Gilles's song suddenly startled me back into the present moment. The sounds that fell from his mellifluous and full-blooded voice arose steadily from the depths of his ancient Indo-European soul. They seized my heart. The combination of the ongoing harmonium drone, together with the vocal sounds that arose from it, spiraled around me in the midnight air and directed my attention immediately toward the center of my chest. I became aware of a searing sensation in my breastbone, a piercing through. I dropped my jaw and gasped for air. The sound was acting upon me like a finely tuned drill, first searching out an entry point in my chest then pricking through the surface of the skin, pursuing its one-pointed way down into the fleshy part, snapping through bone, on down into the marrow, on and on through blood vessels, muscle and, finally, right into the softest and most inaccessible regions of my wounded heart.

I was at a loss to participate in any way imaginable. I was wholly immersed in a great listening net that hauled me up through an ocean of grief—my personal grief, and also the sorrows of the whole world and the sufferings of humanity since the Fall; the suffering of a world driven by territorialism; and closer to home, the suffering of my family struggles.

Then came the words of the song to drive the sounds still deeper. Gilles sang slowly, watching me with a smile upon his face. These were no ordinary words. Gilles had composed a song inspired by an epic Indian sacred text called the *Bhagavad Gita,* in which the great warrior hero Arjuna is in dialogue with Krishna, the God of Light and Lord of the Universe. They are in a life-or-death dialogue on the battlefield of human conscience. Arjuna has been called upon to face the unimaginable prospect of having to slay members of his own family upon the battlefield. He is understandably resisting this sacred call to duty. Meanwhile, Krishna patiently comes to his aid to remind him of the sacred law of Unconditional Love. Rather like Abraham in the face of God's calling him to slay his own son, Arjuna is required to demonstrate a benign disinterest toward his family, surrendering all attachment to them to the point of having to kill them. The test is to surrender all attachments of whatever kind and also all attachments to the success or failure of the war in question. I had read this text many times but I had never absorbed it so deeply.

As Gilles's music continued, I had the sensation that I was disintegrating. My boundaries were down. My spine felt as if it were melting. Suddenly my whole body was trembling and weeping in a helpless profusion of mourning sounds. The lid of all my longing, guilt, shame, loneliness, and separation was off. It was an excruciating catharsis of my soul yet hauntingly beautiful at the same time. Gilles persisted with this singing process until I was entirely spent. Silence fell upon the room. I sat there in this darkened space with just candles and breathing sounds around me. Many members of the group had fallen asleep.

Gilles looked at me half laughing and whispered, "Now it is your turn to sing."

"Me? No way!" I was finished, an empty carcass. There was nothing inside me, and no one left to sing. I was in a state of bereavement and pleaded to pass my turn on to somebody else. He continued laughing softly then simply replied, "Follow me." The music began again with the same raga, but this time with a slow introduction, followed by free improvisation around the notes of the raga. Now there was no battle-field, and no choice either. I simply had to surrender to the sound. But would anything come out? Then something unexpectedly graceful happened as I yielded to his request. Something opened within me to the simplest, most effortless outpouring of love that I had ever known. I let go all thought, emotion, friction, and fear—allowing the sounds of the melody line to lead me through the darkness. Time disappeared. We could have been singing for hours or as little as a single moment.

When we stopped singing, everyone was sitting up, wide-eyed and awake. This experience opened a door for me behind my famil-iar "safer" vocalizing. This was my first experience of the awakening power of my voice.

If this was my first major encounter with the transformative power of my voice, it wasn't until I actually travelled to India, inspired by dreams of the Indian saint Anandamayi Ma, that I encountered a depth of communication that I can only describe as *sound before sound*.

Homecoming

When I met Harilal Poonja, I had just six days left of my stay in India. Those few days marked the end of a life-changing journey there.

I had travelled through northern India in the steps of Anandamayi Ma, the great luminary commonly known as "Ma." I was feeling ful-filled and very peaceful after several weeks in Rishikesh, known as the land of the *rishis* (holy beings). My main intention for being there was to connect more deeply with the presence and teachings of Anan-damayi at her ashram in Haridwar. Anandamayi had passed away in 1982 but her spiritual presence was profoundly felt there. I gave con-siderable time to interviewing Ma's dedicated followers, monks and nuns, many of whom had travelled with Ma and received her teachings directly for decades.

I immersed myself in hours of devotional chanting alongside spiritual dialogues on nonduality and the realization of the One Self. This collision with the divine feminine was electrifying. It dismantled my ego-mind and released decades of tension, altering my fields of perception on all levels. It changed my life utterly and was clearly a preparation for my meeting to follow with "the invisible guru," as he was originally known.

"Poonjaji," or "Papaji" as he was affectionately called, was an engineer by profession. Yet his childhood was preoccupied with an intense hunger to "see God." When I met him in 1990 he was receiving people in his son Surrendra's house in Lucknow, north India. It was a small building on a noisy street, and it seemed to accommodate a large number of children and relations. On arrival, my partner and I were ushered into a tiny living room on the ground floor, where the radiant Poonjaji was waiting for us, beaming from ear to ear, with a remarkable vitality. He was very tall and athletic-looking. His face was kind and finely sculpted. He welcomed us with such openness and generosity of spirit, like long-lost friends. Most striking was his ordinariness. He felt just like my grandfather welcoming us in to tea. There were no airs and graces, no incense burners, no decorations, no rituals of any kind. A small group of five of us had gathered to meet him.

Poonjaji was a student of the great saint Ramana Maharshi, a master of *advaita* (nonduality). *Advaita* literally means "not separate." One Self is all there is. This understanding originates from the ancient wisdom texts or Vedas, handed down by great souls, sages, or yogis over thousands of years. Poonjaji was steeped in this lineage. He began by addressing some practical questions to one of the men, asking him from where he had come, how the journey was, and so on. As he continued to stare at him with his penetrating, benevolent eyes, he asked the visitor if he had a question, and what might this question be?

There was a silence. The teaching had begun. It involved a rigorous process of self-inquiry based on one question: "Who are you?" The aim of asking this question is to return your mind to its source and ultimately to awaken to a direct experience of who you really are. As the evening progressed, my turn came to respond to Poonjaji's intense self-inquiry process. I tentatively asked him about the path of devotional practice (bhakti yoga). Poonjaji rebuffed my question, saying that "visions and chanting are for those who are still at an elementary level of understanding, on the nursery slopes of spiritual practice." He seemed singularly unimpressed by my capacity to ask a *serious* question. So I decided to keep quiet. I noticed, however, as the evening continued, that I was feeling a deepening tranquility. It was as if the film screen of my mind were being slowly removed of its own accord, while I was simultaneously aware of a stillness and a peace that was filling me up from the inside out. This felt profoundly nourishing. Toward the end of the evening Poonjaji looked toward me, saying, "This girl is contributing a lot of silence into this room." Yet the silence was everywhere emanating from everyone and every object in the room already.

This was a silence that I had known all my life, yet one that I had rarely acknowledged to anyone. It was my secret world. Suddenly the secret was out, and it was being acknowledged by my new Indian "grandfather" in Lucknow. Poonjaji proceeded over the coming days to transmit and anchor me in this ever-deepening stillness beyond the distractions of my ordinary mind. As he later told me, "Some meditation teachers remove the furniture of the mind; I remove the mind altogether!"

Gradually any residual self-consciousness fell away. "Chloëness" no longer dominated the field of consciousness, and internally the attachment to my old identity was fast disappearing. My ordinary mind had no control over this. Soon I could not think coherently at all. Every word that I uttered was incomprehensible. My nights then became a new drama all their own. Every night I lay wide awake in what felt like a high fever, which seemed to be burning endless layers of my personal identity away. I felt as if I were rolling in an invisible fire. Yet it was not painful or dramatic. It was beyond emotion. I had no illness. My body-mind was sinking into a depth of silence. Any thoughts dissolved as soon as they appeared. A new life sprang into being in me during that short time with an intensity I could not have dreamt of.

My body-heart-mind seemed to have surrendered to an irreversible process. I was kept awake at night by a burning sensation that made it impossible to remain in one position for long. I was moving in a perpetual flow, tossing and turning like a roasting carcass on a spit. Despite the great heat that inhabited my body, I did not feel any pain. My awareness seemed to be caught up in a state beyond my ordinary senses, such that I no longer identified with physical discomfort. All I remember was being awake, alert, and open, without any need to sleep ever again. An aliveness was streaming through me in an unstoppable current of loving presence.

"Inside outside all around us, naked in our song" (*Fierce Wisdom*).

Then I dreamt that Shiva—one of the primary forms of God in the Hindu culture—appeared and engaged me in a seductive dance. Dressed in a brown robe, Shiva entered a room where I was sitting, my face hidden behind veils. As Shiva entered, I parted the veils from my face to watch him. He moved in a slow swaying dance toward me, smoke pouring out of his neck, and he began chanting in soft tones, "Shiva, Shiva, Shiva!" When he was within a few feet of me, I realized this was all an illusion. Even Shiva, the god of gods, could not liberate me. At this moment, a sword manifested in my hand; I lifted it up high then swung down strong. The dream blanked out, and there was nothing but darkness, an imageless landscape. I woke up. The night continued with the tossing and turning as before.

Poonjaji had invited me for an individual session the following morning. At 7 AM I was ready to rise. I felt completely refreshed but apprehensive about my meeting. I put the night behind me. I took a rickshaw to Poonjaji's house, where he greeted me and introduced me in a formal way to all the women in the household, after which we ascended the little stone staircase to his room. It was a tiny space dominated by a huge beneficent photograph of the great saint of *advaita*, Ramana Maharshi.

Poonjaji sat behind a table and looked sternly at me. "You are now ready for the final assault," he said. My ego was delighted on hearing this, and I was full of expectations of a dramatic final experience in which all traces of my old self would be extinguished. I waited. Nothing happened. Silence. Then Poonjaji suddenly looked at his watch and said that he wanted me to accompany him to the doctor in a few minutes. What did this have to do with the "final assault"? I was deflated.

Yet my ordinary mind was unaware of the enormous internal changes that were taking place. The pure delight I felt in Poonjaji's presence was catalyzing a profound and spacious awareness, giving rise to extended states of sublime joy. Suddenly he asked about my night. I told him about my Shiva dream, and he looked at me with delight, his eyes lighting up like a child hearing a fairy tale.

"From now on I will call you Shakti. Shiva cannot exist without Shakti. Without Shakti, the active principle, the divine feminine energy behind the universe, there can be no Shiva. Even Shiva, the god of gods!" Then he continued, "Today is the day of your incarnation. Everything that has gone before is past, finished. Your destiny, past karma, past hopes and aspirations are finished, complete . . . from now on I will call you Shakti. And you must reflect on the meaning of Shakti. It is a nameless name."

I spoke to Poonjaji about my dreams and visitations from Anandamayi Ma. She had been spiritual advisor to Mahatma Gandhi and Nehru, amongst many others in her twenty-four ashrams. I told Poonjaji how I had made a pilgrimage to her ashram before arriving in Lucknow; how I had met some of the great souls there who had lived with Anandamayi when she was alive. Poonjaji looked at me and smiled gently: "I feel as if some divine hand has brought you here. It is She, Ma, Maha-Shakti [Great Shakti], unconditional Love, Mother of the Universe."

Every now and again, he would place his hand on my shoulder for support while we walked around. I waited for the right moment to return his attention to that "final assault" he had alerted me to with such urgency. But nothing was going to happen. After sitting in the doctor's clinic for what seemed like hours, Poonjaji took me to the Botanical Gardens and then to the zoo to sit in silence in front of the lions and tigers, absorbing their primal energy. I began to feel a more osmotic relationship with the energy of everything around me, especially as it coursed through the veins of the plants and animals. We walked slowly back to his house. Once he stopped, looked at me very seriously, and said firmly, "Be mad with the mad people, and be foolish with the foolish, but do not forget the inner silence. Not for one instant! You are That—*Tat Tvam Asi*."

When we returned to his room, he told me that during the night all my *samskaras* (psychic impressions) had been burned away, revealing the true nature of pure being within me. In the next breath, he started talking about the train timetable, and asked me which train would be best for us to take back to Delhi later in the week. His facility in shifting his awareness effortlessly between mundane practicalities and sublime reality was a teaching in itself.

As the day progressed and the silence deepened, I began to realize that the so-called *final assault* was a revolution taking place within me, emptying me of all thought. Hence I could see and feel this all-inclusive energy from the inside out, spreading everywhere, unifying everything. How was this possible? Was he a magician manipulating some irreversible hypnotic state? Since falling into the hands of this remarkable person I was being gifted with a transmission of love beyond any understanding of it. My old conditioning was dying and I felt blessed by the invisible grace of pure being.

Chloë Goodchild and Poonjaji "Papaji" (1990). Photo by Roger Housden

The next day, Poonjaji took us to lunch with a doctor and his wife, two of his devotees. On our way there in the scooter-taxi he sat opposite me, smiling with a vibrant ecstasy while simultaneously observing me with his mysterious impersonal glare. By now I was immersed in such a state of interior peace that nothing of the chaotic noisy turmoil of urban Indian traffic and street activities affected me. Everything and everyone was simply there, as was I. There was no conflict, and no struggle anymore. When I opened my eyes Poonjaji was always laughing at me, saying, "She is in deep *samadhi* [sublime peace], can you see?"

When we arrived at our destination, Poonjaji cross-examined me to see how distracted I had been by the everyday hustle and bustle of our journey.

"How much noise did you hear? Which noises disturbed your concentration?" He was suddenly very earnest and direct. "Can you keep this silence in the UK when you are fully involved in your activities?"

When I was unable to speak more than a few words Poonjaji started to laugh and laugh again. His laughter affected everyone caught in the fire of his presence. I remember little more that day than waves of laughter and waves of silence. I also remember an exquisite smile of compassion upon Poonjaji's face, which lasted for the taxi ride back to our hotel. I was filled with such joy and peace that softened and relaxed every muscle in my face, body, and being. I had never felt such deep relaxation. I felt so fresh and young all of a sudden. I was thirty-six years old.

Before I left him, Poonjaji asked me if I had any questions before I returned to England. When I could find none, he simply responded by saying, "Do not waste time with purifications, rituals, ceremonies. What is taking place within you will take care of itself. Eventually, everything that occupies your ordinary mind will go once and for all. Keep your attention on silence. Retreat deeply into yourself and let no one and nothing disturb that."

I was reminded of a Rumi poem:

After all the certainties, the visions,
This final aloneness
That you flower in

—TRANSLATED BY ANDREW HARVEY IN *Love's Fire*

On the morning of my departure, I went to see Poonjaji alone. He told me how, as a child, he had disappeared into the jungle to find God. "I was driven by an inner fire. That force has constantly accompanied me. It is still here. I have never been alone. Even now, that force is alive in these old bones [more laughter]. And you [pointing to me] know this fire!"

This "happening" all those years ago brought with it an inner fire and a freedom from thought control that was constant, unstoppable. What I came to call the Naked Voice was awakened here, and with it a whole new cycle of life.

After the many years of singing, excavating, engaging, navigating, and constantly transforming the full spectrum of my emotional life from sadness into anger, grief, rage, confusion, helplessness, into lust, longing, passion, fierce love, gentleness, tranquility, ecstasy, quietness, expressing and releasing these birds from their cages through one musical mood then another, I had finally happened upon a deeper sound awareness within, which stopped my singing dead in my tracks. My naked voice was the source of all sound. A soundless sound within. Sound before sound.

From the intensity of this happening I began to hear this nakedness resounding in every human voice, whether it was people chattering on a train, my child's daily questions, the news presenter on the TV, dinner conversations with a friend, or a voice session with a student. And I have come to recognize how this source of our sound awakens within us the naked truth of our human condition, signaled by our voice and awakened through the energies of love. And it is right here that the essential ingredients of a new language of consciousness exist, rooted in being, a language that by its nature can transform the fear language of a *me-centered* reality into the wisdom language of a *being-centered* reality. Your singing voice is the most efficient, fastest, most direct and powerful access I know to this direct encounter with your self.

Once back in the West, this all-pervading presence continued to fill my days amidst the many activities of work and mothering. Yet this naked sound of my own self had an inner momentum of its own. To begin with, the desire to sing outwardly was no longer there. "Singing" had become internalized as a felt vibration in every cell of my body, pervading my whole being. It was a resonance rising up through me, whose inner music was far more penetrating and real than all my outworn, historical voices could ever touch. Yet somehow this new sound awareness was of their essence. And through it, by some alchemical act of grace, I had happened upon my own authentic spirit.

I was totally embodied, a bubbling spring sounding from the source of existence, awakened by the energies of love streaming through me. Gradually a deeper open-throated naked song began to flow through me. This newfound voice awakened a more effortless singing within and all around me. And I felt as if I were sitting inside the giant ear of the universe. It was more beautiful than I could ever have imagined. This transmission of unconditional love received from my Indian grandfather in Lucknow brought about an encounter with my self, a self-initiation process whose imprint has remained with me.

From this happening I started to sound out again. I soon discovered that authentic singing, or *sounding my self*, by its very nature had the power to shift my consciousness in an instant from being in control to being out of control. Many times I have had the privilege of witnessing a voice student who, after discovering his or her true sound, is surprised by its energy and resonance. And always the question, *"Who was that?"* Once we are asking, *"Who is singing? Who am I?"* the journey can really begin, and a new language of consciousness can evolve from here. And I am back in the *advaita* self-inquiry process, asking "Who am I?" or "Who are you?", communicating from emptiness before thought.

This sound intelligence of yours can only be initiated by your *heart-brain*. Your rational *head-brain* only knows about how to "pull yourself together," "snap out of it," or "get a grip" while attempting to erase your negative emotional state by imposing a positive state upon it. This superficial approach serves only to suppress the negative emotion for a limited time while you accumulate more negative tension inside. However, your intuitive heart is able to listen, accept, and embrace the full spectrum of your emotions, including the negative ones.

Invite them all in laughing! says Rumi (Coleman Barks version).

Your unconditional heart knows how to welcome and embrace all your musical emotions, however they sound or show up, with a benign disinterest—witnessing them while simultaneously encouraging them to express their moods directly and nonverbally from wherever they are located in your body-field: from your belly, center of the chest, head, etc. Nonjudgmental awareness is an essential skill in this transformative process.

In the early days, and with the support of this new sound intelligence, I found that nonverbal singing was the most effortless, empowering way to engage with the more challenging subterranean territory of my soul. I found that I could explore and navigate dark or negative emotions—catalyzed by an old storyline or personal issue—courageously and without judgment. The nonjudgmental ground of my singing process disoriented my ego's power to hold on or resist. Subsequently I started noticing just how powerful my singing heart is. It has an uncanny capacity to seek out, uproot, and unearth the negative stories or emotions blocking my truth. The old emotions magically changed into a new authentic music moving through me that made me feel embodied, present, and connected.

I started to explore this alchemy of sound with individuals, inviting them to embrace and express their negative emotional states. Nonjudgmental listening to this singing process built the initial trust, confidence, and loving presence required to provide a supportive environment in which every emotional state is embraced and accepted without resistance or fear. The nonverbal sound power was such that it could liberate the singer from any emotional glue into a lightness of being previously not known.

So where did all that weight of negative emotion go? It didn't "go" anywhere. It simply remembered and transformed itself from its unconscious, inaudible hiding place into its own authentic and audible voice. Emotional expression is after all just the sound of energy, the energy of love, the sound of love coming in.

Since that "no-mind" awakening in India, I have shared this sound intelligence through the Naked Voice practices in diverse ways. It is your transforming intelligence of sound that will reveal the wisdom of your human soul. It is through your sound intelligence that you can embrace and transcend your rational mind, opening your heart to a way of living and being that is cocreative, interconnected, multifaceted, all-inclusive.

Sound intelligence is self-knowledge through sound.

It is a *fearless music* latent in everyone. It is sound wisdom.

I am you are we are
a wisdom older and deeper
than the polarity of all conflict
a vibration moving through
the cells of every human being
whose resonance
is fierce courage
whose sound penetrates
the heart of compassion
the energy of effortless being
your naked voice is
a direct way
home

Chloë Goodchild, a portrait (1991). Photo by Roger Housden

4.6 Seven Sounds of Love

How I Love You, How I Love You
—"How I Love You," *Fierce Wisdom*

The Seven Sounds of Love are gateways into your Naked Voice. They provide a body-centered singing map—inspired by the seven energy centers in the body—using vocal practices that awaken the energies of love within us. Long before I knew anything about energy centers or musical chakras, I was captivated by Julie Andrews's rendering of the "do re mi" exercise with the von Trapp family in *The Sound of Music*. At the age of eleven I went to see that movie eleven times! Little did I realize that two decades later I would be exploring the same vocal exercise in India, but this time described as the *saptak,* meaning "seven steps." These seven steps are really musical intervals which, when sounded, interconnect the seven energy centers of the human body from the root to the crown, activating the ascending-descending force in the body. As with Do Re Mi Fa So La Ti Do, there is a specific sound or *swara* for each of the energy centers as follows: SA (root) RE (pelvis) GA (solar plexus) MA (heart) PA (throat) DHA (third eye) NI (back of head). In India, each musical sound of the scale is considered to be a mantra and can be practiced alone as a meditation.

In the same way that the seven sounds are used to pitch a tune correctly, these sounds can be used as the musical stepping stones to harmonize mind, body, and soul. Whereas Do Re Mi is a largely mental exercise taught specifically for the benefit of learning to pitch notes and sing in tune, the *saptak* offers a much deeper language of listening in which you can embody each musical note, integrating the seven elemental sounds with their emotional color.

Singing the Seven Sounds of Love is like walking into a garden of flowers. Each one has a unique fragrance, expression, and intensity. Sung together they provide a unique body-centered sonic practice and a vibrational framework within which you can start to create courageous musical conversations of all kinds, with yourself and with others. These *seven sounds* are essentially "vocal homeopathy" for the brain, body, and soul. They catalyze an alchemical process that, with practice, rewires your brain and transforms your reactive mind by the simple act of expressing your emotional energy supported by these sung sounds.

What I love most about these musical sounds is that you do not have to be a trained musician for this singing practice. The sound awareness and listening skills you have been developing with the sounding of the AUM, Seven-Chakra Mantra, and Heart Sutra along with One Breath, One Voice and the other more spontaneous singing exercises will now give you confidence to start attuning yourself to your emotions and then to locate where they are held in your body, and ultimately, to give them new vibrational and sonic clothes. The impact is empowering as your singing voice aligns with the essence and flow of your emotional life, its shadow and light. You soon discover how to engage and embrace your previous emotional longing and striving, transforming it into the symphonic aliveness of your singing soul. You will also find that it's impossible to remain fixed in a negative emotional state for long. Once you discover the music of your emotions, you can start to exchange the sound of your reactive thoughts for new creative musical options.

Discover the Seven Sounds as Vibrational Medicine

I was first introduced to what I now call the Seven Sounds of Love, or *saptak,* in India in 1985 by Gilles Petit. In my early years working with him, our improvisation practice was always preceded by physical exercise: breathing *(pranayama)* and vocal practices that strengthened our capacity to sing from the belly. This in turn strengthened our sounding of the SA from the root of the body, as well as built a substantial energetic core, or *chi* energy. This took time to develop and sustain and was always accompanied by a practice of the Indian music scale, substituting do, re, mi with the Indian equivalent:

SA	RE	GA	MA	PA	DHA	NI	SA
do	re	mi	fa	so	la	ti	do
1st	2nd	3rd	4th	5th	6th	7th	1st

Over the years I have explored and expressed myself through the subtle microtones and spaces between each of the seven sounds with a greater depth of awareness and listening as the musical notes began to open up a vast uncharted spectrum of feeling inside me, energizing my body, dissolving negative emotion, and freeing my spirit in ways I had never known. Each sound carries a vibrational power that awakens a specific emotional state, a realm of self-awareness and wisdom within us—from the root of the body into the pelvis, the solar plexus, heart, throat, third eye, back of the head, and crown of the head—in the same way that the chakras or energy centers can. This sound work is a *vibrational medicine.*

I have created a simple method using these sounds, with voice and meditative movement, to awaken your ears to the full spectrum of your consciousness. Once learned, the seven sounds provide a stable framework within which you can explore your emotions as reflected through the musical notes and intervals, and ultimately discover how to master your emotions and deeper feeling as the music of your soul.

Journey with the Seven Sounds of Love

This section describing the vocal exercises with the Seven Sounds of Love includes photographs/diagrams of the mudras (meditative hand gestures) and meditative movements for each musical interval of sound, together with beneficial related online practices.

We will be exploring these sounds in three interdependent groups: instinctual, intuitive, and insightful sound:

INSTINCTUAL LOVE—sound to strengthen your belly
Mantric sounds: SA = root   RE = pelvis   GA = solar plexus
INTUITIVE LOVE—sound to strengthen your heart
Mantric sounds: MA = heart   PA = throat
INSIGHTFUL LOVE—sound to strengthen your mind
Mantric sounds: DHA = third eye NI = back of head SA = crown

These three groups of sounds—located in the three main centers of the body—introduce a simple methodology for your emerging sound awareness and vocal practice. The sounding of the Seven Sounds, from the root to the crown, together with their accompanying mudras, helps you to embody your sound and the quality of love that each center inspires. You will then become more conscious of which realm your loving is most easily expressed in (instinctual, intuitive, insightful). Much depends upon the strength and depth of connection with your root sound SA, which is the source of your vocal journey.

These Seven Sounds are vibrational building blocks.

As you gradually ascend SA-RE-GA-MA-PA-DHA-NI-SA and then descend, returning to the unchanging root sound SA, notice which sounds touch you most, which sounds feel familiar, and which ones feel unfamiliar and new. Some of them may leave you feeling nothing at all. Simply notice and enjoy this unfolding journey through your inner garden of love, as you awaken to the light and shadow of your emotions expressed through sound. With practice you will discover how to simultaneously observe and express the emotional energy activated by your sound. You will access the capacity to navigate the highs and lows of your emotional life, gradually discovering how your every emotion contains a wondrous power to transform from negative into positive feeling.

NB: The accompanying photographs associated with these sound practices will clarify and support your practice.

Instinctual Love: Energy Centers 1, 2, and 3: Root, Pelvis, and Solar Plexus

Root chakra	SA: I LISTEN
Pelvic chakra	RE: I OPEN
Solar Plexus chakra	GA: I GROW

1. **SA**—SOURCE OF LOVE—I LISTEN—ROOT

Qualities: Earth, unmanifested love, emptiness, darkness, Earth's core, humility, nothingness, primordial being.

Sound Movement and Mudra Practice: Stand with your two feet together, eyes closed, immersed in an interior feeling of dark warmth and deep restfulness. Your awareness is one hundred percent interior, focused on your root (Muladhara) chakra. Your left hand is closed around your right, your right hand curled around the left thumb. We call this "the sword inside the sheath," protecting the root chakra. Strengthen your vertical axis as you sink your awareness deeper and deeper into the earth beneath your feet. Your shoulders are relaxed, and likewise your feet are relaxed, not clinging to the ground. Breathe deep, let go of all exterior preoccupations, and bring your awareness to the unchanging, the unmanifested reality, the source of your existence. Let your awareness sink deep down to your feet and to the ground beneath you. Smile and disappear into emptiness. This is at once the most simple and the most impossible task because, in returning to essence, you are returning to a state of emptiness, prior to the birth of ego or a "separate identity." Standing in SA is a return to the source of your essential nature.

SA BEING (Root chakra)

2. **RE**—SEXUAL CREATIVE LOVE—I OPEN—PELVIS

Qualities: duality, birth of the ego, relationship, sexual love, emerging light, polarity, separation-union.

Sound Movement and Mudra Practice: The image of the movement from SA to RE is one of a young shoot bursting through the earth. Open your eyes, feet, and hands simultaneously. As you open your hands, from bud to flower, let them face the world in front of you at the level of your pelvis. As your hands open you are awakening to the revelation of light as it arises from your root to fill your whole pelvis. As your hands open, feel the presence of light in your palms especially, beaming out light from their center. Out of the unmanifested darkness of SA, the sound of RE arises. A unique new form is created from formlessness: *your very own self!* An extraordinary energy is required for this opening to occur. How is this possible? When will it happen? Who is moving when it does happen?

RE OPENING (Pelvis)

As you deepen your attention and practice you will become increasingly awake to the effortlessness of this movement out of emptiness.

To begin with, you "do" it as if "you" are "in charge" of the decision to move from being nothing to being someone. It is easy to underestimate the power and mystery of this apparently simple movement, and yet as you learn to experience it by continual repetition, you will begin to access the mysterious interface between being nothing and becoming something. You will begin to discover that in truth you have no control over this movement from SA to RE or indeed any movement at all. Within this movement the opportunity exists to discover what is meant by saying "I do nothing" and "I am," as opposed to "I am so-and-so," i.e., a singer or an actor in control of my universe. The musical interval RE is all about RElationship and REvelation, the revealing of yourself as a being both separate and in union with the source of existence. RE is the birth of that wondrous phenomenon you have come to know as ego, or your "separate identity." RE comes from the original Sanskrit words *svah,* place, and *sthana,* ego.

3. **GA**—INSTINCTUAL LOVE—I GROW—SOLAR PLEXUS

> Qualities: sun energy, erotic love, jewel in the belly, strengthening chi energy, prana life force, *duende,* personal power, "my" will, nourishment, protection, loyalty.

Sound Movement and Mudra Practice: Sounding GA, slowly raise your open hands up to waist level in front of you, in a spirit of receiving, and then absorb invisible energy into your hands. Slowly draw your hands back, forming two soft fists of energy, softly held, while resting your elbows on the tops of your hips. The sound and movement of GA are about gathering fuel for the inner fire. Sounding GA generates a feeling of inner stability in your belly (or *hara* in Japanese), nourishing your core and filling your lower abdomen with light. GA recharges you with new lifeforce energy and calms any emotional imbalance in your nervous system. Sounding GA gives you the capacity to transform all your negative instinctual me-first emotions into the fearless music of positive human feeling.

GA is the center of the nervous system, the heart of your instinctual energy, and the realm where the whole range of your raw emotions continually rises and falls. This instinctual realm has been misunderstood and abused for millennia. Yet with attention and loving presence, the vibration of GA reveals our capacity to communicate and to love without being driven by the desire to dominate or control, and ultimately to transform our fear of death. Sounding and moving with GA offers you the skill to develop a strong and healthy instinctual nature in which the music of your personal power, protection of your species, steadfastness, and compassionate stable leadership may grow. Left to its own devices, this same instinctual energy can create an unconscious war-field of divisiveness and negative opposing emotions, which, if the realms of SA and RE are also silent or vulnerable, will drive and sustain the illusion of a supreme personal will, otherwise known as "my will." This leads to relationships that are in a constant state of

GA GROWING
(Solar Plexus)

reactivity, fixated on the distorted soap opera of a life governed by "I am right, you are wrong," the "us and them" game. This tragi-comedy tends to dominate most relationships from the personal to the global arena. As you continue your practice with SA-RE-GAAAAAAAAAAA you will begin to feel your own natural inner fire strengthen as the benefits of the GA movement balance what can otherwise be a soggy emotional realm of undealt-with per-sonal issues. Sounding GAAAAAAAAAAAAAAAAA brings enor-mous energy and aliveness into every cell of the body, stabilizing, harnessing, and conserving your emotional energy in the estab-lishment of loyal, trusting, self-sustaining relationships that are re-spectful and protective of your personal needs and of those in your community.

Intuitive Love: Energy Centers 4 and 5: Heart and Throat

Heart chakra   MA: I GIVE
Throat chakra   PA: I SHARE

4. MA—DEVOTIONAL LOVE—I GIVE—HEART

Qualities: devotional love, bridge between earth and heaven, offering, longing, belonging.

Sound Movement and Mudra Practice: The shift in awareness from GA to MA, from the third chakra to the fourth, is immense. It is one that humankind is desperately trying to learn to make, both at the microcosmic and the macrocosmic levels. MA is the source of all words for mother, mater, matter. The sound MA opens up a spaciousness in the heart. Slowly bringing forward your soft GA fists from where they have been resting on your hips, open them out in front of you at the level of your heart, in a gesture of offering until your palms are open and facing upward in a spirit of receiving from the sky. As your hands open, you will notice a wealth of new feeling filling your chest center, awakening the immensities in the soul across a far-reaching spectrum of love's longing, from the eroticism and intensity of romantic love to the subtle self-containment of devotional love and service, and back again. Moving from GA to MA opens the potential to move from a state of "me" and "my will" to "thou" and "thy will." MA expands your awareness beyond the self-centered "me-first" needs for security and personal power in GA into a new realm in which your heart, rather than your stomach, leads your awareness from an instinctually driven consciousness to an intuitive one, enriched and informed by your intuitive heart. The physical movement of opening your hands in a gesture of offering can have a profound impact on your previous "me-centered" reality, awakening a wider field of awareness in which your relationships with yourself and others are open-hearted and "being-centered."

MA GIVING (Heart)

5. **PA**—ALL-INCLUSIVE LOVE—I SHARE—THROAT

> Qualities: true speech, companion love, self-actualization, leader, brightening the world, receiving, giving, uniting heaven and earth, unifying the vertical and horizontal axes of the body.

Sound Movement and Mudra Practice: Once the belly is strong and full of pure chi, the intuitive heart is opening, and devotional awareness is arising, PA can sound out loud, resonant, and clear from the throat center. PA is in essence the voice of your resounding true humanity. A healthy PA is a healthy ego capable of expressing itself clearly from the heart. PA is the expression of yourself as a public figure at the height of your human potential, capable of manifesting your vision in the world as inspired and informed by everyone's best interests. A healthy PA is a self-actualized, self-aware communicator, a grounded and stable

PA SHARING (Throat)

personality inspired directly from the source. From the devotional offering hands of MA, open your arms out wide, perpendicular to your body, to form a cross. The open-handed gesture of PA exposes the whole body in a mudra that is at once vulnerable, fearless, and free to receive and give simultaneously. In PA the vertical and the horizontal axes are in balance with each other. The vertical line of energy rises from the feet to the sky, representing your direct engagement with spirit, and the horizontal plane sends a line of energy between left and right sides of the body, through the heart, embracing the whole world with light. Your hands are facing the sky, and your fingers are pointing as far away from your ears as possible, as if some invisible force might be trying to pull them off! This awareness in your hands helps to strengthen the vertical-horizontal interface within your body as you stand sounding PAAAAAAAAAAAAAAA.

INSIGHTFUL Love: Energy Center 6: Third Eye

Third Eye chakra   DHA: I SERVE

6. **DHA**—WISE LOVE—I SERVE—THIRD EYE

> Qualities: insight, compassion, sword, illusion-cutter, Diamond Mudra, Heart Sutra, fearless wisdom, divine uncertainty.

Sound Movement and Mudra Practice: If PA is the self-actualized communicator of truth identified with the successful and professional delivery of your "product" in the world, DHA takes the carpet from under your feet and whispers to you in the night, "You are more than this" and "You are not who you think you are." DHA takes you beyond the secure boundaries of the family social compound. DHA has you waking up in the night and wondering who you are beneath the veneer of social responsibility and public face. In PA you found yourself completing your personal therapy and inviting your therapist to dinner to acknowledge the completion of a cycle. In DHA you find yourself picking up the phone one morning and, without knowing why, saying to your staff,

"I won't be available for a while. In fact, I have to go on leave for an indefinite period. Can we make arrangements accordingly?"

In DHA the focus of your awareness is raised from self-identification with your public persona to a deeper self-inquiry that requires more interiority and spacious awareness. Sounding DHA raises your attention from the throat to the third eye, opening the capacity to cleanse your mind from an existence driven by reactivity and outer expression to an existence focused on the qualities of discernment, compassion, and fearless wisdom. The shift in awareness from PA to DHA can be profoundly disorienting, even shocking, to the one who has been so identified with outer circumstances and action as being the only reality. DHA cuts deeply through the illusions related to "being somebody."

Moving from PA to DHA, bring your open horizontal palms up above your head, letting your head fall back to watch the movement of your arms pointing up toward heaven. Then join the palms in a prayerful mudra while slowly bringing them down in front of you, remaining in this prayerful mudra as your joined palms point like a

DHA SERVING
(Third Eye)

sword in front of you. Your elbows are open and there is a protective empty space created between your prayerful hands and your chest. Your eyes are wide open. Imagine that your hands are an invisible sword with its long shining blade pointing into the far distance. Your gaze is focused on the far distance, far beyond anywhere you have ever been. This posture is an ancient one for the purpose of cleansing the mind and heart. It is called the Diamond Mudra.

Ecstatic Love: Energy Center 7: Back of Head

Back of Head chakra NI: I SURRENDER

7. **NI**—MYSTICAL LOVE—I SURRENDER—HEAD

> Qualities: letting go, awareness to back of head, hair spiral point, mystical awareness, self-surrender, divine frenzy, looking heavenward.

Sound Movement and Mudra Practice: From the Diamond Mudra bring your hands, still in prayer posture, up above your head as if creating a crown or church spire above you. Your awareness similarly rises up from the third eye to the back of the head, as you breathe into the top of your lungs, sounding NIIIIIIIII (pronounced "knee"). This unearthly sound is so unlike any other sounded before. It doesn't seem to come out of the front of the face, but rather as if you have an invisible mouth where your hair spirals out at the back of your head. The sound NIIIIIIIII emanates from there, its ethereal tone lighting up and energizing the brain cells, bringing a light-headed feeling and a spacious awareness that can unground you if your SAAAAAAA is not strong enough. NI is the realm of ecstatic love and mystical revelation. NI is the complementary pole with the earthly revelation of RE in the pelvis. In NI you can hear the inner voice calling you to your eternal home, once again, to the original source of your being. Many people walk around in NI—head in the clouds—all their lives, longing to return home, longing for freedom from the burdens of this earthly life, longing for union with their true nature. The ecstatic musicians—lovers of God—from every ancient tradition have all been touched by the doorway into heaven, whose portal is NI.

Such an initiation into this mystical realm is challenging until we have first awakened the six Sounds of Love leading us to an understanding and embodiment of the seventh musical interval. When grace intervenes, NI opens the crown portal SA into an awareness of Universal Love. The Crown SA thus completes the journey from the root to the crown.

NI SURRENDERING
(Back of head)

Universal Love: Energy Center 1: Crown

Crown chakra   SA: I AM

I. **SA**—UNIVERSAL LOVE—I AM—CROWN

> Qualities: fulfillment, interconnectedness, oneness, union with the Beloved, compassionate service, planetary mind, completion of cycle, grand finale, hallelujah.

Sound Movement and Mudra Practice: In the Western world we consider this note as number 8 or the octave note, thus completing the *musical octave,* i.e., eight musical notes. In the Indian system the seventh musical note NI is the ultimate note of the *saptak,* or the seven steps of the musical scale. It is resolved in the crown chakra with a return to the first-named musical note SA. In Indian music SA is the universal unchanging first note. SA is associated with the root chakra, and again with the crown chakra. In truth, SA is the essence of all other sounds, in the same way that white is the essence of all the colors of the rainbow.

Sounding the top SA, open your whole stance, opening and stretching your arms and hands out and up to the sky above your head, to embrace the whole universe, sounding SAA-AAAAAAAAAAAAAAAA.

SA LOVING (Crown)

The Seven Sounds of Love

Sa Re Ga	Impersonal	Dependent	Instinctual
Ga Ma Pa	Personal	Independent	Intuitive
Pa Dha Ni	Transpersonal	Interdependent	Insightful

SA   **Crown of Head—Universal Love**
       Reaching for your highest ideal*

NI   **Back of Head—Mystical Love**
       Pointing toward heaven*

DHA   **Third Eye—Compassionate Love**
       Sword/Diamond mudra*

PA   **Throat—Inclusive Love**
       Brightening the world*

MA   **Heart—Intuitive Love**
       Offering flowers, devoting yourself to others*

GA   **Solar Plexus—Instinctual Love**
       Gathering energy*

RE   **Pelvis—Conditional Love**
       Spreading light*

SA   **Source—Unconditional Love**
       Standing in emptiness*

* Shintaido energy movements, Shintaido.com
Sounds of Love. Illustration by Anne Tyrrell

Conclusion

Enjoy sounding the Seven Sounds of Love. Once you are familiar with the energy movements that accompany each musical note, you will begin to discover how you can embody your naked voice and express yourself in new and unexpected ways, unifying body, heart, and mind to collaborate and communicate as one. The energy field of your body is the vessel for the sonic architecture of your soul to blossom and flourish. Listening more deeply, start to notice how these seven simple sounds create musical intervals that open your heart and empower your experience of love in all its forms: instinctual, intuitive, and insightful.

As you give voice to a whole new spectrum of sound and human feeling, remember to continue asking yourself, "Who is singing?" Let your witness consciousness support the evolution of your sound as you discover your most precious human emotions as a unique music, directly expressed from your soul without censorship, analysis, or negative judgment.

Many people, when asked, will tell you that they do not love their voice. Our social conditioning with its intellectually dominated education system has tended to leave the majority of people focusing on what is "wrong'" with themselves and their voice. The focus in music education on competitive performance and entertainment destroys the joy of sound and song for many at school, who come away with memories of being thrown out of the choir and being told to shut up, be quiet, or just mouth the words. Your relationship with your real voice, that naked sound singing inside you over years and years, maybe lifetimes, can no longer be ignored. And once you have had some practice with sounding your soul, there is no end to the creativity and wisdom you can find there. Your relationship with your voice—spoken and sung and all the spaces in between—can tell you everything you need to know about the sound of who you *are*. The startling truth is that you are—the resonance of your being is—much deeper an d more beautiful than your personality and rational mind could ever fathom. Singing with your naked voice ignites a power of longing, a longing for somewhere you have never been, for something that you cannot name. Singing "naked" generates an energy that can turn all the madness of your fear and your terror of death into a madness of an entirely other kind: the madness of love beyond any understanding of it.

4.7 Singing Between Worlds: The Woman Who Died Singing

You could always hear her approaching, this dark Sumerian Earth Goddess. Her unapologetic and strident gait set her apart from most of her contemporaries, those well-behaved daughters of the patriarchy.

When we met, Magdalena was a buxom gypsy-woman in her sixties, a belly-laughing feisty crone who had the nerve to let go of the politesse and security of her social compound and to cross the uncertain threshold of life's wilderness. No more reference points. She had thrown all the maps away. Here was one of life's adventurers, a woman in search of her own true voice, the sound of her real self. No trimmings, no sweetness and light, no beat-about-the-bush. "Let's get straight to the heart of the matter" was her constant refrain.

Magdalena wore many stories in her wizened face. And her genuine warmth and friendliness shone through the wrinkled fatigue, communicating a courageous character. She was someone who had bravely overcome the major trials of her own personal battlefield. She had received no traditional singing "training," yet there was something intent and earnest in her penetrating gaze and infectious laughter that communicated an indomitable spirit. Magdalena was one of life's treasures, a passionate prayerful soul driven by a longing to sing out and to be free of all residual ties. She simply needed allies to hear her sing out the song of her life. Her rich ancestral singing repertoire and heritage covered the Caribbean, Latin America, France, and parts of Eastern Europe and Africa.

Her singing voice, raw and open-ended, poured out of her like a wild mare galloping across the plains, unstoppable, a torrent of red-hot, primal, wild, feminine energy. Her ample breasts dangled and shook loose from her shoulders as she swayed. She always smiled mischievously through her ever-widening motherly face, full of wonder, her twinkling eyes seducing us all as she sang freestyle.

Magdalena was one hundred percent woman, a gift of Gaia. She carried this gift quite naturally without any feminist axe to grind or victim ghosts left inside the cupboard. She was unapologetically and relentlessly herself. She came to work with me in the early Naked Voice years when I was leading a one-year training course in the wilds of south Devon, in the UK. Magdalena assumed the role of "high priestess" within our singing community; she kept a constant watch over us and our group room. She transformed the room into our temple of song, adorning the workspace with flowers, cleansing it with frankincense and myrrh fragrance and with meditation candles. This was how she expressed her devotional heart.

Magdalena was salt of the earth: practical, openhearted, and well rooted, with no time for airs and graces. One might find her stomping around the retreat center in restless anticipation of what new voices might fall from her mouth the next time she was given a chance. She was always ready to jump in to play God's fool, to try anything new. As our work together progressed, she came to love all aspects of it: the contemplative voice, the silence, and the inner-sound practices inspired by chants, and the aligning power of the Seven-Chakra Mantra. She even decided to embark on a long solitary retreat between our courses. This was a profound time of change and transition in Magdalena's life, and it was a privilege to support her on this sonic adventure.

She slowly became virginal again, in the original sense of the word—self-contained, a woman no longer dominated by habitual human needs and desires. She was ready to step with confidence and a renewed faith into life's pathless way, alone.

Most of all, Magdalena loved the Seven Sounds of Love. She reveled in the ever-changing elemental and emotional colors that she could squeeze out of each musical interval, especially when she learned how to slide microtonally between one note and the adjoining one. First there was the dark sensuality from SA (root) to RE (pelvis), then the instinctual fiery power of GA in the solar plexus, and the impassioned longing sound catalyzed between SA at the root and MA in the center of the chest. The all-inclusive presence of PA rang out from the base of her throat like a victorious clarion call that shocked and delighted her simultaneously. And when she sounded DHA, the sixth musical interval, I could literally feel her compassionate spirit open like a flower, infusing the whole room with unconditional loving kindness that made my skin tingle. The musical interval NI, the seventh mystical note, was new territory for her. It requires shifting one's sound awareness to the back of the head, and Magdalena initially found this quite disorienting. She approached this shift with an adolescent apprehension and a sense of awe.

This simple structured way of ascending and descending the musical scale while locating the musical intervals in the main energy centers of the body was unexpectedly appealing to Magdalena. Given that she was not a trained musician, it offered a very accessible entry into the musical architecture of her soul and provided a sound foundation that anchored her wild spontaneous singing.

"I have cleared all my intimate relationships," she announced one day, "and I am ready to fly the nest. I have decided to travel to India to research this Indian vocal work more seriously!"

Her first and last stop in India was Varanasi (formerly called Benares), the city of Shiva, god of creation and destruction. Varanasi is considered by Hindus to be a most auspicious place to live, and even more so to die. Magdalena had no conscious knowledge of this when she decided to go there. Her love of singing had ignited a fascination for Indian vocal music as a spiritual practice. So now she wanted a more disciplined vocal and meditative routine. She established herself in simple accommodation near the banks of the Ganges and made contact with Monique Lacombe, a classical teacher of the most ancient Indian vocal style called *drupad*.

A couple of months after receiving a letter from Magdalena that said "I've never been so happy in all my life," I got a phone call from Monique to say that Magdalena had died. What? How could this be? I was choked with bewilderment and disbelief. I stood there for an eternal moment absorbing this new yet impossible reality. Then a stream of questions poured forth. "How did she die? Where is her body now? What happened?"

There was a long pause.

"Chloë," Monique said in a hushed tone, "I was privileged to be present at Magdalena's passing. She died right in front of me during her singing lesson."

"What? How come? Surely not!" I stammered.

Another long pause. "Yes," Monique continued, "our mutual friend Magdalena actually died singing. And having witnessed this, I pray that I am blessed with the same passing."

I kept silent.

"Magdalena was a beginner in one sense with the singing voice, but nevertheless . . . she still knew how to move into the next life!" Monique said. "We had been chanting the AUM for a while, and then talked about ways to continue the practice with the Indian scale. I had been teaching her how to slide from top SA down to DHA. Slowly, Magdalena stood up to sing; she took in a long in-breath, then an unexpected miracle happened before my eyes. As I watched Magdalena and listened, I saw her awareness slowly rise up from the root of her body and on up into the third eye. Her eyes rolled back, she looked up to the crown, and with that she sank down to the floor with a simple groan and left her body. I tell you now that she somehow knew, and was ready to leave this world. She left without pain, and without struggle."

A month or so later, Magdalena's family and friends celebrated her life with a ritual memorial service on the grounds of the Devon retreat center she had lived in before leaving for India. It was a profoundly moving ceremony in which I, our energy-movement master Masashi Minagawa, and the group of students who had accompanied Magdalena throughout her Naked Voice introductory one-year training all came together to sound her name one more time, and to pray, chant, and sing for her with all her favorite music. The rain fell softly on our shoulders as we sang her name and planted a tree in her memory. We sang the three mantras central to the Naked Voice: AUM, the Seven-Chakra Mantra, and the Heart Sutra. As we chanted the Heart Sutra for her one last time—"Go go far beyond, far beyond, the wisdom is" *(om gate gate paragate parasamgate bodhi svaha)*—with Masashi accompanying our chanting with his noble body movement of Tenshingoso, the rain clouds finally parted and a great light shone directly down onto the assembled gathering like a heavenly blessing celebrating this courageous woman's life, fully lived to the last breath. I read my favorite Rumi death poem in which he describes death as humans' "wedding with eternity." From the mystical point of view there is no death: death is an illusion. Death itself is already dead.

ON THE DAY I DIE

On the day I die, when I'm being carried
toward the grave, don't weep; Don't say

"He's gone! He's gone!" Death has nothing
to do with going away. The sun sets and

the moon sets, but they're not gone.
Death is a coming together. The tomb

looks like a prison, but it's really
release into union. The human seed goes

down in the ground like a bucket into
the well where Joseph is. It grows and

comes up full of some unimagined beauty.
Your mouth closes here and immediately

opens with a shout of joy there.

After this I sang a song, "I Am Not I," inspired by a poem of Robert Bly. I sang solo with my harmonium as I visualized Magdalena's soul singing effortlessly into her newfound freedom, a freedom beyond the visible.

I am not I, I am this one, standing beside me whom I do not see,
Whom at times I manage to visit and at other times I forget,

The one who forgives sweet when I hate
The one who stays indoors while I take a walk
The one who remains silent while I talk
I am not I, I am this one, the one who remains standing
When I die, I am not I, I am this one.

—*Naked Heart*

At the end of this song, we all stood together in a deep and reverent listening presence, each of us reflecting on Magdalena's soul in the silence of our own heart and the privilege of having travelled with her for a short yet essential moment. When the time arrived, we slowly opened eyes, moved, and connected gently with each other, speaking in quiet tones, smiling, some very sad, embracing, others fulfilled and privileged to have been present. A Zen monk moved toward Masashi to share lineages. Children began to play and laugh and dance in the space, shifting the attention from death into new life.

Chapter 5

Your Soul Voice

5.1 The Seamless Thread:
Unifying Silence, Speech, and Song

So far I have shared—through simple structured vocal practices, storyline, and reflective teachings—some new and surprising ways to start engaging, exploring, and expanding your heart's voice. You may have also begun to integrate the way you listen to and express your naked voice. This is the first part of Naked Voice exploration, where—with the support of your deep listening, sound-awareness skills, and the elemental and emotional range of your voice discovered through the Seven Sounds of Love—you are equipped to sail out of the safe harbor of devotional chant and simple improvisation into the ocean of the unknown heart. There you will be able to engage with the wilder and messier subterranean music of your emotional life. I am presently most excited and passionate about this new territory because it is here where many people are challenged as they attempt to embody their true voice.

There lives within the depths of every human being an inviolable longing for peace. This longing can only be satisfied through a direct encounter with your true nature, without censorship of any kind. Once heard, this connection with your true self is stronger than the fear of separateness and death. It is the healing salve that paves the way home to the source of our true being. Your naked voice is a seamless thread unifying your sung, spoken, and silent presence into one song.

You are about to uncover the deeper unknown parts of yourself, and you will also learn how to navigate, dance, and engage more freely and masterfully with the different elements of your nature.

Your relationship with your darkest wounds is every bit as important as with your daylight visions. Holding both of these will enable you to heal, grow, evolve, and transform through the logos of your awakening soul. The writer Ben Okri describes it beautifully in his book *A Way of Being Free:*

> We are all wounded inside in some way or other. We all carry unhappiness within us for some reason or other. Which is why we need a little gentleness and healing from one another. Healing in words, and healing beyond words. Like gestures. Warm gestures. Like friendship, which will always be a mystery. Like a smile which someone described as the shortest distance between two people.

Okri reminds us what is most important right now when he writes in the same book, "It's not the size of your voice that is important: it is the power, the truth, and the beauty of the dream."

Your naked voice wants to lift your life, to enchant, to transform. So I invite you now to walk through a new door to explore fresh ways of dissolving the "disconnect" between your speaking and your singing voice. My understanding is that this disconnect—or rather, the belief in the illusion of a disconnect—has seriously disrupted the essential flow between the human head and heart. This disruption can sabotage the potential for a much richer and seamless interweaving of your personal, interpersonal, and transpersonal powers of communication.

Yet I have been privileged to witness many practitioners over the last thirty years experience the transformative power of their naked voice directly, so I know that all that is required is a simple rewiring process enabling you to remember this seamless communication without judgment. It is accessed somewhere in the space between your spoken and sung voice. Once touched it is like a wondrous power that melts your frozen frontiers with a fierce and gentle unconditional love.

This may sound ridiculously naïve and idealistic to the cynical or skeptical mind. And it's not usually possible to restore the full spectrum of one's consciousness overnight. However, with the support of the Seven Sounds of Love, we can apply skillful means more subtly and deeply as we begin to dissolve the boundaries between heart and head. In so doing, we will gradually uncover a long-forgotten depth of communication older and deeper than the polarity of all conflict.

If we are to evolve as human beings, we must access new ways to switch on the whole light bulb of the brain and awaken *all* the energies of love—instinctual, intuitive, wise, ecstatic, and universal—and thereby open up the belly, heart, and head brains, unifying right and left, East and West, releasing a communication that flows effortlessly, naturally, spontaneously, inventively, all-inclusively as one *undivided wholeness*.

There have been many books written on the voice, either as a speaking *informative* business tool or as a singing *performative* entertainment tool. There have also been some beautiful books written about the voice as a *transformative* spiritual tool that allows access to the higher realms of truth. The Naked Voice embraces all three as one interconnected communication.

Throughout the course of this book, we are investigating and distilling these three inextricably linked dimensions of communication into one. I trust that by now you have let go of the old "I'm not a singer" myth. Our school music system rarely encouraged singing beyond the learning of classical or folk songs, usually pitched in inaccessible keys. However, your natural singing voice has the power to restore an immediate connection with your soul, or even with a community, in ways that can take the rational or analytical speaking voice much longer. Once you rediscover your singing voice at this subtler level as a *transmitter* and a *transformer,* you will discover your voice as a catalyst of conscious communication. You will be able to integrate the once-separate worlds of silence, speech, and sung voice.

My meeting in the 1980s with poet and modern-day shaman Nicholas Twilley inspired this experiential research into the cross-fertilization of spoken and sung voice. In a way that was complementary with Masashi Minagawa's energy movement, Nicholas supported me in the evolution of the Naked Voice teachings. In the early '90s, the three of us formed an alchemical trio, combining our respective disciplines of sound, energy movement, and rhythm. And we have co-facilitated many individuals and groups together. Ex-lawyer, self-made man, Nicholas is one of life's originals. Following his fleeting role as manager-roadie of Freddy Mercury, rock star of Queen, Nicholas became a Tibetan Buddhist practitioner of dzogchen, a shaman, world percussionist, visual artist and poet, the shepherd of a flock of alpacas, father of seven, and devoted husband. Over the years he enhanced and intensified my listening awareness through world rhythm, notably African, Asian, and Middle Eastern drumming, fueled by a strong commitment to the extended family and the spirit of the tribe. Nicholas's allegiance to indigenous rites of passage led him to pioneer trainings and apprenticeships for individuals and groups in wild nature for many years in England and Wales.

When I first met Nicholas he was already a long-time student of the Tibetan Lama Namkai Norbu, whose book *Mirror to the Light* had already touched my inner life. It was with Nicholas that I discovered the musical and multifaceted realms of trance as a conscious meditation practice. In our co-facilitated trainings we are constantly evolving and investigating listening practices to quicken the heart of the practitioner and awaken a creative expression. The long hours of deep listening together for days, months, and years forged in ourselves and our collaborations an auditory consciousness that links instinct, intuition, and insight in a respectful and empowering response to each person's needs, direction, personal circumstances, nervous disposition, level of intention, responsibility, courage, and imaginal, musical, and artistic talent.

This intensive research took place during residential retreats as well as performative local and world gatherings. Our students came

Nicholas Twilley,
a portrait (1999)

Nicholas Twilley,
a portrait (2002)

from all walks of life, many of them newcomers to the idea of voice as a spiritual practice. Nicholas lends his constant presence and patient ears to each person's issues or questions, supporting their endeavors with subtle instrumental soundscapes and sonic textures—sometimes infinitely gentle, other times provocative and chaotic—as each practitioner discovers the unexpected pathways through which to access, improvise, and navigate their inner journeys.

It is with gratitude that I now look back over the evolution of our collaborative work. We have touched the source and forged a substantial language of listening, love, and emotional power that has broken through the false notions of sacred versus secular, and sung versus spoken communication. We have cocreated a living new language of love, informed, performed, and transformed by a unique relationship with sound in all its forms that I have come to call *sound consciousness*. Sound consciousness arises from an intimate and unified relationship with sound—in whatever form it shows up—as a seamless thread of communication in which everything arises from and returns to silence. The alchemy of sound generates soul communication: a spoken and sung bridge into every heart.

The Seamless Thread: Bridging the Spoken and Sung Voice

The following vocal practice dissolves the veil between the speaking-singing voice and empowers you to move between the worlds as one unified voice that no longer distinguishes between head and heart communication. This exercise is about expressing not impressing yourself or anyone else. Stay close to the emotion and feel of each word you express.

1. First ask yourself what you most love about your voice.
2. Witness your emotional response to this question, as you courageously listen more deeply to your heart's response, as you ask your soul, what **five qualities** do I love about my voice today?
3. Breathe in two, three, four and out two, three, four as you let the qualities arise.
4. Examples may be "flowing," "passionate," "connected," "penetrating," "sensuous dark velvet."
5. Once you have your five qualities, take one at a time and start building a phrase that embellishes that quality, placing the word in a longer sentence. Let your voice speak as in the first person. For example, "I am flowing like a river." Explore how your voice utters this phrase slowly, quickly,

impatiently, loudly, softly, letting the phrase rise and fall in pitch, rhythm, and tone.

6. Tune in with the pitch of your speaking voice as you express the word "flowing." After much experimentation, open your heart and soul as you listen more deeply, and without judgment or self-sabotage, to the musical energy, feel, and tone of your spoken sound.

7. Without effort, let your spoken sound slide immediately, without any break, into a pitched singing tone.

8. Explore this practice with the other qualities you have chosen.

9. Weave the phrases together and express the deeper musical and melodic nature and tones of your soul, speaking into singing as one.

5.2 Diving Deeper into Spoken Song

There is a place I know
Only I can go
And no one else can go there for me
Yes—no one else can go there for me

> —"On the Other Side of Here,"
> *Thousand Ways of Light*

The simple melody of this song above, along with its lyrics, has opened the door wider for many people who want to dive deeper and more courageously into the spoken song of their soul, fueled by the *Who am I?* and *How can I find out?* questions of life. I have shared it in many Naked Voice workshops, and the following story reveals how it showed up, as well as why and when you can use it to empower your life through your own spoken song.

I was in a New York recording studio and just coming to the end of a vocal session with my friend Gabrielle Roth, founder of The Moving Center. I was singing on her next CD. She looked at her watch and said,

"Well, Chloë, we still have some recording time left. We finished earlier than I thought. How about you just improvise freely and we'll leave the record button on?"

"Sure," I replied.

This was my favorite recording style. This was also the last time I recorded for Gabrielle before she passed. She had been a remarkable loyal friend and passionate champion of my music ever since we met. Gabrielle's last words to me on the phone before her "wedding with eternity" were, "Your music brings me closest to heaven." I treasure her dancing soul. May the unique legacy of her mighty calling continue to rock the world.

Gabrielle's sound engineer had chosen a dark, subatomic drone sample for me to improvise over. As I settled into the womb-like recording booth, I allowed this drone sound to anchor my attention. I aligned myself and asked the life-long question I always ask when I am singing into the unknown: "Dear soul, what would you have me sing?" and I waited for inspiration.

"*Let go of all thoughts of imaginary things*" came the reply, and so I let be what would be and started sounding nonverbally, then whispering-speaking and then speaking-into-singing.

As the music of my soul took over, the sound started to flow out of me. I suddenly had a vivid memory of a voice workshop in which the song "There is a place I know" was born. I was working one on one with a female participant in the presence of the rest of the group. She was trying to find the sound or words that would empower her to walk over the threshold into a new cycle of her life. The lyrics of my song "There is a place I know, only I can go . . ." appeared out of nowhere in that moment. They were an intuitive message in response to her journey, and as I started to sing them it was as if I were simply mouthing words that were already voicing themselves inside her soul. The words combined with the melody line simply followed her, supporting and sustaining her focus as she began to navigate an unknown future.

With the passing of time it became clear that this song was fulfilling its purpose. Its gentle introduction expressed a childlike, nonthreatening innocence that began to build confidence, anchoring her in the grounded, warm, lower-belly sounds. The song then took a sudden and unexpected leap upward only to cascade down onto the words "And, no one else can go there for me." This phrase was then repeated to reinforce the listener's resolve, embracing the whole full octave once again with an affirmative paradox, "Yes, no one else can go there for me!"

The aim of this simple song when repeated is to strengthen the listener-singer's intention to respond to the call of their new journey. I am glad to say this song had the desired outcome, as the whole workshop gradually joined in to reinforce the woman's experience. Everybody recognized that they were resonating with her experience. Our collective awareness expanded beyond the boundaries of time, and we were transported into the beauty of presence together. All in its own timing, the song gradually faded to a quiet humming of the melody line, and finally into a deep and restful contemplative silence. The work was done.

I was facing a new cycle of life of my own, here in Gabrielle Roth's recording booth. Not surprisingly, this same song came into my mind. I began singing it over and over with the same liberating impact upon my own singing soul. I have sung this song in so many places at similar transition points. I know of few other activities that can, within minutes, inspire the same depth of silence, calming the mind and nervous system and opening the contemplative heart into effortless being.

5.3 Sound into Soul Communication: Spoken-Song Conversations

Now it's time to walk your talk. The following practices introduce ways to facilitate your sound into soul communication by reconnecting your spoken and singing voice more effortlessly without censorship. The Seamless Thread practice from section 5.1 is a great preparation for your Sound into Soul Communication. Ideally, you will use a handheld recorder for the following practices.

Spoken-Song Conversation, Practice I

Let your speaking and singing voice blend and merge as you sound out freely, fueled and activated by your presenting emotional state. Allow your words to interweave with your nonverbal sound, back and forth. Then as you feel more connected with the emotional energy in your sound and where it is coming from in your body, sound from there with greater intention. The aim is to dissolve any gaps or impasses between your spoken and your sung voice and to unify the two as one interconnected voice. As you sound forth nonverbally, connect more deeply with the energy in your sound. Let it rise within you, enlivening your whole body-field. Gradually, as your sound opens and flows in this practice, your heart song will emerge. And as you begin to hear it singing inside you, don't doubt it in any way—simply let yourself sound it. Explore moving between speaking-into-sounding-into-singing it. Breathe more deeply, hear your sound more deeply, receive and express your sound with greater attention and intention as it expands, expressing and allowing the feeling of the sound to communicate itself in new and unexpected ways. Follow it, allow it to carry you away, to open new doorways into the unknown sonic landscape of your soul. Be ready for anything. Play! Enjoy!

NB: After recording this process, listen to the recording and notice melodic phrases or words that recur or that especially touch your soul. Gradually the emotional fragments of your soul song will reveal themselves to you like glistening pieces of hidden treasure, showing up in the form of melodic shapes, rhythms, and resonant or dissonant sounds in your soul's garden.

Spoken-Song Conversation, Practice 2: Writing Uncensored

Now commit the same spontaneous process to paper. This time let the imaginal voice of your soul pour forth its feelings, as text, from your unassuming pen. Like a brainstorm, or an uncensored word association, let the words flow without any attempt to censor your feelings in any way at all. Here is an example of one of my Spoken-Song Conversations:

You already know I know you know that every act, every decision, every obstacle that stumps you, stands you up, sticking you inside the muddle of your mind is just your inner lover patiently waiting once again to find you, enfold you in its arms while whispering over and over its eternal refrain, silently smiling inside your face now, listening again, awaiting a new moment, remaining patient slowly to rewind your mind and find you once again. Yes in this slippery split second that strikes only once every thousand years this simple secret, swaying like a leaf in the wind, is gently saying I love you this much, to wake you up, painstakingly shake you up, pummel your edges, stir you in the cauldron of your dreams, spin you round relentlessly, make you senselessly clench your raw fists wringing out the wrathful mismanagement of your mouth until even NOW out of nowhere suddenly your spirit is heard everywhere singing like a mighty bird. Your voice once heard and now again you already know its primordial rune, this mindful music, this fathomless tune where once at seven years old and still now your child is dancing you joyously home.

NB: Once the words are down on paper, record them without censoring your expression in any way. Enjoy what and who is revealed through your emerging soul sound. Reverse the process. Express a stream of spoken-song conversation directly onto your recorder first. Then write it down afterward.

Here's another one, distilled from an original longer version.

This is when the Spoken-Song Conversation begins to reveal the essence of its message more clearly, after several versions:

who sings my voice?
yes me this choiceless one
i have no choice.
who seized my soul?
i never wished
to be a
fish in a bowl
who swims me naked?
sings me whole
why **you** my
upstream force
against the tide
my
invisible swimmer
swimming guide
now tell me . . . open wide
what fish

in its left mind
would seriously choose
that ride?

—*Naked Heart*

Spoken-Song Conversation, Practice 3: Song of Your Soul

Once you have developed confidence with Practices 1 and 2, you will become more masterful at expressing and communicating a more embodied naked-voice improvisation as you allow your emotions to find and express their own music more effortlessly.

This time, start with a simple question like "How do you feel? And how does that sound?" or "How does your feeling sound?" or "How does your sound feel?" All questions end up in the same place. Starting with simple melodic phrases, you slowly tread into deeper emotional waters, exploring more subtle combinations of sounds and sound intervals. Simple improvisation is a first step away from the familiar, away from the safe structures and symmetry of bar lines, of neat and tidy melodic shapes, well-known tunes with clear-cut beginnings and endings, and into the potential chaos and the uncharted realms and radical aliveness of your heart's authentic voice. What often occurs at this stage is that you experience deeper upsurges of emotion after singing freely and alone for a while. These emotions, which are the doorways to ever-deeper feeling, are usually unexpected or even foreign to the singer. They might confuse and frighten at first. You may become overwhelmed by feelings of grief, sorrow, fear, or anger. What to do?

The simple answer is nothing. Simply be present with this emotion, accepting it totally and allowing the silence out of which it arises to embrace it. You will slowly discover that this silence is an anchor while you continue to sing without needing to push the emotion away or to pull it toward you. So the whole process of sounding your soul song can be meditative and intensely felt at the same time. Sometimes it is pleasurable, sometimes painful, but always held within a larger context of abiding, unchanging stillness. You are beginning to integrate the self-observing mind of the scientist with the subjective emotion of the artist. Right-left brain. One Self, the Song of your Soul.

As you come closer and closer to expressing your authentic soul song at the heart of all true communication, you will now also begin to discover through this profound sound experience how to communicate consciously, supported by your *sound awareness* and *sound intelligence* skills. Gradually you will gain more and more confidence to sing and transform the previously turbulent, disturbing, or distracting emotional forces of the ego. This *sound into soul communication* provides a valuable practice in accessing and transmuting a previously disturbing emotion into a clearer and deeper positive feeling.

The more deeply anchored you become in the stillness of your own self-observing witness consciousness, the more courageous you will be to face and embrace the wildest emotions that show up with the sword of your naked singing voice, while maintaining a sound awareness of the original unchanging presence of silence from the source.

With practice you will be so well rooted in this unchanging stillness sourced from the unchanging sound of SA within the song of your soul that you will be free to abandon yourself totally through your naked sound, as it transforms all surface or "disconnected" emotions into the true resonance of who you *are*.

This process of self-surrender through sound can also happen unexpectedly, like an act of grace. I have been privileged to witness this many times. A fine example of this experience occurred once with a third-year college student who came to a weekend course that I was conducting in a British university. This student, whom I'll name Echo, was an extremely earnest, highly intentioned, achievement-oriented student. She was an accomplished violinist and pianist. Yet, more than anything else, she wanted to be able to sing well. And she could not sing in the upper register. She was "blocked" in the throat, and for several years she had been to see doctors and therapists, none of whom could help. Halfway through the course, she came to me and said that she was not sure she could stay any longer. The pain of experiencing another failure with her voice was more than she could take. We sat together in the lunch break in silence, simply "being" with her anxiety and apprehension. Something in her decided to stay for the afternoon session.

I invited the group to explore the music of their emotions. They had already tasted the benefits of the One Breath, One Voice approach (section 2.4). I had also introduced them to the Spoken-Song Conversation practices. One individual after another expressed, released, and transformed their own particular emotional blocks through sound. Echo's turn came, and she began to sing. Her so-called "voice problem" manifested itself. As we stood side by side for a while, I suddenly looked up and saw some round lights placed in the ceiling which were beaming down upon us. In an intuitive flash, I suggested that she should focus her attention upon one of the lights and imagine that there was a presence beckoning to her, drawing her up and beyond herself, inspiring her into sounds she had never sung. There was a moment's pause, and then something beyond her conscious reasoning opened like a flower and said Yes to this challenge.

Suddenly, as if out of nowhere, she was soaring like a bird with her voice, higher and higher, released at last from the bondage of her inhibiting "vocal story." It was a moment of grace. The tone and frequency of her voice was transported into a golden resonance as it seared through the air. Echo had travelled far beyond the boundaries of the ordinary self to receive this transformational gift. The voice of Echo's personality had ceased to dominate her authentic and *naked* voice. She was open.

When this liberation occurs inside you will feel deeply nourished and naturally at home in yourself again. A profound sense of gratitude and reverence for life is released into the body-mind following such moments of self-healing, forgiveness, well-being, and fulfillment. It's also a connection with something larger.

5.4 Naked Song:
Collaborations with Coleman Barks

There is some kiss we want with our whole lives . . . "You don't get nervous in public performance, do you?" famed Rumi translator Coleman Barks asked me at the end of our first lunch meeting in San Francisco during a 1997 conference called "The State of the World Forum." We had met there accidentally. I was giving Naked Voice workshops in San

Francisco and had some time to participate in part of the conference. Coleman gave a recital of his versions of Rumi, accompanied by an ensemble of world musicians, including Jai Uttal and Geoffrey Gordon, and with Zuleikha, the sacred-movement artist. It was a breathtaking presentation of spoken and sung word, culminating in a wondrous spectacle of Zuleikha's Sufi whirling.

At the end of the evening I was encouraged to go and say hello to Coleman. A few months previously I had sent him a letter requesting permission to set some of his poetry to music. He had replied with a postcard that said, "Fly naked with the poems and with your soul sound!" I moved awkwardly forward with a girlish shyness and entered the gratitude queue awaiting to express appreciation in a stream of superlatives to a buoyant yet bashful Coleman Barks, whose radiant openheartedness, generous laughter, down-to-earth Southern drawl, and modest reception of people's praise was very touching. Finally it was my turn to offer my appreciation.

"Hello, Coleman, you may not remember, but I am Chloë Goodchild. I am the one who contacted you a few months ago, for permission to set your Lalla poems to music."

"Chloë, yes! The songbird from England!"

It was both startling and delightful to suddenly be with him in person. We agreed to meet the next day for lunch in the hotel hosting the conference, and there began a friendship that was to have a profound influence over the subsequent decade of my creative life and my research into the healing bridge between the spoken and sung voice.

Our lunch meeting evolved into a car journey to Oakland to meet Coleman's beloved Sufi soul brother, the great Egyptian *oud* (lute) player Hamsa El Din. On the way there, he lost the directions, but this was of little concern. "How about that!" he exclaimed. "Two mystics, lost on the path!"

We eventually arrived at our destination and were greeted by Hamsa's wife, who graced us with tea. Coleman and Hamsa embraced, two Sufi brothers, mutually respectful, blessed to be reuniting again. Once we had settled in, Coleman pulled out his Rumi poems, Hamsa opened up his oud, and we began to simply improvise together. I listened for a long time before I allowed the naked voice to arise from the deep sonic vibration of the oud's strings, as it supported the softly spoken words. Within a very short time, we were enveloped in deep listening as we interwove our spoken-sung voices, uttering words, singing, and playing upon the simplest of secret melodies, disappearing and reappearing inside the diversity of each other's music. Our connection was timeless, with no need for social airs and graces, for sharing of background or foregrounds—in fact only interested in the one unifying ground that had brought us together through the sacred word. I had never improvised with two intimate strangers in this way before.

At the end of our vocalizing together, a deep unfathomable ordinary presence pervaded. Finally, our closed eyes opened, and we glanced at one another like three kids. Hamsa and Coleman acknowledged each other with a sudden friendly glee and brotherly sweetness as they had done many times before. Hamsa then looked at me and smiled, saying, "I like your sound." Coleman suddenly exclaimed, "We don't need to rehearse, do we? Let's record something together!"

This heartening celebration of silent, spoken, and sung word heralded many more creative collaborations. We created a collection (a CD or album) called *There is Some Kiss We Want with Our Whole Lives,* along with giving many live performances. Our collaborations took us on journeys to different countries of the soul as well as the world.

> There is some kiss we want with our whole lives
> The touch of spirit on the body
>
> —RUMI

Part III

TRANSFORM
YOUR LIFE

Sound Wisdom

Chapter 6

Your Naked Voice

6.1 The Singing Field

Out beyond ideas of right and wrong doing
There is a field
A singing field
I'll meet you there

—FROM RUMI, SUNG ON *Thousand Ways of Light*

Your naked voice is fast evolving into a transformative conduit for spirit. I have previously described this vessel as your "house of song," revealed through the body's seven energy centers. This naked voice of yours is a gift of grace that can awaken, empower, and heal the lives of others too. It is from this naked core of your being that a deeper "field" of energy or aliveness can be found and accessed—a spacious field of awareness that dissolves all separation and makes us aware of our connection with the web of all life. Part III of this book invites you to experience this all-inclusive field as a music singing within you and all around you. I call it a *singing field,* and we are about to explore what or who it is that generates this field of energy as vibration, sound, and song, a *singing energy* that inspires us to hear the diversity of our voices as one and from there to cocreate a new sound-led language of consciousness, sourced from the unique song within every human soul.

> This we have now is not imagination, Not a sorrow or a joy or
>   an elation,
> Those things come and they go, This is the presence, that
>   doesn't.
>
> —Rumi

What we have been discovering is how our sound has the power to release us from the imprisonment of duality. What we have been discovering throughout this book is that sound is not some entity or thing that is separate from who we *are*. Sound is our very existence. The whole world is sound. Our very existence is made conscious through sound. WE ARE SOUND. Our whole life—breath, body, heart, mind, soul, relationships—is made possible through sound. Our relationships, colleagues, friends, lovers, communities, our global family comprise an all-vibrating, singing, dancing *field of sound*. And it is this sound that births the field of energy that we ARE with the support of our sound-awareness skills. Our Naked Voice reveals who we are as *sound-conscious* human beings discovering our life as music. This sound awareness energizes our aliveness, which, once we tune in with it, can be transmitted through our naked voices into the world around us, back and forth. It's magnetic, it's infectious, it's a singing circuit. Our human body-field is an evolving, resourceful, resonating circuitry of energy, vibration, color, and light.

In the words of the master Indian musician and teacher, Hazrat Inayat Khan in his essay "The Silent Life":

> Creation begins with the activity of consciousness, which may be called vibration, and every vibration starting from its original source is the same, differing only in its tone and rhythm caused by a greater or lesser degree of force behind it. On the plane of

sound, vibration causes diversity of tone, and in the world of atoms, diversity of color. It is by massing together that the vibrations become audible, but at each step towards the surface, they multiply, and as they advance they materialize.

Hazrat Inayat Khan goes on to explain: "Sound gives to human consciousness, evidence of its existence, although it is in fact the active part of consciousness itself, which turns into sound. The knower becomes known to her/himself, in other words, the consciousness bears witness to its own voice. It is thus that sound appeals to man. All things being derived from and formed of vibrations have sound hidden within them, as fire is hidden in flint; and each atom of the universe confesses by its tone, 'My sole origin is sound.'"

Sound and music have bridged generations and cultures for centuries, offering a unique and, as yet, not fully tapped resource for the evolution of inner-outer harmony and peace. Sound can create a harmonic resonance capable of unifying the most unlikely groups and situations.

The beauty of shared sound and song is that it's free, everyone can do it, and it provides an accessible way to build self-esteem, dissolve friction, and generate forgiveness, healing, happiness, self-knowledge, and conflict resolution. As you have experienced, singing from the heart ignites an aliveness that awakens the energies of love. Its presence can have a surprising and unexpected impact on everyone.

The following stories from my life are moments when I first discovered this groundbreaking power of sound to awaken consciousness and touch wisdom—beyond ideas of right and wrong doing—in what I call "a singing field," a place where the whole spectrum of human longing and belonging is welcomed, received, heard, and honored.

Singing in this way becomes the interconnective tissue of a community or culture, inspiring us to:

Accept and sound our feelings without fear.
Listen and communicate without negative judgment.
Embrace and sing through the emotions of our shadow.

Integrate and transform our terror of an external "enemy."
Shift from a "me first" to a "we first" understanding.
Generate mutual respect and harmonic resonance.
Create cooperative and compassionate relationships.
Empower conscious leadership and service in the world.

My anthem "Singing Field" is very much inspired by Rumi's vision of a field "beyond ideas of right and wrong doing" (Coleman Barks version). The "field" image is of course prevalent in all the new science and quantum conversations about interconnectedness and realms of energy and light, pointing toward the evolution of a "planetary mind" (Teilhard de Chardin). However, "Singing Field" as a melody-line arising from my soul first visited me in the late '90s while I was singing in concert at the Thomas Berry Hall on Whidbey Island, off the coast of Seattle. I had decided to improvise freely with my musicians around the adapted words inspired by the Rumi poem "Field," and suddenly a new constellation of Coleman's original poem manifested as follows:

Out beyond ideas of right and wrong doing
there is a field, a singing field, I'll meet you there

The line simply appeared out of nowhere while I was improvising different musical phrases. Then the melody locked in and refused to change its musical shape or rhythm. I was powerless to sing anything else. It just felt right. Suddenly everyone was joining in, singing it with me, as if we had all been singing it for years! From that moment on, that melody and song became known as the Singing Field anthem. I have sung it all over the world ever since, from local to global gatherings. Its message is now central to the Naked Voice teachings.

The concept of a singing field has since evolved to become a unique meeting point where our Naked Voice workshops take place. The singing field—inspired by its anthem—is now a metaphorical conduit for the Naked Voice work. It is created wherever two, three, or more gather to engage in the Naked Voice deep listening and vocal practices.

I want to emphasize that this singing field is not a performative, entertainment type of singing, for there are no separate "performers" or "audience members" in the Naked Voice community. Everyone is responsible for the sound awareness, which in turn is determined by the depth of the shared listening. The intention of this sonic field is therefore to access a quality of presence arising from the source of the sound itself—silence.

An entirely new quality of sound can arise from this depth of stillness and conscious listening. This sound is medicine for the soul, and everyone feels it. It's a presence that generates and unifies the personal, interpersonal, and transpersonal dimensions of our nature into an undivided wholeness or oneness. This field has the power to uplift and transform left-brain strategic talk and heady diplomacy into a new realm of communication fueled by the fire of the compassionate heart.

Have you ever tried to have an argument, angst, or conflict of any kind with someone who is consciously singing? Or alternatively, has anyone tried to pick a fight with you while you were singing? It's a disarming experience at the very least, and challenging to sustain. Try it and find out!

Great orators or leaders or teachers often inspire their followers by the spirited resonance or musical tone in their voice. They also enjoy using humor and laughter to dissolve the conflicted mind. American comedian Swami Beyondananda (otherwise known as Steve Baermann) is an example of one such teacher who disarms the mind through humor. For example, here's one of his irresistible one-liners:

The universe has got you surrounded,
so you might as well surrender!

And surrender we must. In this time of global chaos and spiritual crisis, many of us living in relative safety may feel that we are powerless to respond to the prevailing uncertainties and devastating news assailing us from the media. What to do? We are being called to surrender our attachment to and identity with the old archaic systems of separateness, institutional violence, and "an eye for an eye" so that we can prepare for a greater shift in humanity's destiny. The singing field provides a sanctuary, an unusual meeting place where we can learn to listen and remember together how to courageously surrender to the responsibility that is our shared song.

Looking more deeply, we realize we are not "in" the singing field. We *are* the singing field. In fact, our human body itself is a singing field. Understanding this is essential, because in realizing ourselves as fields of energy—personal, global, and cosmic—we can make the evolutionary leap from a heady intellectual "I think therefore I am" to a heartfelt intuitive "I sing therefore I am" and even more deeply to "I AM," or AUM, the sound of the universe. AUM was the first sound we shared together at the beginning of this book.

I AM—AUM Sound Practice

Just take in a big breath right now and sound out the AUM a few times. Listen to the silence that follows. Feel that silence singing in every cell of your body, every organ, muscle, bone, and blood vessel, right down to the subatomic particles emitting light from every cell. Hear the presence of the AUM vibrating in the space around you and rippling out into the room and building you are in right now, and on throughout the whole building, and on further out into your local community, country, planet, universe, cosmos, and beyond. Breathe and listen to this mysterious secret sound, the sound of who you are.

"AUMmmmmmmmmmmm"

I once had a wonderful Indian singing teacher named Karunamayi (compassionate mother) who told me a simple yet powerful story. One day she just looked at me and said, "You know, Chloë, people in the West, they say OUCH. They reinforce the feeling of pain through that sound. But if you transform OUCH into AUM, the pain disappears!" She started laughing and laughing. A great story! Try it and hear.

The awareness of a universal field of energy that connects us in creation is growing. Some, such as Stephen Hawking, have even referred to this field as the "mind of God." Thanks to the internet there is a growing movement of people who are seeking out and sounding out their original songs. Filmmaker Michael Stillwater's projects "Song without Borders" and "In Search of the Great Song" are examples. The global musical internet community of musicians "Playing for Change" is another. The United Nations recently called on rock singer Bob Geldorf to regenerate his "Feed the World" song in an effort to counteract the fear and terrorism around the Ebola crisis using collective sound and song.

Looking more deeply, the cultural historian Thomas Berry wrote in his book *The Great Story*: "To attain peace among the nations in any dynamic or enduring form requires not simply political negotiation, but a new mode of consciousness. The magnitude of this change is in the order of a religious awakening or a spiritual rebirth . . . A change is needed in every phase of human life."

The Naked Voice research is now uncovering how these new modes of consciousness can be heard and accessed through the sung voice, inspired by what I call the musical modes of consciousness. That is the subject of my next book on "Sound Evolution."

Meanwhile, our awareness as sound-conscious human beings has to extend beyond self-consciousness into this new sound consciousness, a we-centered, all-inclusive, cooperative music in which the individual and collective ego, soul, and spirit collaborate consciously to orchestrate ourselves into a symphony of Love governed by the principles of sound as outlined in the early stages of this book.

"Sound," said Edgar Cayce, "is the medicine of the future." That future is *now*. An increasing number of people are calling out for a new myth to share and give voice to, one that redefines our true role as humans, awakening us to the sacred task of living more authentically, consciously, reverently, and responsibly in this interconnected universe. As our global village moves through the devastating impact and terrifying uncertainties of environmental destruction, climate change, energy depletion, world poverty, and the horrors of fundamentalism, a radical awareness is called for to transform our relationship with ourselves and each other.

This must no longer be only an intellectual ideal—it must be an embodied reality, rooted in a direct experience of oneness or unification.

The human voice is a gift of spirit. Witness the compassionate use of the human voice as a sounding board, lifting humanity to a new level of consciousness, by such spiritual leaders as Martin Luther King, Jr., Mahatma Gandhi, Aung San Suu Kyi, Nelson Mandela, Stevie Wonder, and thousands of other voices emerging. Your voice too can be a visionary mouthpiece for the spiritual revolution, a bridge for interconnectedness, capable of awakening the energies of love and the real conscience of the human spirit.

Witness also *The Singing Revolution* film, one of the most inspiring twentieth-century accounts of how the nonviolent use of collective singing was activated on a national scale to liberate the Estonian people from more than a hundred tortuous years of Nazi and Stalinist invasion. Estonia sustains one of the biggest folk libraries in Europe. It was the annual Estonian Festival of Choral Music that constantly revived the people's spirits each year despite the dehumanizing attempts of nihilist forces to disempower the Estonians. And it was this choral singing power that ultimately enabled Estonia to overcome and transform a century of tyranny by outside forces. Following *perestroika*, these extraordinary "ordinary" Estonian people were finally able to gain some leverage for their vision to reclaim their country; and it was through the unbroken attention to the shared sound and singing of their inspiring melodies and choral music that they successfully and nonviolently sang the Russians out of their country in the late '90s!

I once had a former environmental minister make a prescient statement following his first experience of our shared sound and singing—culminating in the Singing Field anthem—at an environmental conference. As we exchanged places on the platform he looked at me with a stunned expression and said, "If we had singing like that at all our Party Political conferences, it would change politics overnight!"

Having recently begun to introduce The Naked Voice Singing Field practices in Chile, I have started to engage with another remarkable musical force d'esprit demonstrating the transformative power of collective music-making in South America: that of "El Sistema," a classical music *tour de force* founded by visionary José Abreu in Venezuela. It all started a few decades ago when the economist, musician, and orchestral conductor had a dream in which all Venezuelan children would have the same musical experience as he had had.

To the first eleven children who turned up to José's first music rehearsal, he made a promise that he would turn the orchestra into one of the leading orchestras in the world. He committed to liberating the arts, and music especially, in Latin America from being a monopoly of elites into a human right for ALL people. In the organization of El Sistemo there exist no class distinctions. It is quite simple: if you have the *vocation* and the *talent* and the *will* you are taken on board and given the greatest opportunity, which is to move people's souls and be moved in your soul by music. The Youth Symphony Orchestra of Venezuela did just that, and then as they began to travel they started to move people in their deepest souls in Europe, with standing ovations at all the concerts.

The "new mode of consciousness" that you and I and the world community are being called to requires every man, woman, and child to wake up and share responsibility for restoring and unifying our diversity into our original song of oneness.

Time is of the essence.

6.2 International Policymakers Share Their Sound

One is one and one world turning
Naked in our song
One is one the heart is burning
Naked in our song

—"Naked in Our Song," *Fierce Wisdom*

I was invited to introduce the work of the Naked Voice at a three-day conference organized by an independent nonpartisan organization, for a large group of international policymakers. There I was privileged to meet some remarkable and courageous individuals who were willing to forget their separate or opposing political positions for a moment, and to share human friendship through the power of voice. It was an unforgettable experience and one that opened doors on the transformative impact of shared sound as an effective catalyst for conscious leadership and peace-making.

More than thirty countries were represented, from the U.S. to Eastern Europe to the Middle East. Their focus was space-based satellite weaponry, or the "Star Wars" question. They were informed that I would be giving them a "musical surprise" on the last night.

For three days I watched and witnessed this group of suited gentlemen thrash out their anxieties and defense plans: high-tech warfare tactics and high-wired strategic prowess were displayed on slide-projector screens for the implementation of stronger defense measures worldwide. As I listened to the technical jargon, I was struck by the apparent ease with which they used aggressive phrases like "launching the killing vehicle" while demonstrating—at the simple push of a remote-control button—the total annihilation of a vast sector of the world. As the days proceeded this bravado escalated, only to be calmed and deflated at intervals by the quiet presence of the one leading woman facilitator orchestrating the dialogues.

"An eye for an eye" was the underlying assumption fueling most of the communications. As is my practice, I began to listen to this techno-defense jargon as a dynamic music, whose staccato rhythms slowly escalated into an ongoing and largely unrecognized frenzy of despair between the respective countries. Unfolding before my ears and eyes was a confirmation, in microcosm, of the vast, unredeemed "divide and rule" beliefs still driving our world decision-making.

From the perspective of the Naked Voice, whose aim is to transform the negative emotion of an individual or group into a positive human feeling through their naked sound, I heard in these staccato communications a music of terrorism. Knowing that in a couple of days I was to present and share my understanding with them, I began to jot down the technical jargon as it spurted forth from the mouths of this highly sophisticated and eloquent group of displaced noblemen.

The more deeply I listened to their rage and terror, the more I found myself falling into an interior listening awareness beneath this mental battleground. I traveled into the personal history of these men and to the circumstances in which they fell victim to carrying the world shadow. As I reflected more deeply on the nature, vibration, and quality of their communications, I began to feel empathy for these soldiers of pain and for the intensity of their despair in the face of a so-called "enemy" as they tried to "fix" things in the name of a so-called "peace." The increasing intensity of their emotional distress played out through the rhythm, volume, pace, and pitch of their voices as the hours passed by.

It therefore seemed both appropriate and essential on my first direct meeting with them that I would thank them for what they had taught me about our shared terror of death. After dinner on the appointed evening of their "musical surprise," I began by offering a sung improvisation inspired by all the technical jargon that they had been using in the previous days. This opening presentation was surprisingly effective in activating their attention, as they listened to this unexpected semiverbal interpretation of their strategic plans, freely expressed through sung voice and sound. My initial aim with this was to pry off the lid between the participants' heads and their hearts. A stunned silence followed this simple improvisation, which gave me the space and time to thank them for giving voice so graphically and unapologetically to the profound uncertainty that most humans feel in the face of death. Caught unaware in this new interpretation of the conference, their bodies nevertheless began to relax and open, as did the quality of their listening.

It then seemed quite natural to pose my first question, which was out before I could do anything about it. Its apparent naïveté threatened to estrange the group, yet it seemed strangely purposeful and appropriate:

"As we have been investigating the best ways to protect ourselves and our loved ones from the finality of death, may I ask how many of us have actually been present at the death of a friend or a loved one?"

There was a long and disorienting pause. Their startled faces revealed the years of left-brain indoctrination as they endeavored to access and absorb this unexpected right-brain question. Not one individual responded with a yes or a no.

"Well," I continued, "my father has just died, and I sang with him while he was dying. We sang 'thy will be done' together. As an Episcopal bishop, he had always wanted me to make a sung version of the Lord's Prayer. The rebellious child in me, while adoring my father, nevertheless had rejected formalized religion in my teenage years and left home in search of a way that integrated body and spirit. I had never honored his request. So now was my moment."

These men stared at me aghast. Who was I? How dare I disarm them so? What kind of "musical surprise" was this supposed to be? It certainly was not the usual entertainment one might expect for a gathering such as this!

Beneath their surface reactions I could feel that they were nevertheless still on board and ready for the ride. So I continued: "Throughout the course of my life, singing has given me a way to face my own personal terror of death. It has enabled me begin to see through the finality of death and beyond.

"*May death itself die!*' say the great masters of the perennial wisdom. As my beloved father and I sang, choked, and cried our way through the Lord's Prayer in the last intimate, holy moments of his life, I realized, as we approached 'thy kingdom come' that he was no longer holding on to anything. His frail physical form was no longer fighting to stay alive. In a final wave of energy, and a roaring call, his singing softened into a gentle whispering fire, as he struggled to throw off the garments of his flesh and enter the majesty of his own kingdom. What he revealed to me in these final utterances was the inner freedom that he had devoted his life to. As he let go of eighty-eight years fully lived and loved, with eyes wide open, his last breath was followed by a silence so peaceful I shall never forget it."

I looked around the group.

"So," I continued, "as death is the presenting issue for this conference, shall we practice dying together?"

At the thought of this, some defense representatives from the middle of the world made for the door, clutching their glasses of port. Two minutes later their expectant faces reappeared around the door, having placed themselves at a safe distance from the center of any forthcoming action. I scanned the room for willing playmates as I spoke more about my fascination with sound and its potential to open doors and dispel boundaries between people of opposing beliefs. I spoke of my work with victims of trauma and prisoners of war, then returned to the present moment.

"We have an exercise called One Breath, One Voice. In one breath, you sound out as if this is the first or last breath of your life. You take the deepest in-breath, and without any thought, you simply pour out your heart and soul, to the sound 'Ah' for as far as the breath will take you. Having emptied yourself of all breath you then stay for a moment in this emptiness, until the next breath involuntarily pumps back into your body. Would anyone like to join me?"

"OK," I replied, and without another moment's thought I breathed in and began calling out, full-throated across the room, wailing and crying for my life, for the whole world, summoning the Deities, mountain-hollering and soaring, my voice rising and falling in undulating waves of energy and a timing all its own. Finally the breath died away and I was empty in the presence of forty amazed and apprehensive gentlemen of war.

Will she breathe in again? In that uncertain moment, my next breath jerked back into my body, and everyone sighed with relief. Clearly no one was going to follow this bizarre demonstration of the human life-force. Nevertheless, a simple encounter with humanity's deepest fear, that of death itself, had been momentarily glimpsed. We moved into safer territory. The group began to relax. Neckties were being loosened and tight dinner jackets taken off as the impact of a substantial dinner and wine softened the thresholds of resistance.

The next exercise, "Offering," was an invitation to open oneself up and make a gift of one's voice and sound to another in the circle. In a gesture of offering, with hands opening up and out, accompanied by a freely improvised song or nonverbal singing, I invited each country to make their way, one at a time, across the center of the world, offering their sound as a gift to another participant on the other side of the circle.

"As you offer yourself up to the sound inside you, follow the sound

across the circle until you arrive in front of someone on the other side."
I first demonstrated this simple gesture of offering and trust. It was
clear from the resonance of the group that everyone was much more
willing to respond to this. I scanned "the world" for a volunteer. Everyone had their eyes cast down, nervous about being the first. Suddenly
we were a schoolroom of awkward teenagers. Then my eyes lighted on
Italy!

"Italy!" I exclaimed, "the most musical culture of Europe. Will you
lead us?"

His head was down while simultaneously nodding negatively from
side to side. Yet an irrepressible smile gave the game away, and with it,
an uncontrollable burst of applause and support from the rest of the
world, with cheering and clapping, and "yes, come on, Italy, you can do
it!" from around the circle in a kaleidoscope of languages.

The Italian representative quietly surrendered and agreed to participate. Silence and awe swept instantly around the world as the participants watched their brave fellow statesman slowly breathe in, lift
his head, and open wide his arms to sing forth. What followed I would
not have dreamed possible, yet it happened. This gentleman expert of
strategic defense was suddenly as one transported into La Scala or the
Sistine Chapel! His voice became a conduit for the divine feminine to
pour through, showering her blessings upon the unsuspecting world
all around in Latin and Italian. A stream of Ave Marias emerged, devotional in tone, operatically expressed, in one seamless, ecstatic voice
and sound of love. His body moved slowly and majestically as he flowed
across the room. He landed in front of Canada, who, initially dumb-
struck, then staggered helplessly back across the center of the world, in
a new direction, sounding out from the depth of his soul, surprising
himself with a stream of unexpected utterances making his offering
to Norway. Norway received the torch of sound, and moved himself
to tears with his own sound, finally arriving in front of another statesman. So the web wove itself, from one side of the world to the other,
over and over until every country had been visited, acknowledged, and
honored with sound.

As the group dispersed later that evening after the sharing of many songs, one of the policymakers, who had expressed much skepticism for this work initially, took me aside. In a hushed voice he murmured, "If we have another war, I want you on my submarine."

6.3 Peace Talks: Singing in the Rain for the Dalai Lama

Om Tare Tutare Ture So Ham

—"OM TARA," *Fierce Wisdom*

Earlier in these pages I set the scene for the Dalai Lama's visit to Belfast, Northern Ireland (see section 3.6). The following story—which took place during the Dalai Lama's Irish visit for the Peace Talks—revealed to me just how profoundly sustaining and protective the collective recitation of sacred mantra can be, especially when sung in the most uncompromising situations imaginable! The scene this time was a rainy parking lot in Belfast, Northern Ireland. The event was part of a series called "The Way of Peace," organized by the Christian Meditation Movement, founded by the mystic, monk, and meditation teacher Father Lawrence Freeman. It was a privilege to sing for the Dalai Lama's visit to Ireland.

I arrived very early in the morning with my small ensemble of musicians to perform at the appointed venue: a car park, which was designated as a neutral ground between the Roman Catholics and the Protestants. I had been invited to provide the music for a mediation initiative aimed to bring together the Roman Catholic and Protestant communities in a spirit of reconciliation as never before in the presence of the Dalai Lama. So it was right here in the heart of one of the world's most troubled war zones that I was to discover the infectious and transformative power of sacred mantra in the presence of several thousand people from diverse religious faiths and political persuasions.

In honor of the Dalai Lama I dedicated our performance to the Buddhist Goddess of Compassion, Tara. I chose this mantra as the most appropriate one for the conditions we were in because the word *Tara* happened to have significance both for the Tibetan Buddhist world and the Irish. *Tara* is a Celtic Goddess who presides over *Tara,* the sacred hill of Ireland. So I sensed that this meditative music would provide us with a nonthreatening opening and a solid foundation to sing from.

A makeshift platform and stage had been erected for the arrival of the Dalai Lama, together with the two distinguished leaders of the Protestant and Catholic churches, Canon Barry Dodds and Father Gerry Reynolds. I had brought four other musicians, including the Gaelic singer Deidre Ni Chinneide, flutist Tim Wheater, world percussionist Nick Twillley, and saxophonist Ed Jones. I had also asked my Japanese energy movement instructor, Masashi Minagawa, to join us in creating a peaceful ground for our presentation. We were required to create a calming musical atmosphere for the crowds already building in this car park while awaiting the arrival of the three religious dignitaries. The idea for our music was to create a strong, nonpartisan, and inspiring musical atmosphere while the Dalai Lama and his two religious companions took a long slow stroll down the so-called Peace Walk through this car park. They would eventually arrive through the Peace Gates to where we were singing. The Peace Gates were tall metal gates that usually divided the opposing sides, but which were opened for official state visits of this nature.

It was 8:30 AM when we arrived, and the place was already littered with security guards and police. The atmosphere was extremely tense because the security guards had just been told that there was dissension between the two religious sides. The word had got around that the stage was a few feet closer to one side than the other! We had no choice but to proceed to our allotted performing ground amid the cacophony of radiophones, police sirens, and mounting voices of the crowds. A security guard came rushing up to me to explain the exit strategy if violence broke out!

"It's just possible that when we open the Peace Gates, the children from the opposing sides may start throwing stones at each other, and they may start throwing stones at you, Chloë, OK?" he told me. With this dilemma out his voice turned into more of a high shriek. "We have a security car, and we can get you all out of here in twenty minutes, I promise, alright?"

We all looked at each other, breathed in deep, and braced ourselves to begin. The crowd had reached a thousand easily by now, and there were more coming in. There was a bank of policemen and paramilitary with guns held high holding back the crowds.

The rain had turned to a drizzle and was strangely comforting as it showered our faces and bodies in a misty coolness as we opened our voices and instruments to sound of the Tara mantra.

I internally connected with the sacred feminine presence of Tara's vast, compassionate energy and visualized her showering blessings everywhere, healing the terrible years of bloodshed, melting deep-seated beliefs, relaxing opposed fixed positions, breaking ancient angst, dissolving entrenched separateness and fear language.

First, I could hear the Tara mantra singing from within, then the melody was out and the musical instrumentation harmonized and enhanced it so serenely:

Om Tare Tutare Ture So Ham
Om Tare Tutare Ture So Ham

Already my body-mind began to relax as the spiritual power of the words allowed the melody and the presence of this archetypal feminine deity Tara to flow through the cells in my body, dissolving my own apprehensions of this historical killing field that we were all called to.

I have no idea how long we sang, but I remember the same security guard coming up to me some time later and thrusting a piece of paper in my hands which read "HH Dalai Lama is moving slowly, so please just keep going! It may be another twenty minutes before His Holiness and the other religious leaders arrive. We actually have no idea how long they will be!"

My eyes had been closed so as to focus deeply on the sounding of the mantra; I had almost let go concern of the unpredictability of this situation, offering it up and letting the spirit of the moment take over. So when I opened my eyes to see a line of paramilitary with their guns dropped to half-mast while they were stretching their ears to hear what we were singing, I knew all was well, for the time being. So I closed my eyes again, and the mantra increased its volume as we all moved into a new musical gear together, improvising and enjoying the healing power of *Om Tare Tutare.*

By now the crowds had joined in, as the simplicity of the chant and the reference to Tara had filtered through, indicating that they could relate to this and that they were happy to sing along. I closed my eyes again, smiling and grateful this time, as my voice and sound took on a momentum and increased volume of its own.

Om Tare Tutare Ture So Ham, Om Tare Tutare Ture So Ham

Once the instrumental textures were well established and improvising joyously, I added my own lyrics with a new vocal melody all its own that soared, bringing a more Western flavor to the original chant.

Woman of the wisdom tree, Goddess of humanity
Singing of the unity we long for.

Soon I added more verses, interweaving them like islands and ocean with the trance-like melody:

Mother of eternity, Goddess of humanity
Singing of the unity we long for.
Om Tara Tutare . . .

Fierce and gentle wild and free, Naked in her majesty
Singing of the unity we long for.
Om Tara Tutare . . .

More time passed, and by now I and my musical partners were all deeply focused, sounding as one, harmonizing and embellishing the main melody and cocreating a *field of sound* that integrated the Tibetan Buddhist formal melody line with a groove and a Celtic folk lyricism that was more accessible for the huge crowd of listeners. There was a sense of all-inclusiveness everywhere, thank God. We were all travelling together, united by a deeper sound beyond the horrors of political history. My eyes were closed again as I enjoyed sensing the deepening peace and harmony within the audience. More time passed and we virtually lost all concern about when the Dalai Lama would arrive. Tara had stolen everyone's heart, and her presence returned us all to a time before the history of war, sharing her grace everywhere, as we all began to taste the possibility of compassionate energy in our veins.

Then at last, after an hour or so, the moment came for the Dalai Lama and the two religious leaders to arrive through the Peace Gates. And something extraordinary happened. First of all, the sky cleared, as if the deities had pulled two curtains back while His Holiness stepped into the car park, smiling, laughing, bowing to everyone, striding along free as air, as if he walked through Irish car parks every day of his life!

Suddenly there was brilliant blue sky and sunshine, and as our music intensified, the crowd starting clapping, cheering, and sounding the Tara mantra ever louder. What was most startling for me when I opened my eyes was to look down and see the children from the opposing sides—the ones who were supposed to be throwing stones—looking up into my face while sweetly singing beside other victims of the war in wheelchairs, everyone singing loud and strong as if this was the easiest thing in the whole world, and we were one vast, extended family—which we were for a timeless moment in time!

Om Tare Tutare Ture So Ham
Om Tare Tutare Ture So Ham . . .

His Holiness had by now mounted the steps onto the stage with his two religious brothers, and they came to the front of the stage together. Then something wonderful and entirely outrageous occurred, which no one but the Dalai Lama would have been able to pull off. Both religious leaders had wonderful beards. His Holiness without any thought looked at them both and spontaneously took hold of their beards and started banging their heads against his! This brought the house down. Everyone loved it, and it catalyzed a burst of applause, laughter, and cheers. Then the gathering came to a deep silence, and the Dalai Lama looked at the two religious leaders, then again at the crowd, and said how honored he was to be here in the midst of the Christian community of Northern Ireland. Then he paused and thought for a while, and whispered in low basso profundo tones that reverberated out across the attentive crowd gathered there, saying, *"I can understand why there is opposition between different religions, but I cannot understand why there is such fighting between people of the same religion!"* and then his wild fiery laughter shot out into the bemused crowd as people unexpectedly joined his laughter, releasing decades of collective tension in the shortest span of time. Finally, everyone settled again and returned to a deeper listening, having heard the Dalai Lama's profound and simple wisdom message, slowly absorbing and accepting it: silence and a peace passing all understanding. We were one.

The three men took their seats for the ceremony that followed.

The Dalai Lama (center) and Christian leaders Father Gerry Reynolds (left) and Canon Barry Dodds (right) (The Way of Peace 2000)

6.4 Healing Sound, A Holy Ground: Flying Over New York on 9/11

Jars of spring water are not enough anymore
Take us down to the river

—"Jars of Spring Water," *Fierce Wisdom*

"Ladies and gentlemen, grave news!"

These stern words from a disoriented pilot sent shock waves through our United Airlines plane flying from the UK to San Francisco. The date was September 11, 2001, and it was about 10:30 AM. Our pilot was clearly disturbed as jumbled words stumbled out of his mouth in an attempt to explain what was going on. It was impossible to understand him, and so everyone started calling out in a cacophonous chorus, "Stop, start again, we can't understand you!"

Were we about to crash-land? No, but thousands of others had just fallen victim to an unimaginable deathtrap in the heart of Manhattan. I looked out the window and could see nothing but soft clouds and endless white space. Had someone invaded the cockpit? No. So why grave news? We had recently cleared New York around 9:30. Our United Airlines flight was never to reach its West Coast destination. Right now our pilot was flying us toward the Canadian border, as all the U.S. air terminals had been closed down for security reasons.

He had waited an hour or so before announcing to us that the World Trade Center had been struck by a United Airlines plane and the Twin Towers had just gone down.

We must have narrowly cleared New York before the explosion.

Air stewardesses were trembling while trying to suppress panic and keep a grip, their eyes wet with bewilderment, uncertainty, and fearful apprehension.

Meanwhile the rest of the passengers suddenly turned into a fast-talking, openhearted group, sharing truths and fears about friends and relations living in New York City. Within minutes we became intimate strangers, a long-lost community rediscovering itself after decades of searching. It was like a Naked Voice workshop with a difference. People started pouring out their hearts to each other, crying, laughing, questioning, speaking the unspoken in great haste just in case we ourselves might become the next victims of a further terrorism.

We were in another United Airlines plane after all.

"I am so grateful to be alive" was my mantra and constant refrain. I was also glad that I was able to resource myself from a deep stillness within as I listened and responded to the terrified conversations taking place all around me. What touched me most in this crazed situation was the ordinary-extraordinary ease with which everyone began to open up to each other. Prior to this dreadful news, most individuals had been sitting in their own closeted worlds, completely unavailable to their neighbor. Within minutes of receiving the news everyone miraculously began to open up, making themselves available to give and receive. It is often said how war-time inspires the closest communication between human beings, but *how much longer* do we have to wait before we can share all that is beautiful in the human spirit without depending on the catalyst of war or some other apocalyptic crisis?

New lyrics started to emerge that eventually turned into melodies and made their way into my next album, *Fierce Wisdom*. They brought me great solace during this devastating historic moment, thousands of feet up in the sky, flying somewhere over North America. These words have been sung over and over in our singing fields around the globe. They are inspired by the teachings of Anandamayi:

How much longer will you wait at a wayside inn?
The wanderer the exile home coming home
One Self is all there is

—*Fierce Wisdom*

I was on my way to sing and teach near Vancouver, Canada. But I had left my musical harmonium in San Francisco and was planning to pick it up, and to spend a day or two with friends there before flying on to Vancouver. As our plane flew us in circles, awaiting new landing instructions, we were finally redirected to Edmonton, Canada.

The world was in chaos and media was madness. The same horrifying morning scene of the United Airlines plane striking the Twin Towers was played over and over on TV screens everywhere, from the airport to our hotel bedrooms. It was like watching some horror blockbuster movie come to life. This was reality TV like we had never seen it, and we were caught right in its wounded heart.

My own family, thousands of miles away in the UK, was wondering where I was and whether I was still alive. We were told that all internet and phone communication was unreliable, most likely impossible. Sitting in a stupor in my hotel bedroom and watching the images of this human fatality on a vast scale, I began to go deeper within myself to connect with these dark collective forces as they lived in me, within my own shadow unconscious. First I remembered how New York City was once described to me as the city of Shiva—the Hindu god of destruction. But Shiva's destruction is not literally negative. In the Hindu tradition Shiva's role is to destroy the distractions of the ego-mind, the illusion of separateness, negative desire, ignorance, and ultimately death itself.

Staring more deeply into these nightmarish scenes before me, I became aware of the terrifying power of the dark Mother of the world, the Black Madonna, the primordial voice of the defiled Earth, the abused and tormented feminine.

And from my lips came the words, *"This is the fierce wisdom of the Great Mother. And she will continue killing until humanity wakes up!"*

In my diary I wrote myself a question:

How can my sound engage with and respond to this fierce wisdom?

Not long after, I received a call from my record distributor to say that my CD music *Sura* was being played in a mainstream department store all over New York City. This came from one inquiry made by a dear friend to the owner of this major fashion store. Suddenly it was possible to make one simple contribution through my music in response to this profound horror. I thanked God for the healing power of this music to assist in the slow process of restoring ordinary peaceful human relations in the streets of Manhattan.

Soon I started to hear a new music simmering inside me, called "FIERCE WISDOM." The lyrics—"How much longer will you stay at a wayside inn, the wanderer, the exile, home coming home"—would mark a climax point in the music that would take the listener on a human-divine journey of longing and belonging. My aim was to create what I called a *vibrational medicine* for a world in spiritual crisis.

The following days gave hundreds of us displaced individuals more opportunities for standing in queues, letting go all our social armoring, making new and unexpected friendships. While in conversation I remembered the Dalai Lama, whose eternal message, "my religion is kindness," was a healing balm, clear and simple, played out on TV screens everywhere at regular intervals.

As security measures became tighter by the second, the message from Canada to this bewildering influx of international travelers was constantly warm and welcoming. Amidst the mayhem of the milling crowds, we were asked to be patient, as we might conceivably be in Edmonton "for the foreseeable future." What to do? Thy will be done. Surrender all expectations and attachments to outcomes. I remember standing in an eleven-hour queue in Edmonton's airport after being awoken at 4:30 in the morning to be told we would be on a 9 AM flight to San Francisco that day. This queue was at least half a mile long, and we moved forward about two feet every hour, due to the newly enforced and very detailed security checks. There was nothing to do but treat this new queuing ritual like a meditation walk while surrendering into a timelessness beyond the suffering of expectation.

My diary reminds me of my ultimate appreciation for this treacherous confrontation with our world shadow. A couple of days following September 11th, I wrote: "I am becoming aware of human innocence pervading this whole sorrow-filled dream. The capacity of thousands of people in the airport to cooperate with this unknown journey into who knows where is simply astounding. People are perhaps just too tired and stunned to panic or express their rage or angst at these endless long delays. As a result, a more humble response is possible, evident in some places and surfacing. The new transitions required of us to cross unexpected borders and to move in unintended directions is becoming a meditation in deep acceptance. This allows for a deeper inner shift from 'my will' into 'thy will.' Original intention has to be abandoned in the face of a new journey and destination. Focusing on the present moment is the only reality here. Simple communication can drop deeper and begin to intermingle with serious discussions about why we are here on Earth, and where on Earth we are going."

A composed gentleman, Mr. Singh, director of a huge wireless communications company, was in a queue moving along slowly beside me. He stood in the line serenely and quietly, engrossed in a fat white book entitled *Indian Philosophy*. Perfect! For several hours we were able to exchange knowledge and deepen our respective experiences of the nature of being, dualism, nondualism, and the exploration of Eastern and Western perspectives.

After a couple of days of leaving and returning to the hotel from the airport, the U.S. terminals were opened again and I finally arrived in San Francisco. Our plane was the first to arrive there following the reopening of the borders. The airport was like a ghost town. I marveled at the silence in the skies above the airport—an awesome unearthly silence, which must have found its way across the whole continent for a brief and precious moment.

Several days later—having reunited with my harmonium—I was finally aboard a ferry driving at top speed to my Canadian retreat center off mainland Vancouver, where fifty or so of the most naked voices I have ever encountered plunged into the welcoming depths of the dark Mother realms, where in an unstoppable outpouring of soul, from early morning into the night hours, we sought out new sutras for rebirthing our world. This was a huge moment for everyone to share. It was clear for all present that there inside the naked voice of the soul was a holy ground of healing from inner to outer, personal into global. This was the deepest blessing, a place to fall down on the ground, melting the gates of hell in an inescapable act of open-heart surgery, crying from the depths for redemption and forgiveness. There—in the presence of this field of seeming helplessness and uncertainty—the candle of the spirit could slowly burn away the sorrow of loss and disillusionment while the devotional and wild spontaneous naked ocean of song poured out continually back and forth across the frontiers of longing and belonging, known and unknown, separateness and union, until an awesome stillness finally returned.

Out of the sorrow and despair of this shared gathering, the music of *Fierce Wisdom* was born in one unbroken stream out of my mouth and onto CD. An international event at the Royal Opera House in London was its launching pad the following year. The event was called "Transforming September 11th."

Chloë Goodchild singing at *Fierce Wisdom* premiere, London (2002)

Jars of spring water are not enough anymore
Take us down to the river
The face of peace
The sun
Om tare tutare ture so ham!

—"Jars of Spring Water," *Fierce Wisdom*

6.5 Fierce Wisdom: Transforming September 11th

Not Christian or Jew or Muslim, not Hindu,
Buddhist, Sufi , or Zen. Not any religion
Or cultural system. I am not from the East or the West,
Not out of the ocean or up from the ground....

—"Only Breath," from Rumi poem translated
by Coleman Barks (*Fierce Wisdom*)

To orchestrate such an ambitious gathering, I teamed up with peace activist Dr. Scilla Elworthy. Our vision was to create a series of unusual public dialogues on stage, supported and sustained by a musical atmosphere that would inspire a nonthreatening context for deep listening and respectful communication.

Scilla convened the peace builders and celebrities who attended from all over the world. She instilled a confidence in the gathering that convinced them to come and demonstrate conflict transformation in action. This involved working with a supportive team to create an organic preparation process that included running a day seminar to deepen everyone's understanding of the event ahead of time.

My task was to create a musical environment that would integrate both spoken and sung voices on stage, establishing a stable bedrock for compassionate conversations to unfold between representatives of historically opposing groups. The proceeds were to fund a new global initiative, Peace Direct, to promote and empower nonviolent initiatives, communication tools, and skills worldwide.

"Transforming September 11th" was "performed" over three nights in the presence of peace activists, religious leaders of all faiths, charitable organizations, sociocultural visionaries, celebrity artists, authors, film-makers, poets, actors, and comedians. It provided a nonpartisan context for humanitarians to come together, to share intense emotions, and to awaken conscience. The music inspired openhearted listening and enabled visionaries to share new nonviolent maps and initiatives for planetary peace. Celebrity artists such as Steven Fry, Julie Christie, Juliette Stevenson, Ben Okri, Mark Rylance, and many more spoke out through poetry, prose, and song. It was a high-security risk situation demanding the utmost care and attention to detail at every level of organization, presentation, and performance.

Fierce and *Wisdom* were the two words I had instinctually heard arising directly from Mother Earth on 9/11. The musical message of my *Fierce Wisdom* album was newly born, and I had shared it with Scilla at her home. I had composed, sung, and recorded this new vocal odyssey in the aftermath of the 9/11 disaster. It therefore offered an appropriate ambiance for this unusual event that was neither theater, festival, nor conference but something entirely new.

Fierce Wisdom was composed and developed over one singular and unchanging note: A below middle C. It is regarded as a healing note with a very calming vibration. A is also the note that orchestral players attune to at the beginning of a concert. The *Fierce Wisdom* music integrated multipart harmonies with solo devotional chant, improvised song, choral anthems, spoken poetry, and ecstatic love song. The aim of this music was to communicate the fierce and gentle wisdom message of the sacred feminine. The lyrics were inspired by the teachings and messages of unconditional love, drawn from Anandamayi and Rumi (Coleman Barks versions). The musical score combined contemporary Western instrumentation with a strong infusion of sacred mantra and mystical poetry from the Middle East, Africa, and Asia.

As the curtains went up, I sang the words of our Singing Field anthem: *"Out beyond ideas of right and wrong doing, there is a field, a singing field, I'll meet you there."* We completed the evening with full audience participation in the same song, inviting them to stand to chant the Singing Field anthem as one voice.

I will never forget the opening line of one of the first speakers—a remarkable Irish peace activist who happened to be a past member of the paramilitary in Northern Ireland. His opening words were stark and shocking: "I used to sing like Chloë until they put a gun in my hand at sixteen."

This black humor stunned the audience into dead silence. It fell from the mouth of one of the most compassionate men I have ever met, who by fate as a teenager was pushed to kill in an act of self-defense. If he hadn't used that gun in his hand at that moment, he himself would have been murdered, or kneecapped in cold blood. His horror story prompted a life sentence. During his prison time he took the opportunity to read every yoga and meditation book he could lay his hands on. This prison sentence was a wake-up call that transformed his whole life and has since transformed the many traumatized lives of war victims in Northern Ireland. His opening lines certainly quickened the audience's ears and catapulted the musical purpose of the evening into action, igniting the *fierce wisdom* message in the hearts and minds of all present, establishing a deep nonjudgmental listening between speakers and opening the hearts and conscience of everyone present.

The *Fierce Wisdom* music begins with a rousing ceremonial invocation, a dynamic choral chant. Its African rhythm, pulse, and feel celebrate and generate the universal and energetic presence of the Sacred Feminine with the words "MAHAMAYA," meaning "The Great Mother" or "Mother of the Great Illusion."

I remember Scilla Elworthy saying to me before we started, "There is top security everywhere and high tension on stage, but if we have any security issues I know you will know what to do!" It was certainly a demanding situation, and I was relieved and delighted when each evening passed without any threatening drama. The music, along with the intention of everyone present, succeeded in creating a balanced environment in which each of the public speakers was relaxed enough to share and exchange truths from a depth of listening that diffused any reactivity, habitual opinionated views, or "an eye for an eye."

Fierce Wisdom demonstrated its musical power as an all-inclusive hymn of life, transcending boundaries of culture and creed. I now invite the music to speak for itself, as you listen to *Fierce Wisdom*, an odyssey of the soul sung by the singer soloist who embarks on a quest to overcome and transform her longing for inner-outer peace on Earth.

NB: My lyrics include wisdom messages inspired by one of the greatest embodiments of the sacred feminine on Earth, Anandamayi Ma. I allowed her words to inspire my music and lyrics, its melodic moods and messages, expressed through the chants, poems, songs, and anthems. They are supported by an instrumental ensemble that includes percussion, violin, saxophone, synthesizer, and spoken and sung solo vocals. You may access music samples here:

http://thenakedvoice.com/fierce-wisdom

6.6 A Wisdom Older and Deeper: Ireland

Thousand arms of compassion
Thousand wings so bright
Thousand blessings for our children
Thousand ways of Light
          —Thousand Ways of Light

"Chloë, we have heard about your work, and we want *to change the resonance of our city.* Can you help?" This earnest request from a local authority in one of Ireland's cities presented a new challenge to explore the potential of the singing field as a force for urban harmony. *Thousand Ways of Light,* a choral singing-field training, was the first initiative created to explore new ways to transform the resonance of the community. And *transform* it did, yet not in ways that we first imagined. This was an innovative leap. I knew from science that if you take the square root of one percent of the population, that can be enough to significantly impact, and possibly transform, the resonance of a whole city. Dublin was one million strong, so that meant we had to constellate a choir of at least one hundred people to make any significant impact on the community.

My dedicated Naked Voice Ireland organizer Catherine Walsh and I sent the message out to our Irish database, inviting hundreds of "singers" and "nonsingers" alike to come together on a monthly basis to share the Naked Voice sound-awareness practices and musicianship skills with me and eight trained Irish facilitators. My core team, Masashi Minagawa (energy movement master) and Nicholas Twilley (world percussion), would teach within the occasional residential weekends. The Thousand Ways of Light Training was named after my album of that name. One year later, one hundred people, many of whom had never sung in their lives, had found their naked voice and were doing the sound and movement practices together, in their own ongoing self-managed groups, or at home, at work, in the street, in their communities, as well as a whole group in several concerts.

This choral field was very inspiring and empowering for many people; some even called it "life-changing." What interested me was how the Irish singing field generated its own self-organizing interconnected network. The members have now become so cohesive and committed that small or large groups can be called upon anytime to witness, sustain, and support each other to care for and strengthen members of the community in crisis. The original eight Naked Voice facilitators have become "singing-field catalysts," who now oversee the singing field in Ireland beyond the original stomping ground of Dublin. The Irish singing field members are also known to show up at funerals and transform the prevailing sadness into a deeper communion through their simple soul sound.

You too will have begun to experience by now how your very own body-field is a singing field. Whether you are alone, walking in nature, in the presence of family and friends, in a community choir, in a flash mob, in your office at work, at the bus stop, on the train, or in a ceremonial setting, everywhere offers itself as a place to engage the sound values of the soul.

How willing and ready are we to communicate with our fellow human beings and share oneness more organically and effortlessly? The buzzing drone of bee wings, the flapping of bird feathers, or the high-frequency songs of a dolphin pod—these are all sounds that can energize and unify a whole group, informing or reminding each one what their specific role is, what their direction and purpose is, whether it is to make food, clean up the nest, nourish and caress, keep watch, venture out hunting, inspire new directions, expand the horizons, or build harmonious relationships.

As for many of us, the *community* I have dedicated my life to includes a *local* as well as a *global* dimension, extending from my personal family life into my local community and on out across the worldwide web into the far-reaching cosmos. Sound incorporates all these realms as one humming, thrumming, interconnected intelligence of life. It is thanks to my conscious relationship with inner sound, soul song, and soundmaking that I have been able to interact with this omniversal symphony of life as one. And we have hardly started!

I owe my deepest gratitude to Ireland for the grassroots developments of the Singing Field. It was in the 1990s that I began to really focus on the naked voice as a radical tool for conscious living. I was blessed to be able to lay down anchor in the Emerald Isle in 1994 shortly after my return from India. And it was in Ireland that I was able to plant seeds, birth my voice, and grow The Naked Voice teachings. Eventually I was asked by committed practitioners to create a training for individuals to become Naked Voice facilitators. Many of them are now mentors to the new Naked Voice trainees. Since the early days in Ireland, a decentralized international singing field has evolved in Europe and North and South America.

It was an immense relief to find in Ireland a culture whose oral singing tradition, like the Estonian folk culture, was so strong as to have withstood the most intense decades of oppression, famine, and war. Here was a culture that could demonstrate that there is no suffering too great for human song, and where there was nothing to lose by daring to release your lamenting angst, your grief wail, your fighting tooth and nail for recompense, for justice, or at least some acknowledgment, some kind of peace from "the troubles." In the Celtic Isles it became normal to shout from the rooftops, to let your hair down, speak your truth, say it exactly as it is from the heart. Here were a people who didn't think twice about staying awake into the early hours singing devotional chants, interwoven with Gaelic songs and primal sound.

Like sacred fools they would dare themselves to open into uncertainty, further, wider, and deeper than ever they imagined possible, dare themselves to scare themselves, to jump off the edge of the known, plunge into the abyss of raw flesh, skin, blood, and bone, the subterranean unknown of the soul.

I was privileged over many years to witness, midwife, process, challenge, and wonder at the sheer courage of hundreds of individuals who took the big dare to reveal their naked voice, to heal the long-held traumas of centuries, of ancestral repression, sexism, political torture—to let go, let it all go, follow a new calling, celebrate a new cycle, rise again, raise a toast, laugh, howl the final frozen fear away, shriek out, fall, drown, swim to the surface again and again, float away, sink and rise again and again, to fly into the courageous realm of new dreams.

The Naked Voice Ireland evolved and blossomed through ups and downs over two decades into a fluid grounded community whose strong foundation rested on a loyal commitment to listening—listening without judgment or fear. This is a singing-field community, without roof or walls. A gathering place where discovering the unique song of every soul was everyone's birthright and everyone's goal.

Ireland is a culture akin to India and Italy for me. These are cultures where thoughts originate and communicate themselves from the center of your chest; where thoughts are instinctually *felt* then filtered through the mind before they pour out of the mouth; and where the human body-field is undoubtedly, without question, a singing field. And yes, there is much accumulated wounding in Ireland too, the messy fall-out from a repressive religious regime and the horrors of wars past and present. Yet beneath all this, I found golden soul treasure there in that Celtic land, always singing its secret song from the heart. The Irish soul holds an inviolable knowing that no wars can ever defile.

After many moons of arriving and leaving and arriving in Ireland to lead introductory weekend voice workshops, public concerts, and residential retreats, I began to cocreate simple sonic structures, vibrational maps, energy-movement forms, mudras with accompanying sutras, and musical chakras to straighten our backs and strengthen our emotional and spiritual stamina; to rewire our brains and entrain ourselves through sound practices that aligned the spine with the heart so that the mind could start to find a point of inner-outer balance.

We are conditioned and unconditioned; we are both at the same time

—"Both at the Same Time," *Fierce Wisdom*

These were magical days of deep listening and fine-tuning of our ears and our souls. We were like singing bowls; we listened in ones and twos and threes until the trees sang around our knees as we rested in the long grasses after mealtimes. At the end of all our sound practicing—energizing our bodies with sonic codes and sacred vocalizing—and after all the wild spontaneous play of singing on an open stage, in the evenings came a deeper call. We were drawn into a well of listening within ourselves that gradually drew us deeper down into another reality prior to any conceptualization. It was as if our very sound itself was a portal drawing us homeward to the magnet of our existence, and on to the source of silence itself. Here was a wisdom that was uncompromised, transparent, and clear.

And so it was in Ireland that The Naked Voice message was born as "a wisdom older and deeper than the polarity of all conflict." In this wisdom:

THE HUMAN HEART IS THE MESSENGER OF THE SOUL

The human ears are the antennae of the brain.
The human body is the music of the mind.
The human voice is the mouthpiece of the spirit.
And when heart, soul, ears, brain, body, and soul are working in
   unity, compassionate communication arises and the spirit is
   freely expressed and shared.

These are the essential catalysts and conductors of openhearted, all-inclusive listening, in which every voice is heard, honored, and respected without judgment. When all these qualities are present, a harmonic resonance is established between human beings and a singing field, wherever two or three or more are gathered together.

From this understanding I was able to introduce a simple practice that embraced the energetic, elemental, and emotional essence of The Naked Voice understanding and its collective expression as a Singing Field: The Singing Field Triad.

The Singing Field Triad

The following shared practice is a simple yet highly effective way to unify the three interdependent realms (impersonal, personal, and transpersonal) that you have been exploring in this book. It will help transform your listening, transform your communication, and transform your life.

The Singing Field Triad requires three people ideally: yourself and two others. Each of you takes a turn being a witness, a loyal friend, and a singer at 5- to 30-minute intervals. These roles rotate until you have each experienced them all for the agreed length of time.

1. **The Witness** (impersonal presence) is a silent listener. S/he sees and observes what is going on with a benign disinterest. The witness is nonjudgmental, impersonal, and grounded.

   The Witness abides in the spiritual or vertical axis of consciousness and remains totally silent, listening deeply with a benign objective indifference to every sound uttered by the Naked-Voice Singer. S/he endeavors to hear everything communicated without any judgment—either positive or negative. By doing so, s/he strengthens the faculty of attention called the *witness consciousness* in which you observe yourself, your thoughts, and all inner-outer sensations, feelings, and perceptions without any attachment or reaction (for or against).

2. **The Loyal Friend** (personal presence) is an open, intuitive communicator who is there to serve and encourage the singer in expressing and integrating his/her highest aspirations with their grounded purpose on Earth. S/he listens and responds intuitively with sincere feeling and loving attention, either mirroring the singer's mood or empowering him/her to overcome self-sabotaging self-consciousness and doubt and to express a true naked sound.

   The Loyal Friend abides in the social sphere, or horizontal axis of consciousness, in relation to the Naked-Voice Singer. The Loyal Friend's intuitive heart is the leading quality here. As such s/he responds with deepest feeling and a respectful positive regard for the very best expression that the Naked-Voice Singer is capable of.

The Loyal Friend knows how to respond and empower the singer with sensitivity and support—spoken, sung, or silent—encouraging him/her to access and give birth to their most authentic and naked utterance. Contrary to the Witness, the Loyal Friend is in a completely subjective intuitive relationship with the Naked-Voice Singer. The aim of the Loyal Friend is to listen in a way that invokes the most profound expression from the Naked-Voice Singer.

3. **The Singer** (transpersonal presence) sings with the intention of totally liberating him/herself through sound in a spirit of total abandonment, spontaneity, and presence while consciously endeavoring to unify body, heart, and soul. Supported by an impersonal objective Witness and personal subjective Loyal Friend, s/he expresses him/ herself from the source of being—exploring, welcoming, embracing, and transforming the conflicting modes of his/ her nature into one seamless thread of song.

The Naked-Voice Singer represents the expression of our most essential nature, unfettered by self-consciousness or fear language of any kind. The Naked Voice is in direct communion with the source of his or her nature and is able to draw on all the worlds: earthly (instinctual), heavenly (intuitive), and beyond (cosmic). The Naked Voice draws sustenance directly from the source or root chakra, expressing itself across the full spectrum of human feeling, from the most gentle and still to the most impassioned instinctual power. The Naked-Voice Singer is informed by the deep observational listening of the Witness and the faithful loving support of the Loyal Friend; and s/he stands everywhere and nowhere, is neither attached to nor detached from what s/he is singing. S/he may choose to express him/herself in any style: silent, spoken, or sung. The Naked-Voice Singer is ultimately the embodied expression of full-spectrum consciousness.

The Singing Field Triad is a musical matrix that offers a profound and radical way to heal the divide between your inner-outer voice, restoring presence and compassion in your life. This matrix ultimately heals the broken thread between our silent, speaking, and singing voices into one unified sound.

Silence	Inner Voice	Witness	nonjudgmental listener
Speech	Outer Voice	Loyal Friend	cocreative communicator
Song	Naked Voice	Resonant Human	compassionate leader

Details of Setting Up the Singing Field Triad

An appropriate space must be found for the exercise, preferably somewhere quiet and uninterrupted by everyday demands. The Loyal Friend is timekeeper, responsible for informing the Naked-Voice Singer when they are 5 minutes and 1 minute from completion of their singing time. The participants then hold hands and stand in silence, bringing their full awareness to their feet so that they are rooted in the ground and ready to listen from the deepest awareness. It can be favorable to share one long unchanging sound together—SA or AUMmmmm, for example—before the start of each new session as well as at the end. There is no conferring, discussion, or feedback until the very end of the process, when all three participants have sung. If the group size is larger than three—four or even five—then have two Witnesses at least in each constellation. If the group size is five, you can have two Witnesses and two Loyal Friends.

NB: There is only ever one Naked Voice singing at any one time. At the end of the process when everyone has sung, the group can then sit down and witness each other's experience.

Sounding a New World into Being

The world is sound
sound heralds your existence
your life is birthed through sound
sound is the resonance of who you are
sound awareness inspires the breath of your life
vibrating every cell in your body-mind
sound is the heart song of your awakening soul
the energies of love, the unique music of your spirit
sounding your naked voice is a direct experience
the key to your soul, the house of your song
your naked voice is a vocal map of your true identity
a sacred geometry—harmonic resonance
your sound intelligence, an all-inclusive knowing
your naked voice can be forgotten & remembered in an instant
deep listening, forgiveness, self-acceptance
gratitude, humility, conscience sing its grace into being
transforming your longing into belonging
your separateness into a singing field
a homecoming beyond belief
a wisdom older and deeper than the polarity of all conflict

Transform Your Life

Listen—Communicate—Live

You my child, and you my lover
father mother sister friend
You are my son, you are my brother
You're my Life my Voice my ...
You're my Friend

— "You," *Thousand Ways of Light*

In the 1980s, I wanted to change the world. In the 1990s, I discovered that there was no *separate world* to change. I suddenly woke up to find myself, the world, and the cosmos as a dynamic interconnected web of Life, a universal intelligence expressing itself through sound energy and light.

My naked voice was as close as I could come to exchanging this understanding with others. It inspired a direct encounter with my Self. When I shared it—especially by singing—the *nakedness* of my vocalizing began to touch a similar "knowing" in others. Listening more deeply, it became a portal into stillness, presence, silence before sound. So I began to explore my deepest feelings with this inbuilt sonic laboratory that was to become the most intimate and trustworthy friend of my life.

May you also discover your unique voice as the mouthpiece of your own true self. In this book I have introduced you to practices that release your voice from being a victim of habitual, reactive thinking; to becoming a vessel of self-empowerment, authentic and creative expression, catalyzed by nonjudgmental listening. You have begun to explore ways to move your vocal identity from an inhibited self-consciousness, to a deeper state of being, inspiring conscious communication and spiritual dialogue. With mindful attention and spontaneous passion, you can now continue to discover how your naked voice will assist you to express and to integrate your highest ideals with your grounded purpose on Earth.

The naked human voice is everyone's signature song and birthright. When it is shared with others as a *field of sound* or a "singing field," it ignites its collective healing presence as a compassionate singing.

If we can breathe, we can sing. If we can sing, we can love. We live in a world that for centuries has longed to make the shift from a Love-of-Power to the Power-of-Love. The Naked Voice awakens this Love-without-condition, unconditional Love. It is a Light shining brighter and stronger in our hearts, and when we see, hear, and sing it together as one song, it becomes a harmonic resonance, a symphony of Love reaching far into the cosmos.

Thank you for inspiring me to write this book, and for your daring to courageously explore your unique sound through the naked voice practices. May *The Naked Voice: Transform Your Life through the Power of Sound* assist you in revealing the original song of your Being.

I leave you with a message from the naked voice of my soul....

And all the while a silent laughter sings
As wind through an open window saying
Be deeper still
Be deeper still
Sound from zero
　　—"ZERO," *Fierce Wisdom*

I wish you every fulfillment and joy with your naked voice to transform your life, and sound a new world into being.

Chloë Goodchild
Spring 2015

Further ongoing practices are available online at The Naked Voice Online School (thenakedvoice.com), where you will gain access to a diverse range of restorative and transformative sound, vocal music, audiovisual practices, live webinars, trainings and retreats taking place in Europe, the USA, Canada, South America and beyond. Everyone is welcome to join our all-inclusive expanding worldwide **Singing Field Community**.

Reading List

A selection of the books that have inspired me:

Sound Energy, Voice, and the Body

Aoki, Hiroyuki. *Shintaido*. Novato, CA: Shintaido of America Publications, 1982.

Aoki, Hiroyuki. *Tenshingoso and Eiko*. Shintaido of America Publications, 1989.

D'Angelo, James. *Seed Sounds for Tuning the Chakras*. Rochester, VT: Destiny Books, 2010.

Davies, Dorinne S. *The Cycle of Sound*. New Jersey: New Pathways Press, 2012.

Frazer, Peter. *Decoding the Human Body-Field*. Rochester, VT: Healing Arts Press, 2008.

Wren, Barbara. *Cellular Awakening*. Carlsbad, CA: Hay House, 2010.

Deep Listening through Sound

Berendt, Joseph Ernst. *The World Is Sound, Nada Brahma*. Rochester, VT: Destiny Books, 1987.

Easwaran, Eknath. *The Upanishads, A Selection*. Tomales, CA: Nilgiri Press, 2009.

Goodchild, Chloë. *The Naked Voice, A Memoir*. London: Rider Books, 1993.

Khan, Hazrat Inayat. *Music*. Claremont, CA: Hunter House, 1974.

Khan, Hazrat Inayat. *The Music of Life*. New Lebanon, NY: Omega Publication, 1998.

Khan, Hazrat Inayat. *The Mysticism of Music, Sound and Word*. Delhi: Motilal Banarsidass, 1994.

Michael, Edward Salim. *The Law of Attention: Nada Yoga and the Way of Inner Vigilance*. Rochester, VT: Inner Traditions, 2010.

Ni Riain, Noirin. *Listen with the Ear of the Heart: An Autobiography*. Dublin, Ireland: Veritas, 2010.

Paul, Russill. *The Yoga of Sound*. Novato, CA: New World Library, 2004.

Steindl-Rast, David. *The Music of Silence*. San Francisco, CA: Harper SanFrancisco, 1995.

Thich Nhat Hanh. *Heart of Understanding*. Berkeley, CA: Parallax Press, 2009.

Tomatis, Alfred. *The Conscious Ear*. Barrytown, NY: Station Hill Press, 1992.

Healing through Music, Voice, and Sound Awareness

Campbell, Don, and Alex Doman. *Healing at the Speed of Sound*. New York: Hudson Street Press, 2011.

Crowe, Barbara J. *Music and Soulmaking: Toward a New Theory of Music Therapy*. Lanham, MD: Scarecrow Press, 2004.

Goodchild, Chloë. *Your Naked Voice*. Boulder, CO: Sounds True Audiobooks.

Goodchild, Chloë. *Awakening through Sound*. Boulder, CO: Sounds True Audiobooks.

Goldman, Jonathan. *Healing Sounds*. Rochester, VT: Inner Traditions, 2002.

Hamel, Peter Michael. *Through Music to the Self*. Vega Books, 2002.

Hess, Linda. *Singing Emptiness*. Calcutta: Seagull Books, 2009.

Kenyon, Tom. *The Hathor Material*. Santa Clara, CA: S.E.E. Publishing Company, 1996.

Linklater, Kristin. *Freeing the Natural Voice*. Drama Book Publishers, 1976.

Nakkach, Silvia. *Free Your Voice*. Boulder, CO: Sounds True USA.

Shewell, Christina. *Voicework, Art and Science in Changing Voices*. Chichester, West Sussex, UK: Wiley-Blackwell Publications, 2009.

Steiner, Rudolf. *The Inner Nature of Music*. Spring Valley, NY: The Anthroposophic Press, 1983.

Stevens, Christine. *Music Medicine*. Boulder, CO: Sounds True USA.

Sound, Poetry, and the Spoken Voice

Ayot, William. *Small Things That Matter*. www.williamayot.com/book.htm.

Barks, Coleman. *A Year with Rumi*. New York: HarperCollins, 2006.

Barks, Coleman. *The Essential Rumi*. San Francisco: Harper SanFrancisco, 1995.

Barks, Coleman. *The Soul of Rumi*. San Francisco: Harper SanFrancisco, 2001.

Barks, Coleman. *The Glance: Songs of Soul Meeting*. New York: Viking Press, 1999.

Bly, Robert. *The Kabir Book*. Boston: Beacon Press, 1977.

Harvey, Andrew. *Love's Fire*. London: Jonathan Cape, 1988.

Heaney, Seamus. *The Spirit Level*. London: Faber & Faber, 2009.

Housden, Roger. *Ten Poems to Change Your Life*. New York: Harmony Books, 2001.

Lalla. *Naked Song*, translated by Coleman Barks. Atlanta, GA: Maypop Books, 1992.

Oliver, Mary. *New and Selected Poems*. Boston: Beacon Press, 2005.

Rosen, Kim. *Saved by a Poem, The Transformative Power of Words*. Carlsbad, CA: Hay House, 2009.

Warner, Stuart. *Echoes of the First Song*. London: Antony Rowe Publishing, 2009.

Whyte, David. *What to Remember When Waking*. Boulder, CO: Sounds True Audio.

Whyte, David. *The House of Belonging*. Langley, WA: Many Rivers Press, 1997.

A New Voice and Language of Consciousness

Balsekar, Ramesh S. *The Bhagavad Gita, A Selection*. Mumbai: Zen Publications, 1998.

Baring, Anne. *Dream of the Cosmos*. Dorset, U.K.: Archive Publishing, 2013.

Berry, Thomas. *The Great Work*. New York: Bell Tower, 1999.

Braden, Greg. *The Divine Matrix*. Carlsbad, CA: Hay House, 2007.

Braden, Greg. *Fractal Time*. Carlsbad, CA: Hay House, 2009.

Campbell, Joseph. *An Open Life*. New York: Harper & Row, 1990.

Clarke, Lindsay. *Parzifal*. Oxford: Godstow Press, 2011.

Clarke, Lindsay. *The Chymmical Wedding*. Richmond, U.K.: Alma Books, 2010.

Elworthy, Scilla. *Pioneering the Possible*. Berkeley, CA: North Atlantic Books, 2014.

Ensler, Eve. *The Vagina Monologues*. London: Virago, 2004.

Grout, Pam. *E Squared*. Carlsbad, CA: Hay House, 2012.

Graydon, Nicola, and Natalya O'Sullivan. *The Ancestral Continuum*. New York: Simon and Schuster, 2013.

Harvey, Andrew. *The Hope: A Guide to Sacred Activism*. Carlsbad, CA: Hay House, 2009.

Houston, Jean. *The Wizard of Us.* New York: Atria Books, 2012.

McTaggart, Lynn. *The Field.* New York: HarperCollins, 2002.

Lipton, Bruce. *The Biology of Belief.* Carlsbad, CA: Hay House, 2008.

Lipton, Bruce, and Steve Bhaerman. *Spontaneous Evolution.* Carlsbad, CA: Hay House, 2009.

O'Dea, James. *Cultivating Peace.* San Rafael, CA: Shift Books, 2012.

Okri, Ben. *Birds of Heaven.* London: Weidenfeld & Nicolson History, 1995.

Okri, Ben. *A Way of Being Free.* London: Phoenix House, 1998.

Pert, Candace. *Molecules of Emotion.* New York: Simon and Schuster, 1997.

Shankar, H.H. Sri Sri Ravi. *Wisdom for the New Millennium.* Mumbai: JAICO Publishing House, 2006.

Shapiro, Ed and Deb. *Be the Change.* New York: Sterling Press, 2011.

Swimme, Brian, and Thomas Berry. *The Universe Story.* San Francisco: Harper SanFrancisco, 1994.

Tolle, Eckhart. *A New Earth.* New York: Penguin, 2005.

Teilhard de Chardin, Pierre. *Hymn of the Universe.* Harper & Row, 1965.

For a more extensive and comprehensive Naked Voice Reading List, see www.thenakedvoice.com.

Acknowledgments

Gratitude beyond words go to you: my grandparents, Gladys and Douglas, my parents, Jean and Ronnie, my daughter, Rebecca, my extended family, my wisdom teachers, soul friends, mentors, students, and creative collaborators. You have ALL played a significant role in the birth, presence, and evolution of The Naked Voice.

Kazuaki Tanahashi: I bow to you for your generous gift of the *Multicoloured Circle,* energizing the book's cover design.

Andrew Harvey: Infinite love to you, my oldest of friends, for your generous heart, and whose close association with North Atlantic Books opened the door.

North Atlantic Books: Thanks to Doug Reil and my editorial and design/production team: Tim McKee, Hermine Compagnone, Hisae Matsuda, Kathy Glass, Mary Ann Casler, Mary McMurtry. Your deep listening to the nondual nature of this voice work, combined with your focus on clarity and structure, and immense patience, have assisted me to distill the multifaceted nature of *The Naked Voice,* making it user-friendly without compromising its teachings.

Masashi Minagawa and Nicholas Twilley: my Core Naked Voice Team, soul friends, and radical creative collaborators for more than twenty years.

Richard Lannoy: Life-long mentor and guide, I offer you one heartfelt humble thank you. Your original photographs of my source-teacher Anandamayi transformed my life, and gave birth to The Naked Voice. A renowned photographer, visual artist, and writer on Indian philosophy, wisdom, and culture, Richard is author of *Anandamayi, Her Life and Wisdom, The Speaking Tree, Benares, and Fathomless Heart.*

Photographic and Illustrative Credits: Special gratitude to my niece Rosa Fay, daughter of my brother, William Goodchild, and photographer extraordinaire, whose photos of *The Seven Sounds of Love* and their energy movements appear in this book.

Thanks also to Masashi Minagawa for the caliographs of the Heart Sutra.

Thanks to Aliki Sapountzi for the photograph of my singing in Madison Square Garden.

World Family: One vast embrace to all my dear soul friends from the Americas to the Celtic Isles, Europe, Asia, and home to Bristol, London, and my Devon community, who continually bless my life. You know who you are, and I embrace you. Brian and Deirdre Skilton, Catherine Walsh, Kim Rosen *(Saved by a Poem),* and Nicola Graydon-Harris *(The Ancestral Continuum),* your blessed loyal friendship is unconditional nourishment. Nicola, thank you especially for your invaluable support in the early stages of this book, creating the book proposal and beyond! What would I do without you all? I have no idea. Thank you, Coleman Barks, Robert Bly, Don Campbell (1947–2012), Gabrielle Roth and Robert Ansell, Gangaji, Gilles Petit, Graham Brown, Jean Houston, James O'Dea, Jennifer Brown, Jonathan Goldman, Judy Ling, Katherine Cross, Kazuaki Tanahashi, Linda Hess, Lindsay Clarke, Oriane Lee Johnston, Ram Dass, Scilla Elworthy, Ursula King, Tami Simon, and Thich Nhat Hanh for your unique resonance with my vocation, your inspired presence, and your vision in the world.

To all my creative music collaborators, too numerous to name: You have graced my life in unimaginable ways as sound designers and orchestral arrangers, poets, and performers. Notably David Lord, my recording engineer. Also Coleman Barks, Angelo Badalamenti, Sir John Tavener (d. 2013), Adrian Freedman, Alphonse Daudet Touna,

Christoffer de Graal, David Darling, Dhevdhas Nair, Ed Jones, Elizabeth Parker, Gary Malkin, Glen Velez, Helen Chadwick, Jerry DesVoignes, Joan Macintosh, Manickham Yogaswaran, Michael Stillwater, Nicholas Twilley, Nick Pullin, Nikki Slade, Paul Clarvis, Phil Clemo, Rebecca Nash, Sonia Slany, Steve Gorn, Ursula Monn, William Goodchild, and Zachiah Blackburn.

Ambassadors of The Naked Voice presence worldwide: Sounds True, Boulder, Colorado; Annette Peard, Martin Duffy, and the staff of Dunderry Park, Navan, and F2 Dublin, Ireland; Martin Fleming, Isha, Lara, and the staff of Buckland Hall, Conference Centre, Wales; The Alternatives Team, Piccadilly, London; Hollyhock community, Cortes Island, BC, Canada; Rev. Diane Berke and One Spirit, NYC; Wendy Young, Don Campbell, and the Open Centre NYC; Bud Stone, Michel Pergola, and Lynnea Brinkerhoff, The Graduate Institute, Connecticut; Silvia Nakkach and Vox Mundi, California Institute of Integral Studies, San Francisco; Pamela Charad and The Naked Voice Chile; Adalbert LoHim So'Ham, and The Kryon Festival of Light, Germany; Robert Ansell and Raven Recording NYC; Gunakar Grundmann, Silenzio Music, Munich; Phillip Hellmich, director of The International Summer of Peace, USA; Nathan Crane and The Panacea Community, San Diego; Peace activist and author James O'Dea; Steve Dinan and The Shift Network USA.

The Naked Voice World Facilitator Community (www.theNVFA .org): My deepest praise and thanksgiving go to all those who have dedicated their lives to practicing and disseminating The Naked Voice trainings and teachings worldwide, with the indispensible coordination of Tim Chalice (The Naked Voice Office UK), Catherine Walsh (NV Ireland), and The Naked Voice Facilitator Association Mentors, Graduates, and Trainees—my unbounded love.

Index

A

Abreu, José, 224–25

Advaita (nonduality), 13, 31, 52, 164

Alpert, Richard. *See* Ram Dass

Anandamayi Ma, 71–72, 73, 101, 110, 119, 149–50, 163, 167, 244, 245

Andrews, Julie, 174

Ansell, Robert, 205

Armstrong, Frankie, 13

AUM (OM) mantra, 103, 111–18, 222

Australian Aborigines, 4–5, 8–9

Authentic voice. *See also* Naked Voice

    discovering, 5

    of humanity, 72

    power of, xxi–xxii, 13–14

    self-consciousness and, 45, 90

    as teacher, 87–88

    uniqueness of, 1–2, 75

Avon Peace Education Project, 12–13

Ayot, William, 88

B

Baermann, Steve, 221

Balsekar, Ramesh, 52–53

Barenboim, Daniel, 2

Barks, Coleman, 8, 26, 46, 90, 110, 137, 158, 171, 212–14, 220, 244

Bauls of Bengal, 5, 148

Being

    doing vs., 26, 31

    nowhere, 26

Berendt, Joachim-Ernst, 113

Berry, Thomas, xxiv, 146, 223

Be Without Leaving Yourself

    practice, 32–33

Beyondananda, Swami, 221

Bhagavad Gita, 52, 162

Bhajans, 144, 149

Black, power of, 79–80

Blackfeet. *See* Piegan (Blackfeet) Wisdom Elders

Bly, Robert, 86, 135, 137, 196

About Chloë Goodchild

Chloë Goodchild is an international singer and innovative educator. She is the founder of The Naked Voice and its UK charitable foundation (2004), dedicated to the transforming practice of self-awareness and conscious communication skills through spoken and sung voice. Deafness in childhood catalyzed Goodchild's discovery of inner sound and silence. This deep encounter with her inner self triggered a lifetime's experiential research of the voice as one of humanity's most untapped resources for personal and global evolution and transformation.

Goodchild studied music, English, and education at Cambridge and Norwich universities. From the late seventies she evolved her own East-West vocal research, influenced by travels through Africa, India, Turkey, Europe, the U.S., and Canada. Goodchild's encounters with indigenous wisdom teachers, spiritual mentors, and classical music masters ultimately led to a transformative experience inspired by the great luminary and saint Anandamayi (1896–1982). This gave birth to her unique method of sound and voice, which Goodchild eventually named *The Naked Voice* in 1990. Her autobiography *The Naked Voice: Journey to the Spirit of Sound* (London: Rider Books, 1993) tells the story of these formative early years.

About North Atlantic Books

North Atlantic Books (NAB) is an independent, nonprofit publisher committed to a bold exploration of the relationships between mind, body, spirit, and nature. Founded in 1974, NAB aims to nurture a holistic view of the arts, sciences, humanities, and healing. To make a donation or to learn more about our books, authors, events, and newsletter, please visit www.northatlanticbooks.com.

North Atlantic Books is the publishing arm of the Society for the Study of Native Arts and Sciences, a 501(c)(3) nonprofit educational organization that promotes cross-cultural perspectives linking scientific, social, and artistic fields. To learn how you can support us, please visit our website.